Seducing the Subconscious

Seducing the Subconscious

The Psychology of Emotional Influence in Advertising

Dr Robert Heath

WILEY-BLACKWELL

A John Wiley & Sons, Ltd., Publication

This edition first published 2012
© 2012 Robert Heath

Wiley-Blackwell is an imprint of John Wiley & Sons, formed by the merger of Wiley's global
Scientific, Technical and Medical business with Blackwell Publishing.

Registered Office: John Wiley & Sons Ltd, The Atrium, Southern Gate, Chichester,
West Sussex, PO19 8SQ, UK

Editorial Offices: 350 Main Street, Malden, MA 02148-5020, USA
9600 Garsington Road, Oxford, OX4 2DQ, UK
The Atrium, Southern Gate, Chichester, West Sussex, PO19 8SQ, UK

For details of our global editorial offices, for customer services, and for information about how to
apply for permission to reuse the copyright material in this book please see our website at
www.wiley.com/wiley-blackwell.

The right of Robert Heath to be identified as the author of this work has been asserted in
accordance with the UK Copyright, Designs and Patents Act 1988.

Library of Congress Cataloging-in-Publication Data

Heath, Robert, 1947–
  Seducing the subconscious : the psychology of emotional influence in advertising /
Robert Heath.
      p. cm.
  Summary: "Seducing the Subconscious reveals how this brave new advertising world works,
using illustrative examples of advertising campaigns that have been hugely successful without
anyone quite being able to recall what they were trying to communicate" – Provided by publisher.
  Includes bibliographical references and index.
  ISBN 978-0-470-97488-9 (hardback)
 1. Advertising–Psychological aspects.   I. Title.
  HF5822.H37 2012
  659.101′9–dc23

                                                                           2011043014

A catalogue record for this book is available from the British Library.

Wiley also publishes its books in a variety of electronic formats. Some content that appears in
print may not be available in electronic books.

Set in 10.5/13pt Minion by Aptara Inc., New Delhi, India
Printed and bound in Singapore by Markono Print Media Pte Ltd

3   2014

For Pippa

Contents

Foreword

"Advertising may be described as the science of arresting the human intelligence long enough to get money from it."

Stephen Butler Leacock
Crown's Book of Political Quotations (1982)

When people are asked about advertising, they often find it quite difficult to remember any. If pressed, they usually come up with famous old campaigns like "I'd like to buy the world a Coke. . . ," or American Express "Don't leave home without it," or The Marlboro Cowboy, or the Jolly Green Giant. In the UK they might mention the Cadbury's Smash Martians, the Guinness Surfer, Heineken "Refreshes the parts other beers cannot reach," or the Gold Blend couple.

There then usually follows a discussion about how much advertising influences us. Most of us like to think that it doesn't influence us unless we are stupid enough to let it. We believe this because we assume advertising works by persuasion, and persuasion is associated with others (typically our parents) trying to argue us into doing something we don't want to do. Persuasion is a rational verbal process, so if we don't hear or remember what an advertisement says, how can we be persuaded by it?

Many experts agree that advertising isn't nearly as persuasive as it claims it is. In the opening paragraph of his book *Advertising: The Uneasy Persuasion*, Michael Shudson writes:

Advertising is much less powerful than advertisers and critics of advertising claim, and advertising agencies are stabbing in the dark much more than they are practicing precision microsurgery on the public consciousness. (Shudson 1984: xiii)

I agree with Shudson. Having worked in nine different advertising agencies over a period of 23 years, I can testify to just how much chance, serendipity, and stabbing in the dark is involved in the creation of great advertising campaigns. Admen may like to masquerade as experts in persuasion, but in many ways they are little more than gifted amateurs. I'd say the average young person on a date is many times more adroit in the art of persuasion than the average creative team.

But if advertising isn't very good at persuading us, how come those companies that use advertising are amongst the most successful in the world? I think the explanation is that advertising has ways of influencing us we are not aware of, and that *don't* involve persuasion. In this matter Shudson and I are also in agreement, for while he asserts that ads are not very persuasive, he also acknowledges that:

> This does not mean ads are ineffective. In fact . . . television ads may be more powerful precisely because people pay them so little heed that they do not call critical defences into play. (Shudson 1984: 4)

Shudson's source for this idea was the psychologist, Herb Krugman. Krugman's theories caused something of a stir in the 1970s, mainly because they suggested that TV advertising received low levels of attention. This was seen by the ad industry as being too difficult a pill to swallow, and Krugman's ideas were pretty much ignored until the start of the twenty-first century, when I wrote a monograph called *The Hidden Power of Advertising* (Heath 2001).

The Hidden Power of Advertising was based on Krugman's idea that TV advertising could influence us even when processed inattentively. Since its publication in 2001 there has been a steady growth in the number of people who accept that advertising subjected to "low attention processing" can be effective. That said, many of those who work in the ad industry still cling to the notion that advertising works only through persuasion, and works best at high attention.

Although my monograph referred extensively to psychology, it was not seen by academia as being rigorous enough. In order to overcome this hurdle I elected to become an academic myself. I studied for and was awarded a PhD, and I read and wrote articles in academic journals. But the more I researched the subject, the more it struck me that this "other" way in which advertising works, this *alternative* to persuasion, was quite possibly much more influential than persuasion. Many people have expressed worries about how advertising might be influencing us without our knowledge, might somehow be "manipulating" our behavior subconsciously; and now I was finding that their worries were not entirely without foundation.

This alternative way in which advertising works is what I call Subconscious Seduction. I should stress this has nothing to do with the subliminal effects mentioned in Vance Packard's famous book *The Hidden Persuaders*. Packard's claims about messages exposed below the threshold of perception were based on a hoax, and there is no evidence at all that advertising can influence us in this way. No, perhaps even more worrying is that advertising's ability to seduce our subconscious uses elements that are in our full view and easy for us to discern. The problem is that although we are *able* to perceive and attend to these elements, we mostly choose not to.

So advertising's ability to work in this way isn't like subliminal exposure, something we can legislate against or put a stop to. It happens partly because of the way our minds work, and partly because of the way we make decisions. This means that explaining the Subconscious Seduction model isn't a simple story: it involves collecting together and considering complex ideas about how we perceive and think and feel and remember and forget. These ideas have been brought into the public domain only in the last two decades, by academics such as Antonio Damasio, Daniel Dennett, Daniel Schacter, Joseph LeDoux, and Steven Rose. Although these ideas are complex, I have done my best to describe them in language that anyone can understand. I have sought to avoid the situation summed up so eloquently by my great friend the late Andrew Ehrenberg, who once told me: "There is nothing in the world so complex that it cannot, when considered by a group of clever people, be made more complex."

There are many people who I must thank for helping me write this book. Most especially I would like to thank Paul Feldwick and Jon Howard, whose insights first inspired my research. Also, in no particular order, Tim Ambler, David Brandt, Jeremy Bullmore, Wendy Gordon, Arthur Kover, Agnes Nairn, Douglas West, and the dozens of others who have indirectly contributed to this book. Above all I should like to express my gratitude and love to my wife, friend, and subeditor Frances Liardet, without whose support my career as a writer might never have come to pass.

Introduction

"I think that I shall never see
An ad so lovely as a tree.
But if a tree you have to sell,
It takes an ad to do that well."

Jef I. Richards
Retort to Ogden Nash (1995)[1]

Advertising is a huge business, and a huge success story. You only have to look at the turnover of those companies who use advertising intensively (Procter & Gamble, Walmart, Unilever, Kraft, Nestlé, Johnson & Johnson, Reckitt Benckiser, etc.) to know that investing in advertising pays off in spades.

But trying to get under the surface and explain *why* advertising is so effective is surprisingly difficult. One reason is that the companies who use advertising to sell their goods don't have the least motive for letting others know how effective it is. Of course, the ad agencies have a motive for publicizing their success, because advertising is their advertising, so to speak. But they are bound to confidentiality by the people for whom they create the ads, the marketers who pay them, and those marketers much prefer success or failure to remain a well-kept secret. One reason for this is that if their competitors find out which ads work and which don't, then all those competitors need to do is imitate the ads that are successful.

---

[1] http://www.financial-portal.com/articles/article229.html#Selling

---

Seducing the Subconscious: The Psychology of Emotional Influence in Advertising, First Edition. Robert Heath.
© 2012 Robert Heath. Published 2012 by John Wiley & Sons, Ltd.

Competitive paranoia is especially rife in the USA, where more money is spent on advertising than anywhere else in the world. Ask a US ad agency how much their client has spent on a campaign, or how much it has earned them in extra revenue, and you'll find the door politely shut in your face. And if you do manage to find someone who can give you this information, you're more likely to get an injunction than permission to publish it.

There are a few exceptions. The ARF (Advertising Research Foundation) David Ogilvy Awards annually publish a series of case studies which occasionally give you an indication of how successful an advertising campaign has been. But the data are mostly very generalized. They'll tell you how much more awareness was created, or how many people liked the advertising. They might even mention how much sales have increased over a certain period, or how much their share of the market has grown. But there will rarely be anything specific about what the ad campaign actually achieved.

Take for example the 2009 Dove "Real Beauty" campaign.[2] The Ogilvy Awards case study says that "engagement" increased 12%, but since no one knows what engagement is that doesn't really tell you much. It also says that the overall strategy increased market share by 33% in the USA, UK, and Germany. But that was over a 4-year period between 2003 and 2007, and was for *all* the activity that went on over this period (i.e., promotions, distribution drives, sales incentives, PR activity, etc., etc.) What it doesn't tell you is how much the TV advertising earned.

In the UK, marketers are slightly more relaxed about revealing business data, and the IPA Advertising Effectiveness Awards provide a gold mine of hard evidence about how advertising campaigns have worked.[3] That is why you'll find I've quoted many more UK than US case studies in this book. There is much more information to work with, which makes them much better at illustrating how advertising works.

But there's a second reason why marketers are coy about how successful their advertising is. And that is because they often don't know. The industrialist John Wanamaker is famously quoted as having said "Half my advertising is wasted, but I don't know which half." Less well-known is that in an interview in 1998, Niall FitzGerald, then chairman of Unilever, observed that "If someone asked me, rather than one of my distinguished predecessors, which half of my advertising was wasted I would probably say

90% is wasted but I don't know which 90% (Lannon 1998: 20)." Astonishing, isn't it, that we can ferry people to and from the surface of the moon, yet according to the head of the world's second biggest advertiser we still can't work out if an ad campaign has been a success.

One explanation for this confusion is that ads frequently seem able to defy reason. For example, it is widely believed in the ad industry that ads we like are more effective than ads we don't like, because people are more willing to watch them (Biel 1990). So how do you explain the following?

Love or Hate?

Over the past few years a whole raft of what are known as price comparison web sites have grown up in the UK. These sites enable you to check if you can get a better deal on services such as power, telecoms, and insurance. Traffic for these web sites is almost entirely driven by TV advertising, and so they make an interesting test bed for what sort of advertising does and does not work.

On Saturday, January 16, 2010, in the midst of a terrible recession which had decimated profits of the UK's leading commercial TV channel, the UK *Guardian* newspaper published an article with a headline "How to save the TV advertising industry? Simples! Send for Aleksandr the meerkat."[4] The article referred to "Compare-the-Market.com," which had ingeniously invented a fictional web site entitled "Compare the Meerkat." Their hugely popular ad campaign featured an anthropomorphized meerkat called Aleksandr bemoaning that fact that people confused his meerkat dating site with the Compare-the-Market web site on which you could buy cheap car insurance.

"A lot of people have been taken aback by how successful Aleksandr has been," the *Guardian* announced. The article pointed out that Aleksandr Orlov, the meerkat in question, had generating an avalanche of followers on Twitter and Facebook, in the process becoming the must-have children's toy for Christmas 2009. Gerry Boyle, chief executive of media buying giant Zenith Optimedia, was quoted as saying "The huge success of these campaigns in capturing the public's attention has proved those who argue TV advertising is dying wrong."

---

[4] http://www.guardian.co.uk/media/2010/jan/16/aleksander-orlov-price-comparison-ads

So just how hugely successful had the meerkat advertising been? The *Guardian*, quoting Mintel, claimed the meerkat advertising had "propelled" Compare-the-Market.com from being in the low teens to fourth most popular UK price comparison site behind MoneySupermarket.com and Confused.com. Sounds good, but the problem was this also put them behind a web site with an equally high awareness advertising campaign, GoCompare.com.

For their advertising, GoCompare.com had invented a character called Gio Compario, an opera singer who regularly interrupted people's leisure activities by exhorting them to "Go Compare" in a loud operatic tenor voice. Gio Compario had also broken some records in 2009, by being named as the UK's most irritating ad campaign for a *second year running*. It was not made clear which of these two campaigns – the meerkat or Gio Compario – had generated the most attention, but there was no doubt which was liked least and which was liked most.

Which makes it all the more surprising that a little over a year later the UK *Sunday Times* announced that "spending on advertising . . . has driven GoCompare into pole position in what is now a four way fight between Confused, MoneySupermarket, and Compare the Market." Apparently, despite incurring the nation's universal opprobrium, the Gio Compario advertising was a huge success. In other words, the UK's most hated advertising seems to have been a great deal more effective than the UK's most loved advertising.

What this tale illustrates is that simple indicators such as liking or hating ads are not very reliable predictors of ad effectiveness. It may seem logical common sense that an ad you like will work better than one you hate, but ads are expert at defying logic. And here's another common sense example. Surely an ad will not work if no one can recall the message it is trying to get over?

The Curious Case of O2

The UK mobile phone network market is renowned as being one of the world's most competitive, and, as with price comparison web sites, success has always been driven by advertising. During the 1990s, two ad campaigns dominated the market: Orange, with its iconic "The future's bright, the future's Orange" advertising, and One-2-One, with its celebrity-driven

"Who would you like to have a one-to-one with?" Alongside these two high profile brands there were two others that struggled for awareness: one was Vodafone; the other, owned by the UK landline operator British Telecom, was Cellnet.

At the end of the 1990s, Vodafone transformed its fortunes by buying a string of companies (including Orange) and becoming the world's biggest mobile network operator. No such luck for Cellnet. In 2001, the struggling network was spun off and relaunched under the name O2 (pronounced Oh-Two). For some years it ran an unassuming advertising campaign that occasionally showed doves taking off and people dancing, but mostly featured blue water with bubbles bubbling through it and some lilting music in the background. The rather cryptic message at the end was "O2. See what you can do."

O2 spent a lot of money on this campaign, and although people were aware of their ads, virtually no one was able to recall what they were meant to be telling them about O2. Partly this was because the "See what you can do" message in the ads didn't really make a lot of sense to anyone, and partly because there were no dramatic price claims or deals or innovative new product features which might have been worth remembering. The fact is blue water and bubbles are hardly characteristics one might look for in a mobile phone.

So, by 2005, you might think you can guess where each of these brands stood in the UK? Here's the answer. One-2-One had been taken over by T-Mobile, and had 11.2 million UK customers. Acquisitive Vodafone had 14.8 million customers. Orange's famous advertising had secured it 14.9 million customers.

And what had O2's somewhat meaningless water and bubbles achieved for the company? Well, it had resulted in the dying network becoming the *UK's biggest phone company*, with 17 million customers. No, that's not a misprint. O2 had in 4 short years become market leader. More interestingly, it had achieved this success without undercutting other brands on price, without having any particular technical advantage, and without using any exceptional promotional activity. O2 seems to have achieved market leadership using little more than its blue bubbling advertising.

How could this have happened? How could advertising that communicated next to nothing have driven a brand to leadership of such a competitive market? As you read on you will find out, and you will also find out how many other companies have done the same. Because my theory is that the most successful advertising campaigns in the world are not those we love or those we hate, or those with messages that are new or interesting. They are those like O2 that are able to effortlessly slip things under our radar and influence our behavior without us ever really knowing that they have done so. And the way in which these apparently inoffensive ad campaigns work is by "seducing" our subconscious.

Unfortunately, just *how* advertising manages to seduce our subconscious isn't a simple story. It turns out it is able to influence us this way because we, as human beings, are peculiarly susceptible to certain types of communication. This susceptibility is a function of the way in which our minds have evolved, so to understand what is going on it is necessary to become acquainted with a lot of new ideas in psychology.

For this reason I've approached the subject rather as an engineer might. I've started by taking current models of advertising to pieces, and then I've rebuilt them in stages into a new Subconscious Seduction model. In the process I've used cognitive psychology, behavioral psychology, neurobiology, and philosophy as the building blocks. As I go along I've tried to illustrate each stage with case studies of advertising, and at various points I've also included diagrams of how the model is developing.

I apologize if you find this approach a little over-diligent, but I believe it is necessary. After all, many people have vested interests in proving the Subconscious Seduction model wrong: some have built their businesses on the old model, and others are just paranoid that advertising will be shown to be something sinister and underhand. But advertising isn't either of these; it's just a lot more complicated than any of us ever imagine it is.

The book is set out in five parts, and here is a brief description of each of them.

Part One: Taking Advertising Apart

Chapter 1 starts by describing the traditional persuasion model. It quickly becomes apparent that not even those who work in the advertising business are always aware of how advertising influences us. The most common view is that what it does is communicate some sort of persuasive information, which in turn enables us to go out and make a rational decision about what we want to buy.

Chapter 2 looks at alternative ideas, both from within the industry and from related fields such as psychology. The first of these was proposed by the psychologist Walter Dill Scott over 100 years ago, when print and outdoor advertising were the only media available. Scott, like me, saw advertising as able to subconsciously manipulate the mind of the consumer. Unfortunately, despite being lauded by many advertisers at the time, his ideas did not fit with those held by the people controlling the media. Bear in mind most of these media moguls were ex-salesmen, for whom the overt presentation of persuasive arguments was the watchword for success, so it perhaps isn't really surprising that Scott's revolutionary ideas were sidelined and forgotten.

It is a testimony to the conservatism of the ad industry that the second major assault on persuasion did not take place for over 60 years. This time it was another psychologist, Herb Krugman, and his target was TV advertising. Krugman simply couldn't understand how the trivial rubbish that made up most of the early TV commercials could persuade anyone to buy anything. He set about proving that most TV advertising was watched in a state of "low involvement" compared with print ads. His ideas were lent weight by the work of a leading statistician, Andrew Ehrenberg, who showed that it was highly unlikely that advertising changed anyone's attitudes, and therefore equally unlikely that it could be persuasive.

The industry had a huge problem accepting that we don't pay much attention to ads and they don't change our attitudes. So it isn't much of a surprise that the response to Krugman and Ehrenberg was, as with Scott, to express great interest in their ideas . . . and then politely ignore them.

But it seems to be an undeniable fact that we *don't* pay much attention to ads, and in Chapter 3 I start laying out the evidence that supports this assertion. It turns out that we probably spend more time avoiding advertising, especially TV advertising, than we do consuming it. And there are many good reasons why we should behave in this way. First, because we have been surrounded by advertising all our lives, it is no longer a novelty. Second, because everything is so competitive nowadays, we assume that mostly all advertisers will do is assert that their brand is better than all the rest. Third, because brands are *all* pretty good, it seems unlikely that much in the way of evidence will be presented to back up this assertion. In other words, we don't pay attention to advertising because we don't expect to learn anything particularly new and interesting from it, and we frankly have better things to do with our lives.

Of course, by ignoring advertising we assume that it will not have any effect on us. In the second part of the book I start to examine whether or not this is true.

Part Two: The Psychology of Communication

When it comes to the way in which we process communication, our minds turn out to make everything much more complicated than you might expect. Chapter 4 looks at how learning and attention interact when we are processing advertising. It becomes necessary to consider not just where we are directing our attention, but how much attention we are paying at any one time. I also discuss a memory system that enables us to learn even when we pay *no attention at all* to advertising; a mechanism known as Implicit Learning.

Chapter 5 looks at how our learning from communication interacts with our memory systems. Our explicit memory – the one we use to recall things – turns out to be really quite limited. That is why we find it hard to recall advertisements and easy to forget them. But we are also equipped with implicit memory, which is not only inexhaustible but extremely durable. Implicit memory is informed by Implicit Learning, and it stores pretty much *everything* we perceive. It is also able to connect these perceptions with semantic memory, where we store meaning. This is a critically important step in explaining how advertising processed at low or even zero levels of attention might be able to influence us.

Chapter 6 looks at a new way of categorizing learning from communication. I define three different types of mental activity: Perception, Conceptualization, and Analysis. These operate across our three types of learning: Active, Passive, and Implicit Learning. These definitions help us get a better understanding of how we process advertising and store what we process. The most important finding is that Implicit Learning is by far the most common way of processing advertising, Passive Learning is the next most common, and Active Learning happens rarely if at all. In this chapter I also discuss subliminal exposure, which has nothing at all to do with how advertising affects us, and the much more important subject of peripheral exposure, which has a *lot* to do with how advertising affects us.

Chapter 7 examines the problems that arise when advertisers try to get us to pay attention. One obstacle is that the more we attend to ads, the better we are able to "counter-argue" their messages, and the less convincing we start to find the claims they make. Another even more troublesome trait is that, in order to prevent our minds becoming too cluttered, we are equipped with a mechanism called Perceptual Filtering which enables us to ignore those elements we don't want to pay attention to. That of course means that if we don't think we are going to learn anything from an advertisement we can direct our minds to focus on the bits we enjoy and filter out the bits we don't (e.g., the message and the name of the brand being advertised).

But there are elements in advertising that elude these defense mechanisms, the most obvious being those connected with emotion. How we process emotion and indeed how our conscious and subconscious really work are the subjects of the third part of the book.

Part Three: Emotion and Consciousness

Until quite recently psychologists thought that emotions were a result of our thinking. In Chapter 8 I show that emotional processing, far from being the last thing we do, is the first. Indeed, it turns out that emotional processing is a function of an instinctive part of our brain that long pre-dates conscious thinking, and therefore *has* to operate automatically and subconsciously.

In order to understand this it becomes necessary to probe what we mean by our subconscious and what it does. This is dealt with in Chapter 9, and is possibly the most problematic idea you will encounter. Many of those who study consciousness now accept that everything we do with our mind is done at a subconscious level, and that "consciousness" is just an observer. So our conscious mind doesn't behave like a computer, more like a computer monitor. Our thinking goes on subconsciously, and a small part of it – effectively what our minds can cope with – is fed through to the monitor for us to look at. So when we seem to argue with ourselves, what we are "aware" of is our mind reporting an argument that happened subconsciously sometime earlier.

Spooky? Not really. I find this way of looking at ourselves is surprisingly liberating. It explains why we can do things so well without thinking about them – instinctively reaching out and catching a falling glass before it hits the ground, for example – and it explains why we perceive so much more than we think we do. But it also explains why there exists in us a huge vulnerability to certain types of communication, most notably advertising.

Chapter 10 looks at the interaction between attention and emotion, and explains why persuasion-based advertising models don't work. Advertisers think that their creativity makes us like ads more and pay more attention to them. What really happens turns out to be the opposite: the more advertisers attempt to subconsciously seduce us with creativity, the more we like it, the less we feel threatened by it, and the *less* attention we feel we need to pay to it. So the more creative advertising is, the less attention we pay, and the less well we recall the message it is trying to get over.

But the sting in the tail is that the less attention we pay, the *more* effective the subconscious seduction becomes. In other words, by paying less attention we effectively give advertisers permission to influence our subconscious.

Part Four: Decisions and Relationships

In order to understand exactly how our behavior is influenced by emotion in advertising we first need to understand how we make decisions. Chapter 11 examines in detail what psychologists now accept, which is that our emotions act as a gatekeeper for all our decisions. Indeed, the influence of our emotions is so powerful that we cannot make a decision unless our emotions concur with it. And if we don't have time to think about a decision, our emotions will effectively make it for us via our intuition. That, of course, means that emotion in advertising is able to influence our behavior far more than anyone ever thought.

There's more: in Chapter 12 we find that it is also emotion that underpins our relationships, through something known as metacommunication. It might surprise some of you to realize that we have relationships with lifeless entities such as brands, but we do; those who have witnessed the love and attention that some people lavish on their cars will know exactly what I am talking about.

Chapter 13 presents the complete Subconscious Seduction model of how advertising works. This chapter discusses some of the contextual influences that now direct our lives, and combines these with the psychologic learning in Parts Two to Four. I find there are two important ways in which advertising is able to influence our behavior at a subconscious level. The first of these is Subconscious Associative Conditioning. This occurs when something in an advertisement triggers an emotive reaction, and over time subconsciously transfers that emotive reaction to a brand. The second is Subconscious Relationship Manipulation. This occurs when the creativity in the advertisement subconsciously influences the way you feel about a brand. The model that emerges in this chapter is by now quite complex, but, as I said earlier, this is not a simple situation we are dealing with.

Part Five: A Fresh Look at Advertising

In the last section of the book I start to explore the implications of the Subconscious Seduction model. Chapter 14 gives you an idea of just how gullible we all are, and how easy it is for external stimuli of all sorts to influence us. For example, randomly nodding or shaking our heads while listening can change our opinions, and the simple act of filling in a questionnaire with a particular color pen can exert an influence on what we buy. This chapter also explains how we have, tucked away in our subconscious, far more knowledge about the *detail* of advertising than we would probably like to have. And, what is more, because it is in our subconscious, there is no way we can get it out.

Many of the examples dealt with up until now are from TV. Chapter 15 discusses how new media, most especially the internet, influences us. I also address what is perhaps the most subconsciously seductive of all media, the practice of paying to place products in TV programs.

All this invites us to ask if it is right that advertising should be allowed to have so much influence over us. This question is addressed in Chapter 16. It transpires that the question should be: "Is there anything we can do about how much influence advertising has on us?" And the answer is "very little." We can and do ban it for products that can harm us – although not quickly enough and not in enough countries – but the wider problem is that if we ban advertising from one media it simply pops up in another. And if we ban it altogether it might well pop up in places where it can't be monitored and controlled at all. So for the benefit of society, like alcohol, it is perhaps best to have it out in the open where we can keep an eye on it.

In Chapter 17 I explain how you can spot when you are being subconsciously seduced by advertising. In four case studies I show how brands on both sides of the Atlantic have become superbrands using advertising that carries hidden messages. Nothing especially sinister, I hasten to add: just extremely clever.

Finally, I conclude by asking where all this takes us. It won't surprise you to learn that I have a special concern about what Subconscious Seduction might be doing to our children. But I also wonder why this extraordinarily powerful mechanism is not more widely used in public broadcast advertising, where it would be of far more benefit to us.

So I invite you to begin this journey through advertising. I suspect that once you have completed it you will be astonished by how much advertising affects your everyday behavior. And perhaps even more astonished by how little you realized this was going on.

1
Taking Advertising Apart

1

The Persuasion Model

"...there are no hidden persuaders. Advertising works openly, in the bare and pitiless sunlight."

Rosser Reeves
Reality in Advertising (1961)

All of us think we know how advertising works. It's nothing very clever or special; in fact, it's dead simple. Personally, I'm certain this is why we get so angry when we hear about admen earning fat salaries and forever having expensive lunches. What they do, we think, is money for old rope.

Advertising mostly starts with a something some company wants to persuade us to buy. I say "mostly," because occasionally we see governments advertising things they want us to *do*, but for the purposes of this book I'm going to stick to advertising for branded products or services that companies want to sell us.

Advertising like this, for commercial brands, dates back at least 2500 years (Fletcher 1999: 11). But the idea that it can be treated as part of a systematic sales activity is only about 100 years old. We know this because of St Elmo Lewis, a salesman for the National Cash Register Company. Right at the end of the nineteenth century Mr Lewis invented a four-step formula for doorstep selling:

- Get *Attention,*
- Provoke *Interest*
- Create *Desire*
- Finally, get *Action* by closing the sale.

Seducing the Subconscious: The Psychology of Emotional Influence in Advertising, First Edition. Robert Heath.
© 2012 Robert Heath. Published 2012 by John Wiley & Sons, Ltd.

Universally known by the acronym AIDA (Attention, Interest, Desire, Action), this led to the first formal model of advertising ever adopted (Barry & Howard 1990). Many advertisers nowadays still think this is how advertising works.

So, back to this thing the company wants to sell. The first step in the process is to try to think of some sort of message or proposition that will change our beliefs about their product and persuade us to buy it. That message needs to be something that will make us think their product works better than the competitors, or is better value, or is newer or smarter or sexier, etc. I'm sure you get the picture. The company usually devises this message in conjunction with the ad agency. Once everyone is happy that the message encapsulates all the best things they have to say about the product, they go to a couple of even more important people in the ad agency called the "creative" team (they must be important because, rather as in the popular US TV series *Mad Men*, they are paid an awful lot of money for mostly seeming to sit around and do very little).

The creative team then dreams up some daft creative idea to justify the ad agency charging the client lots of money. (I hope you'll excuse my cynicism, but I did work in advertising for a *very* long time.) Often this creative idea seems to have nothing whatsoever to do with what is being advertised, and sometimes it doesn't have much connection with the message the company wants to get over either. Anyway, once everyone is happy with the creative idea they then stick the message onto the end of it and go and make the ad. Next they put it on TV or in a newspaper or onto some other media . . . and sit back and wait for results. "Simples," as the meerkat would say.

This process is so unexceptional you might wonder why it's worth me writing a whole book about it. After all, Claude Hopkins, one of the first admen, did that back in 1923. Mr Hopkins averred then that "Advertising, once a gamble, has thus become . . . one of the safest of business ventures" (Hopkins 1998). Selling through advertising was, for Hopkins, a rational, information-based process, with no room for humor or eccentricity.

But, like all business ventures, as soon as you invent something someone comes along and tries to measure it. In this case the someone was Daniel Starch, and the measurement he introduced was to show people a copy of the newspaper with the ad in it, ask if they had read the ad, and then ask what they had "noted" about it. Starch's "Reading and Noting" system meant that getting us to pay attention to advertising became that much more important.

To solve this problem of lack of attention, media owners back in the 1920s decided to employ experts to write advertisements for their clients. Again, this wasn't exactly a new idea. Take for example, this quote from Richard Addison writing in the *Tatler*:

> The great Art of writing Advertisements is the finding out of a proper Method to catch the Reader's Eye, without which a good thing may pass over unobserved. (Fletcher 1999: 16)

You may be surprised to learn that Addison wrote this not in 1920s, nor indeed in the 1820s, but in 1710. Three centuries ago. Only a little later, in 1759, the famous Samuel Johnson perceptively wrote:

> Advertisements are now so numerous that they are very negligently perused, and it therefore becomes necessary to gain attention by a magnificence of promises, and by eloquence sometimes sublime, sometimes pathetic. (Fletcher 1999: 17)

Now you can see what the role of those creative people who sit around all day seeming to do very little is. "Negligently perusing" (i.e., not paying much attention to) ads has always been seen as the big problem for advertisers, and "eloquence" (i.e., the sort of imaginative stuff that is produced by the creative team) is supposedly the solution.

Of course, it was never seen as that much of a problem when advertising was restricted to newspapers. What changed everything was the arrival of commercial television in the USA in the mid 1950s. Suddenly advertising budgets were big business, and the ad agencies that designed and produced the ads likewise became big business. Commercial TV, by effectively bringing the cinema into our living rooms, revolutionized the creative opportunities open to these ad agencies. And getting people to pay attention suddenly became the focus of *everyone's* attention.

Well, it had to. Commercial TV was hugely expensive, and it only existed because of the revenue it earned from advertising, so it simply had to offer something a bit special. What it did offer was the chance for the message to be accompanied by music and movement and drama and celebrity, all those things we take for granted these days. The early viewers of TV clustered around their sets with rapt attention, much as children who have never watched TV before do now. TV advertising was an almost overnight success, and those companies who invested in it early found their share-of-market rocketing. Of course, our infatuation with the small screen didn't last long, and that just made the role of creativity even more important.

But the overnight success of TV advertising meant it started to attract the attention of all sorts of different groups who wanted to get on the bandwagon. Among them were scientists and psychologists who thought they could make advertising significantly more persuasive by targeting it at our aspirations. They in turn excited the interest of the general public, who were concerned not with the money that could be made out of TV advertising, but with the ethics of what it might be doing to us. A confrontation became inevitable.

What sparked off this confrontation was a group known as "motivational researchers," chief of which was the psychologist Ernest Dichter. Motivational researchers attempted to analyze consumer behavior by tapping into areas such as symbol and metaphor and the Freudian unconscious. Typical of their output was a book published by the research director of the *Chicago Tribune*, Pierre Martineau in 1957. Martineau opened up the opportunity for advertisers to persuade people to buy their products not just by satisfying evident practical needs, but also by exploiting latent and incipient emotional needs – needs that in many cases people were not even aware they had.

The activities of the motivational researchers prompted publication of a book by Vance Packard, a journalist. Packard's book, *The Hidden Persuaders*, became an instant bestseller and set a hare running which is still running to this day. In the opening paragraph he wrote:

> This book is an attempt to explore a strange and rather exotic new area of modern life. It is about the way many of us are being influenced and manipulated – far more than we realize – in the patterns of our daily life. Typically, these efforts take place beneath our level of awareness; so that the appeals which move us are often, in a sense, "hidden." (Packard 1957: 11)

Packard's thesis was that US advertisers were shamelessly exploiting the techniques identified by Martineau to sell us products we didn't really want. The "motivational research" with which they were probing our minds was, according to Packard, "antihumanistic": in effect, an affront to our rights as human beings.

Packard identified Martineau and Dichter as being the leading proponents of this motivational research, but implicated the entire ad industry in this supposed conspiracy to manipulate us. The problem he identified is summarized by his quotation of David Ogilvy:

> I am astonished to find how many advertising men ... believe that women can be persuaded by logic and argument to buy one brand in preference to another, even when the two brands are technically identical. The greater the similarity between products, the less part reason plays in brand selection. (Packard 1957: 25)

Packard felt that manipulating the customer's emotions was taking unfair advantage of them. But, curiously, it was not this that caused his book to have such impact. In his fourth chapter Packard referred to research to find out why a man repeatedly chose a certain make of car, and how under hypnosis he "was able to repeat word for word an ad he had read more than twenty years before" (Packard 1957: 41). Then, having raised our concerns about how vulnerable we are both to advertising and to mind-probing techniques such as hypnotism, he describes an experiment reported in the London *Sunday Times*. This experiment apparently took place in a New Jersey cinema and comprised pictures of ice cream being shown at a "sub-threshold" level – below the level of conscious perception. The result was a "clear and unaccountable boost in ice cream sales" (Packard 1957: 42). It was the first ever widely reported case of subliminal advertising.

We know now that the increase in ice cream sales was due to exceptionally hot weather. We also know that Packard's report was confused with a subsequent experiment set up in the same year by James Vickery, in which the phrases "Drink Coke" and "Hungry? Eat Popcorn" were exposed at 0.3 milliseconds, and supposedly increased consumption of these items by 18% and 59%, respectively.

Vickery later admitted this was a hoax publicity stunt for his new Subliminal Projection Company (Boese 2002). We also know from numerous experiments that subliminal advertising – messages repeatedly exposed at a frequency below around 40 milliseconds – does not have any powerful enduring effect on our behavior and certainly is not able to exert a long-term influence on our choice of brands. But, as I said earlier, the hare had been set running, and it still runs today. Despite subliminal advertising being banned in the UK and USA from 1958, as recently as the 2000 US presidential election the newspapers were filled with a story concerning a TV ad aimed at the Democratic Party candidate (Al Gore) by the Republican Party candidate (George W. Bush), in which the word "rat" had supposedly been inserted subliminally (Heath 2001: 11).

Going back to 1957, the effect of Packard's book on the advertising industry was galvanic. It was a time when conspiracy theories concerning com-
munism were rife, and admen not surprisingly made strenuous attempts to
deny what Packard had supposedly revealed. Rosser Reeves, chairman of the
Ted Bates ad agency and probably America's most influential admen of this
era, made his views clear in his book *Reality in Advertising*. In a chapter entitled "The Freudian Hoax" he wrote (in capitals, to emphasize the point):

THERE ARE NO HIDDEN PERSUADERS. ADVERTISING WORKS
OPENLY, IN THE BARE AND PITILESS SUNLIGHT. (Reeves 1961: 121)

Reeves was a great believer in honesty in advertising, and his tirade
is symptomatic of a widespread belief amongst admen that all they were
doing was pursuing the honest trade of conveying persuasive messages to
the general public, and that there was nothing whatsoever underhand about
their business. As recently as 1999 a leading practitioner wrote in *Advertising
Age* that advertising was nothing more than "one-way communication:
creating and sending messages" (Duncan & Moriarty 1999: 44). What could
possibly be wrong with that?

Of course, creating and sending messages is one thing. In the same way
that advertisers up until the end of the 1950s were fixated by getting us to
pay attention, advertisers from the 1960s onwards were equally fixated by
another task. Getting us to *remember* what we paid attention to.

Reeves was well aware of the importance of this. In his book he stated
"The consumer tends to remember just one thing from an advertisement –
one strong claim, or one strong concept" (Reeves 1961: 34). To solve this
problem he invented the USP (Unique Selling Promise) the "one thing that
would make people buy your product," and the USP is still referred to in
the manuals of nearly all leading marketing companies. But, although the
USP remains in common parlance, Rosser Reeves' name nowadays is almost
unknown. A far better-known name is that of Gordon Brown.

Some say Gordon Brown has been the most influential figure in the whole
history of advertising. That's not because he made ads, or wrote ads, or because he ran an advertising agency, but because he was the co-founder of the
UK research company Millward Brown. And Millward Brown's ad tracking
system was responsible for popularizing the use of brand name prompted
ad awareness as a research tool for measuring advertising effectiveness all
over the world.

How did this come about? Well, Gordon Brown realized that genuine
spontaneous recall of advertising was of little value in a world in which

advertising was becoming commonplace. Aside from anything else, people were being exposed to so many ads that they were finding it harder and harder to recall them. So Brown devised a more sensitive question for ascertaining recall: "We show a list of brands and ask 'which of these brands ... have you seen advertised on television recently?'" (Brown 1985: 57). This measure of brand name prompted ad awareness was coupled with a subsequent question in which people were asked what "details" they could recall about the ad. Together, these two measures encouraged a rather simplistic view of advertising effectiveness to develop. For example, Brown describes an ad that failed to achieve high recall as "a disaster" and one that did achieve high recall "a triumph" (Brown 1985: 57). The result, of course, was that creativity, originally invented in order to make us pay attention to advertising, became tasked also with making us recall both the message and ideally some part of the advertising that delivered it.

So that is the persuasion model. According to most people in the industry, advertising is about communicating simple rationally persuasive messages that change our beliefs and make us buy the product. Creativity is about getting us to attend to these messages, because high attention results in higher recall. Creativity is also about putting something clever or unusual in the ad, because that will increase the chances of some part of the ad being recalled as well. There is no deception, no clever trickery, and no manipulation. Everything is open and above board.

If this is the case – that all advertising is trying to do it to deliver a simple persuasive message, and all creativity is trying to do is make us pay attention and recall that message – then we, the general public, can rest easy in our beds, because if we forget or choose to ignore the advertising message, then the advertising should have no effect on us.

But I believe this persuasion model is misleading. I'm not saying that advertising can't or doesn't persuade us, because occasionally it does. But if this really is all advertising does then the "message-less" O2 advertising would have been a total flop. And so would the advertising in the following case study for the launch of the Renault Clio.

Renault Clio Case Study

Back in 1992 the UK had a recession caused by inflation and currency problems. It so happened that the car manufacturer Renault had scheduled exactly this time to launch its new flagship small car, the Clio. What Renault believed made the Clio special was that it combined the sort of luxury finish you get in a big car with the practical maneuverability you get in a small car. Nothing very new or exciting in that, but it was the best they could come up with.

Renault appointed their long-term ad agency, Publicis, to think up some advertising for this new car. Publicis came up with a wacky creative idea featuring a couple of French aristocrats – a father and daughter – driving around the countryside flirting with their lovers. Apparently Renault hated this stereotypical portrayal of the French. At the time most people in the UK thought the French drove dangerously, so UK car ads tended not to be set in France. Especially you didn't show French aristocrats, when the car was clearly a low price model targeted at ordinary members of the general public. So Renault instructed Publicis to make an ad that was very simple and told people that the Renault Clio was small and practical and luxurious.

I believe this ad ran for about 3 months, and sales of the car were disastrous. The story goes that Renault decided that because of the recession they were never going to sell many Clios anyway, so Publicis might just as well make their original ad and run that.

This ad opened with the two French aristos sitting in the sun on deckchairs outside their chateau. The father (Papa) appears to doze off, and his pretty young daughter (Nicole), once she is satisfied he is asleep, sneaks off, gets into her Renault Clio (watched indulgently by the chauffeur), and whizzes off to meet her boyfriend. But Papa is not asleep. As soon as he sees his daughter drive off he summons the chauffeur to bring his own Renault Clio, and then (to the evident annoyance of the chauffeur who obviously thinks he should be driving him) drives off himself to meet his own lover, bearing a beautiful bunch of red roses.

While this is happening a reassuringly mellow male voice-over tells us: "You may be looking for a car that's small and practical, but you still want a car that feels luxurious. Well now you've found it. Because while the Clio is certainly small, it's perfectly formed."

We cut to Nicole returning some time later to find Papa supposedly still asleep. She sits down saying innocently "Papa?" to which Papa replies equally innocently "Nicole?" Finally, we cut to the car and the male voice simply says "The new Renault Clio."

A sweet and rather silly ad, you might say. Let's analyze it according to the traditional ad industry persuasion model. The message (small car practicality with big car luxury) is clearly explained in the voice-over, and is nicely illustrated by having both Papa and Nicole evidently enjoying driving their cars. The inclusion of the romantic liaisons and the flirting gets the viewer's attention, and if we pay attention to things, we supposedly remember them better. So the creative idea should mean the message is well recalled. Obvious, when you think about it.

The Renault Clio launch was carefully monitored, as was the performance of the advertising. Once the new advertising kicked in the launch became a spectacular success. In the first year alone the Clio exceeded its ambitious sales targets by 32%, and achieved a 7% share of the small car market. In a comprehensive review of the launch, the brand's success was directly attributed to the advertising, which ran for another 6 years and was calculated to have earned Renault some £59 million in additional revenue over this period (Chandy & Thursby Pelham 1993). In fact, the Clio is regarded by the UK motor trade as being the most successful small car launch *ever* in the UK, despite there being a recession. And everyone remembered the advertising; in fact, at the time, people used to comment on how frequently it was on air and how annoying it was.

The only problem is this. When the researchers asked people what they could recall about the advertising, *nobody* could recall the supposedly persuasive message about "small car practicality and big car luxury." Nor did anyone believe that the Clio possessed these attributes. The only thing anyone could remember about the advertising was Papa and Nicole and their flirting.

So how is it that the launch was such a success, when no one could recall the message? Evidently the idea that advertising is just about persuasive message transmission isn't the full story. There must be something else going on.

2

Alternative Ideas

"Our minds are constantly subjected to influences of which we have no knowledge."

Walter Dill Scott
The Psychology of Advertising in Theory and Practice (1903: 367)

As we saw in the last chapter, maintaining the myth that advertising is simply persuasive message communication is the ambition of many who work in advertising and marketing. But alongside the majority were a few pioneers who believed otherwise. One of these pioneers was Walter Dill Scott, the man who is credited with having written "the first serious academic study of how advertising works" (Feldwick 2009: 136).

Walter Dill Scott

The place is the Agate Club in Chicago, a prestigious club for businessmen, and the year is 1901. Walter Dill Scott, Assistant Professor of Psychology at North Western University, has been invited to address a group of eminent businessmen connected with the fast-expanding advertising industry. He would almost certainly have included the above extract from his forthcoming book *The Psychology of Advertising in Theory and Practice* (Scott 1903) in what he said.

From the reports of the meeting the businessmen were delighted with what Scott told them. But it was the turn of the century, and the ad industry was frankly still in its infancy. It was not for another 11 years that a version

Seducing the Subconscious: The Psychology of Emotional Influence in Advertising, First Edition. Robert Heath.
© 2012 Robert Heath. Published 2012 by John Wiley & Sons, Ltd.

of the AIDA model would exert its stranglehold on advertising thinking, so possibly these representatives of the embryonic industry were rather more open-minded than their successors.

Scott's view of advertising was that it was a wayward yet seductive sales tool. Extracts of what he said were recorded in a later article by him in the *Atlantic Magazine*. They include this description:

> One man has roughly estimated that seventy-five per cent of all advertisements do not pay; yet the other twenty-five per cent pay so well that there is scarcely a business man who is willing to stand idly by and allow his competitors to do the advertising. (Scott 1904)

Note that advertising was not seen as a marketing tool at this time. The word "marketing" would not be invented for another 5 years, and when it was, it was as an economic function designed to help farmers target their produce more effectively. It certainly had nothing to do with esoteric sales activities such as advertising.

What singles out Scott from everyone else is that he clearly understood that advertising was "manipulating" the minds of consumers. Later in his speech he stated:

> As advertisers, all your efforts have been to produce certain effects on the minds of possible customers. Psychology is, broadly speaking, the science of the mind. Art is the doing and science is the understanding how to do, or the explanation of what has been done. If we are able to find and to express the psychological laws upon which the art of advertising is based, we shall have made a distinct advance, for we shall have added the science to the art of advertising. (Scott 1904)

In the same article Scott predicted that "successful advertisers will be ... termed psychological advertisers." He particularly identified how advertising could influence one subconsciously through what he called "suggestion." In his book he told the story of how a tailor was conducting what he describes as a "vigorous" advertising campaign in Chicago. "I did not suppose that his advertising was having any influence on me," he wrote, but "Some months after the advertising campaign had begun I went into the tailor's shop and ordered a suit." Scott then got into conversation with the owner, who asked him if a friend had recommended the shop to him, and he replied that this was the case. It was only afterwards, when he could not recall which friend might have made the recommendation, that he realised he had been influenced by the advertising without his knowledge:

> I had seen (the tailor's) advertisements for months and from them had formed an idea of the shop. Later, I forgot where I had received my information and assumed that I had received it from a friend. (Scott 1903: 176)

Interestingly, he observes that: "I doubt very much if I ever read any of the advertisements further than the display copy" (what we nowadays call the headline). So just the brief copy contained in the headline had been sufficient to cause him to go into the shop and buy his suit.

Later in the same book, in a chapter entitled "The unconscious influence in street railway advertising," Scott makes perhaps his most famous observation:

> One young lady asserted that she had never looked at any of the cards in the cars in which she had been riding for years. When questioned further, it appeared that she knew by heart every advertisement appearing on the line ... and that the goods advertised had won her highest esteem. She was not aware of the fact that she had been studying the advertisements, and flatly resented the suggestion that she had been influenced by them. (Scott 1903: 370)

The importance of this quote is that it identifies, presumably deliberately, that advertising can affect many people without them really being aware of it having done so. Possibly that wasn't much of a surprise back in 1903. After all, advertising was mostly restricted to newspapers, hoardings, and ads in tramcars, and I'm sure that these were paid the same sort of scant attention that print ads are nowadays.

As it turned out, in spite of the enthusiastic response Scott received in the Agate Club, the ad industry generally ignored Scott's fascinating speculation about the inadvertent effects of advertising. Instead, they decided in favor of the view of John E. Kennedy, that advertising was "salesmanship in print" (Gunther 1960: 58). And a few years later, in 1910, the industry adopted its own version of the AIDA model, one with the acronym AICA, standing for Attention, Interest, Conviction, and Action (Printers Ink 1910).

The contrast between Scott's observations about the possible subconscious effect of advertising, and AICA's uncompromising categorization of advertising as something that needed to get attention and persuade, could not have been greater. But back in 1910 the ad industry was run largely by ex-sales managers for whom inattention on behalf of the customer was frankly just another word for failure. The nervousness of the industry is illustrated by the writings of Claude Hopkins, head of Lord & Thomas, then the world's most successful ad agency. Hopkins, in an attempt to ape the publication of Fredrick Taylor's best-selling 1917 book *Scientific Management*, published a book called *Scientific Advertising* in 1923. Hopkins' beliefs were that "Advertising is salesmanship ... Fine writing is a distinct disadvantage ... No one reads ads for amusement ... Consider (readers) as prospects standing before you, seeking for information. Give them enough to get action" (Hopkins 1923: 220–222). In other words, when writing an ad, behave exactly as if you were a door-to-door salesman.

So Scott's ideas were forgotten, and attention took center stage for the best part of 60 years, becoming even more important with the arrival of commercial television advertising (Barry & Howard 1990). Of course, once advertising became a national phenomenon in the USA, it wasn't long before cracks started to appear in the neat rational "salesman" explanation of how advertising worked.

One of the first of these cracks appeared in 1962, in the form of an article in the *Journal of Advertising*. The editorial announcing it stated: "[John] Maloney presents surprising evidence against the conventional view that an advertisement must be believed before it can influence attitudes or behavior" (Maloney 1962: 2). This is indeed what Maloney, a researcher with Leo Burnett, found, and he had evidence to back up his assertion.

It is worth at this point explaining the difference between attitudes and beliefs. Beliefs arise from things we are told about products and services, and so are attributes we ascribe to those products and services. Thus, we may be led to believe by advertising that a Ferrari sports car can do 163 miles per hour, or that Bold washing powder washes whiter than others.

The problem here is that we don't buy anything because of beliefs, because beliefs don't satisfy our needs. We don't buy a Ferrari because it does 163 miles per hour, we buy it because we need a car that is exciting and will impress our girlfriend or our neighbors. And we don't buy Bold because it washes whiter than others; we buy it because we need our clothes to be seen to be clean. These personalized ideas that relate to our wants and needs are attitudes. The important bit to remember is that advertising doesn't affect us by changing beliefs; it only affects us if it changes our attitudes.

So what Maloney was finding was that people's attitudes could be changed by beliefs, even if they didn't believe them. Just think of the implications. For advertising to work without being believed sounds innocent enough;

but if people didn't have to believe what advertising told them in order for it to be effective, then the "conviction" part of the AICA model had to be wrong? And if conviction was wrong, AICA was wrong, and advertising had to be something more than simply "salesmanship."

Two years after Maloney's article, Jack Haskins presented some more controversial evidence of flaws in the idea that advertising was salesmanship. Haskins, the research manager at Ford, discovered that "factual–rational–logical" messages were *less* effective at changing attitudes than emotional or non-factual messages. He also found that "recall and retention measures seem, at best, irrelevant to . . . the changing of attitudes and behavior" (Haskins 1964: 7). In other words, rational messages didn't work very well on their own, and remembering what advertising said didn't really matter much. A bit like saying "what the salesman says is irrelevant, it's how he looks that counts." This, as we shall see, is a lot nearer the truth than anyone ever thought in those days.

Nether Maloney nor Haskins had much success in challenging the attention-driven sales model of advertising, but 3 years later a more serious assault started. This time it was from another psychologist, Herbert Krugman.

Herbert Krugman

Herb Krugman started his career in the psychology branch of the US Army Air Force and spent time on the teaching faculties of Yale, Princeton and Columbia Universities. Unlike Scott, he had worked as an advertising researcher in the ad agency Ted Bates, and also as a market researcher for the research company Marplan. Krugman had built his reputation in public opinion research, and it was almost certainly his hands-on relationship with real people that enabled him to drop his first bombshell. In 1965, writing for the journal *Public Opinion Quarterly*, he questioned the effectiveness of mass media, describing the impact of television advertising as "limited," and suggesting that "Television is a medium of low involvement compared with print." (Krugman 1971: 3).

You can imagine the reaction of the advertising barons of Madison Avenue. This one sentence, suggesting as it did that television as a medium was defective compared with its arch rival, print, must have appeared to them to be the equivalent of a maniac holding a sharpened knife to the throat of the golden goose. But other psychologists shared Krugman's feeling that responses to television advertising were not what you would expect from traditional persuasive communication. In the first place, when people were asked about the influence of TV advertising, they said (rather like Walter Dill Scott's "young lady") that they "rarely [felt] converted or persuaded" (Krugman 1965: 350). And, in the second place, the very nature of TV advertising content just seemed too trivial and silly to fit in with what was generally seen as persuasive communication. As Krugman put it:

> Does this suggest that if television bombards us with enough trivia about a product we may be persuaded to believe it? On the contrary, it suggests that persuasion as such . . . is not involved at all and it is a mistake to look for it . . . as a test of advertising's impact. (Krugman 1965: 353)

This article of Krugman's did not excite that much attention amongst the advertising community. After all, he was just a market researcher. But 2 years later Krugman became manager of corporate public opinion at the General Electric Company, the USA's biggest advertiser. Now he worked for a client this meant his ideas had to be taken more seriously.

Krugman's next step was to embark on a series of laboratory experiments into the processes of "looking and thinking and attention and relaxation." His initial work was carried out using eye movement recording to measure the amount each ad was scanned, the idea being that more scanning equates to more active learning. But he at once encountered a paradox: it was true that on an individual basis the respondents who scanned more recalled more, but on a *sample* basis it was the ads that were scanned *less* that were better recalled (Krugman 1968).

To find an explanation for this, Krugman turned to the writings of the celebrated Harvard psychologist, William James (James 1890). James defined two types of attention: voluntary and involuntary. He maintained that voluntary attention could not be sustained for more than a few seconds at a time, and that high levels of attention sustained for longer than this were "a repetition of successive efforts which bring the topic back to mind." Krugman's experiments suggested that people might actually absorb more from ads that encouraged them to watch in a relaxed, passive state-of-mind (involuntary attention) than from ads that attempted to excite them and make them watch in an active state-of-mind (repeated voluntary attention). This was in line with the findings of a 1964 experiment by Festinger and Macoby. Festinger and Macoby found that if a message in a TV advertisement was played on audio accompanied by an unrelated video, then students learned it *better* than if it was played accompanied by a video relevant to the message (Festinger & Macoby 1964).

According to Krugman, "Apparently, the distraction of watching something unrelated to the audio message lowered whatever resistance there might have been to the message" (Krugman 1965: 352). In order to investigate this further, Krugman set up an experiment in 1969 in conjunction with the Neuropsychological Laboratory of New York. Its objective was to investigate the difference between the way that the brain deals with TV advertising and press advertising. It is revealing of the attitudes of the ad industry at the time that this was only the second of Krugman's articles to find its way into an advertising research journal (Krugman 1971).

Essentially, what Krugman did was to connect a subject to an electroencephalograph, or EEG machine, and measure the type of brain waves emitted while they were reading a magazine and being shown some TV advertising. He divided the brain waves into three categories: Alpha waves, which indicate relaxation; "fast" (Beta) waves, which indicate alertness, activity and arousal; and "slow" (Delta and Theta) waves, which indicate boredom. Krugman assumed that the difference between emissions of "slow" and "fast" brain waves would signify the level of interest that the subject had in the media being exposed to her. The more fast waves, the more active and attentive was the processing; the more slow waves, the more passive and inattentive was the processing.

The subject used in the experiment was a 23-year-old female secretary. After allowing her to read some magazines, Krugman exposed her to three TV ads, all the time measuring her brain wave emissions. He found little change in the Alpha waves, indicating that the subject was generally relaxed throughout the test. But he did find a dramatic difference in the slow and fast waves emitted during exposure to the two different media. While the magazine was being read, the proportion of fast to slow waves was about 4 : 1, indicating that the subject was alert and interested. But during the TV commercials the proportions were almost equal, suggesting that the subject's level of alertness was far lower than for the magazines. This was excellent support for his view that TV is indeed a medium of low involvement compared with print.

Krugman's experiment had a number of glaring methodologic flaws. First, there was only one subject involved. Second, EEG only measures activity in the neocortex, so any neural activity taking place deeper in the brain will not be registered. Third, the context of the brain wave measurement was skewed: measurement of print advertising covered reading of the whole magazine, not just the ads, whereas the TV commercials were shown in isolation from any programming. Fourth, the subject was sitting in a laboratory.

As I said earlier, advertisers didn't much like Krugman's ideas, and they didn't believe much of what he found in this experiment either. But I have personally repeated Krugman's experiment using a number of subjects, a more accurate measure of attention, a balanced and more representative context, and a more comfortable environment, and the results were exactly the same (Heath 2009). TV is indeed a medium of lower involvement than print.

Krugman's assertion was a categoric refutation of the received wisdom amongst advertisers of the day, which was that TV watching was a high attention activity, certainly higher than reading a print ad. After all, two senses are involved in TV watching – sight and sound – rather than just one, so surely there is twice as much going on to attract the viewer's attention? But Krugman's findings do make common sense. It is relatively easy to pay attention when you are reading text, because you have control of the time you apply to the task – you can scan a page, paying more attention to the parts you are interested in, and less attention to parts you are not interested in. However, with television, the imparting of information depends entirely upon the way in which the advertisement is made. You have no control over it and (unless you have seen the ad before) no real idea of how interested you are likely to be in it. So television becomes a holistic experience: you cannot "scan" the data selectively, and it is therefore quite easy to believe, as James predicted in 1890, that one might slip into a passive, lower attentive state.

The fact that TV was a low involvement medium was not the only dramatic finding from Krugman's experiment. The accepted theory of the day was that interest in TV ads grew with each exposure: the first exposure might be one in which little attention was paid, but once the ad had been seen it was easier for the viewer to engage with the ad and pay attention. To test this hypothesis Krugman played three ads to his subject three times. What he found in every case was that brain wave activity *fell* with each exposure. In other words, far from paying *more* attention on repeat viewing, the subject paid *less*. What is more, this finding seemed to be true regardless of how important the category was to the respondent. Again, this experiment has been repeated, and Krugman's findings have been validated (Hutton *et al.* 2006).

So what Krugman was finding was that TV advertising was low attention, and that attention diminished with repeat viewing. Interestingly, he did not see this as a shortcoming of television advertising but as a potential strength. He deduced that learning was taking place, but not learning in the traditional sense.

> Our initial EEG data [suggest] . . . television does not appear to be communication as we have known it. Our subject was working to learn something from a print ad, but was passive about television. She was no more trying to learn something from television than she would be trying to learn something from a park landscape while resting on a park bench. Yet television is communication.
>
> What shall we say of it, a communication medium that may effortlessly transmit into storage huge quantities of information not thought about at the time of exposure, but much of it capable of later activation? (Krugman 1971: 8)

Nor did he see in his results a suggestion that this "different" type of learning used in television communication was less effective than press.

> As to the question "Which is better?" we are handicapped by our greater familiarity with active and involved types of learning. Our understanding of how passive learning takes place is still deficient and we are not yet sure how to measure its effectiveness in a fair manner.
>
> Although further work with brain waves is indicated, it should be stressed that there is no evidence or speculative inference here to suggest either print or television is "better" than the other, or that fast or slow brain waves are better than the other. Instead, we have a very great need to understand the differences better and perhaps especially to understand better the significance of slow brain waves. (Krugman 1971: 9)

Krugman was primarily a psychologist and researcher and, perhaps because of this, he never sought to design a model that would help advertisers to exploit what he called low involvement. But he gave plenty of clues as to what such a model should be based on. For a start, he discarded the idea that it should be based on purely verbal concepts. The conventional model, he said is the "verbal, look-before-you-leap, reasonable, or 'rational' model. . . . The future of the low-involvement theory is in the non-verbal area" (Krugman 1977: 8). He also understood the importance of repeated exposure: "The theory of low involvement asserts that repetition of exposure has an effect which is not readily apparent until a behavioural trigger comes along" (Krugman 1977: 9). Finally, he understood the critical importance of distinguishing between what he called exposure and perception:

> It might be helpful to first look at two related concepts to look and to see. These two variables permit a fourfold classification – i.e. one can look and see, look but not see, neither look nor see and, perhaps, see without looking.
>
> Seeing without looking involves the two phenomena of peripheral vision and conscious vision ... looking at an object can only be accomplished within a three-degree arc ... You are not especially conscious of that which is peripherally seen. You don't know that you have seen. Later you may deny having seen. Much of what people call subliminal perception is merely peripheral seeing, i.e. seeing without looking at, without being aware that seeing has occurred. (Krugman 1977: 10)

Krugman's ability to conceptualize these ideas so far in advance of others is extraordinary. As we will see in Chapter 6, his notion that you could be influenced by advertising exposed peripherally and not actively processed would not be validated for another 20 years. And his foresightedness went beyond even the realm of processing advertising into the area of decision-making. In his first publication in 1965, he identified the lack of evidence of advertising changing attitudes as being the one major weakness in convincing people of the efficacy of the medium:

> The economic impact of TV advertising is substantial and documented. . . . Only the lack of specific case histories relating advertising to attitudes to sales keeps researchers from concluding that the commercial use of the medium is a success. We are faced with the odd situation of knowing that advertising works but being unable to say much about why. (Krugman 1965: 351)

Then later he suggested what the editor called in his introduction to the article an "arresting" thesis:

> as trivia is repeatedly learned and repeatedly forgotten and then repeatedly learned a little more, it is probable that two things will happen: 1) . . . "over-learning" will move some information . . . into long term memory systems, and 2) we will permit significant alterations in the structure of our perception of a brand or product [that] fall short of persuasion or attitude change. (Krugman 1965: 353)

In effect what he was suggesting was that advertising worked using some kind of "sleeper" effect. Here's how he sums up his thesis:

> I have tried to say that the public lets down its guard to the repetitive commercial use of the television medium and that it easily changes its ways of perceiving products and brands and its purchasing behavior without thinking very much about it at the time of TV exposure or at any time prior to purchase, and without up to then changing verbalised attitudes. (Krugman 1965: 354)

As I said earlier, hidden away as it was in the pages of *Public Opinion Quarterly*, it was easy for the ad industry to quietly ignore Krugman's fascinating ideas. But in the UK there was another person working on this issue, and finding hard evidence which proved that the persuasion model was flawed. This person was Andrew Ehrenberg.

Andrew Ehrenberg

Andrew Ehrenberg was trained in mathematical statistics, and had been working on consumer panel data. This panel data measured what people claimed to buy, and also recorded what they actually bought. Ehrenberg was finding it very difficult to reconcile these two measures which should, in an ideal world, have been identical.

At the time Ehrenberg was not much interested in advertising, and claimed he didn't really start taking the subject seriously until 1970, when he was appointed by London Business School as Professor of Marketing and Communication, despite in his own words never having read anything on either subject (Ehrenberg 2004). But in 1974 he produced a paper which, even if it didn't overturn the ad industry boat, certainly rocked it quite seriously.

Ehrenberg, like Krugman, believed that advertising was able to work without changing attitudes. His view was that the consumer had extensive experience and in most cases already had extensive knowledge and entrenched attitudes about most of the products that were available. He challenged the traditional notion that advertising could change attitudes and persuade the consumer, asserting instead that "advertising's main role is to reinforce feelings of satisfaction with brands already being used" (Ehrenberg 1974: 33).

At the time Ehrenberg's article was published, persuasion-based hierarchy-of-effects models like AIDA still held sway. Ehrenberg identified four weaknesses in these models:

- The lack of empirical evidence showing sales increases resulting from advertising.
- The persistence of small and medium brands in the face of massive advertising spend by brand leaders
- The fact that brands usually survive even when ad spend is cut.
- The catastrophic failure rate of new products.

Ehrenberg did this by using consumer panel data to establish that most markets have few 100% loyal buyers, and that the majority of people buy more than one brand. He showed that brand users held consistently stronger attitudes than non-users, especially evaluative attitudes. But what he could not find was any satisfactory explanation of how attitudes were changed. This led him to question the core assumption within hierarchy-of-effects models that attitude change precedes and drives behavior change. Although Ehrenberg accepted that the traditional idea that "Awareness → Attitudes → Behavior" made intuitive sense, he found many examples of a sequence in which it was the behavior – the purchase of the product itself – which led to "greater awareness of information to which one is normally exposed … and to change in attitude" (Ehrenberg 1974: 30). All this challenged the convention that consumers were rationally persuaded by advertising to change their minds and their brand allegiance.

As an alternative to AIDA Ehrenberg developed a theory he called Awareness–Trial–Reinforcement, or ATR. Note that he was referring to brand awareness here, not ad awareness. The ATR model was popular amongst advertising agencies, at a time when the sales effects of advertising were seen by many as hard to discern even in hindsight, and virtually impossible to predict. Ehrenberg's model suggested that advertising could create, reawaken, or strengthen brand awareness, and could also be one of the factors that facilitated trial purchase. But he also foresaw a role for advertising in converting trialists into satisfied and lasting customers. And he saw repetitive advertising for established brands as primarily defensive, reinforcing already developed repeat buying habits.

In a later article, Barnard and Ehrenberg (1997) refined the ATR model to accommodate what they called "split-loyal" purchasers (those who regularly purchase more than one brand). Here, the role of advertising was to "nudge" these split-loyal purchasers towards a greater purchase proportion of one brand or another (ATR-N).

But even Ehrenberg's ATR-N model generated little enthusiasm amongst marketers. Discussing the popularity of persuasion models in the USA, one of his contemporaries, John Philip Jones, described persuasion as:

> [The] conventional view of advertising . . . which is all but universally believed in the United States and which sees advertising as . . . a driving force for the engine of demand . . . capable of increasing sales not only of brands but also of complete product categories. (Jones 1990: 237)

Nor did Jones accept that advertising was incapable of changing attitudes: "[Persuasive advertising] increases people's knowledge and changes people's attitudes [and] is capable of persuading people who had not previously bought a brand to buy it once and then repeatedly" (Jones 1990: 237).

Jones' view of the way in which advertising achieved this seemed to have changed little from that of the motivational researchers of the 1960s. He described advertising as using creativity to "insinuate" new information into the minds of "apathetic and rather stupid consumers [by] the use of psychological techniques that destroy the consumer's defences; in some cases these techniques are not even perceptible to the conscious mind" (Jones 1990: 237). This contrasted dramatically with Ehrenberg's view of the consumer:

> Buyers of frequently bought goods are not ignorant of them. They have extensive usage experience of the products – after all, they buy them frequently. As we have seen earlier, they usually have direct experience of more than one brand, plus indirect word of mouth knowledge of others. The average housewife is far more experienced in buying her normal products than the industrial purchaser buying an atomic power station. (Ehrenberg 1974: 31)

Of course, the crux of the argument between Jones and Ehrenberg was over attitude change. Jones saw advertising working by changing attitudes which led to changing behavior. Ehrenberg, as I said earlier, rejected the idea that attitude change must precede purchase:

> It seems to be generally assumed that improving the attitudes of a nonuser towards a brand should make him use the brand, or at least become more predisposed to doing so. But this amounts to assuming that people's attitudes

or image of a brand can in fact be readily changed, and that such attitude changes must precede the desired change in behaviour. There is little or no evidence to support these assumptions. (Ehrenberg 1974: 30)

It is worth noting that it is not just the advertising industry that is closed-minded to Krugman and Ehrenberg's ideas. As recently as 1999 a paper on how advertising works published in the world's top marketing journal considered "only theories that adopt an information-processing perspective," and asserted that "Regardless of their content and the techniques they employ, most [advertising] messages share a common final goal: persuading target consumers to adopt a particular product, service, or idea" (Meyers-Levy & Malaviya 1999: 45).

To illustrate just how narrow minded this information processing persuasion-based perspective is, I'd like you to consider a case study from an award-winning market research paper I wrote in 2008 with Paul Feldwick. This case study concerned a brand of instant noodles.

Telma Noodles Case Study

In 1999, a company called Bestfoods decided to launch a snack food product aimed at teenagers in Israel, called Telma Noodles. The ad agency they commissioned came up with a commercial consisting of a pop song with meaningless gibberish lyrics, accompanying a series of surreally linked and sometimes bizarre scenes. In each scene someone was shown eating the product, but since the lyrics of the song were gibberish the ad contained nothing that could be construed to be a persuasive message about the product.

Research was conducted on this ad amongst teenagers before it was shown. The questions asked were common ones in use at the time, such as "Did this commercial give you enough information about the product?" and "Do you think someone would find this commercial easy to understand?" From these questions, average scores were produced for "ease of understanding," "believability," "relevance," "branding," and "persuasion." Since the whole ad was gibberish, the scores on all these dimensions were not surprisingly pretty dreadful. In addition, research showed that the song was widely disliked and detracted from the product. The research agency suggested the ad should not be used and proposed that "Probably a more simplistic route . . . which emphasises the brand name and benefits clearly would work the best" (Heath & Feldwick 2008: 30).

Heath and Feldwick describe what happened next:

> What is unusual about this case is not the research methodology [but] that, for reasons of timing, the advertiser went ahead and ran the ad. The results were exceptional. It became the most liked ad among teenagers . . . with 93% liking the ad very much – especially the song. Most importantly, the brand took a substantial share of the market. (Heath & Feldwick 2008: 30)

So, rather like the Meerkats, here we have an advertisement that is exceptionally well-liked. The difference, however, is that in the Telma ad there isn't even a message about getting cheap car insurance: there is no message, because the ad is gibberish and totally meaningless. It is a perfect example of Herb Krugman's "trivial and silly" TV advertising. Yet in spite of having no message the ad somehow turned Telma into a huge success.

What the Telma case study does is to bring into sharp focus one of the major schisms that exist between ad agencies and marketers. For most ad agencies Krugman's idea that people don't pay attention to TV ads is heresy, because low attention implies their wonderful work will not be noticed or remembered. So the Telma ad, by being liked and talked about, would be seen by them as a victory for creativity. But for marketers, Ehrenberg's idea that advertising doesn't change attitudes is the worse sacrilege, because no attitude change means there is nothing to measure and no evidence the ad has achieved anything for the brand. The Telma ad, by having no message, would therefore be seen by most marketers as a complete waste of money.

And yet it worked. The brand launch was a success. The ad agency would have been able to use this to argue that recall is the most important thing, and that attitude change didn't matter. You can see now why Ehrenberg's ATR model was so popular with ad agencies; it meant they could stop worrying about getting the message over and spend all their time focusing on creativity that gets talked about.

Except, as Ehrenberg correctly observed, we consumers are not idiots. I'm sure the Israeli consumers didn't go around saying "Did you see that Telma ad the other day, it was complete nonsense, so I think I'll go and try it," because generally we don't mention ads at all in our day-to-day conversations. Krugman was right in saying we don't pay much attention to TV advertising. In fact, we don't pay much attention to any advertising, and in the next chapter I'll explain why this is.

3

Why We Don't Pay Attention to Advertising

"Viewers do not want to see advertising.
They do not want that flow of relief broken;
they resist television advertising"
Arthur Kover
Journal of Consumer Research (1995: 599)

So far we have established that there are schisms in how advertising is believed to work. The traditional persuasion model, beloved of many people in the advertising industry, asserts that advertising is there to get attention and deliver some sort of persuasive message that changes attitudes. Within the industry the ad agencies see attention as being the biggest hurdle to overcome, and ad recall as being the more important measure, and marketers see delivering the message as being the biggest hurdle and attitude shift as being the more important measure. Then there are various opposing views which say that persuasion is the wrong model, and that advertising works without getting attention and without changing attitudes. But the argument that underlies all these different views is how much ads are able to make us pay attention to them.

Going back to basics for a moment, we established that companies advertise because they have some product or service they want us to buy. And a little later we got on to the fact that even as long ago as the eighteenth century people were not very willing to pay attention to this advertising. But then along came TV, and everyone assumed everything would change. Why? Well, instead of having to go out and buy a newspaper, and then open the pages and seek out an ad, all we had to do was sit slumped in our

Seducing the Subconscious: The Psychology of Emotional Influence in Advertising, First Edition. Robert Heath.
© 2012 Robert Heath. Published 2012 by John Wiley & Sons, Ltd.

chairs and the ads would be delivered to us in the middle of the program we were watching. What is more, instead of just pictures there would be action and sound. TV was intrinsically more interesting than print, so it stands to reason that TV ads would intrinsically be more interesting.

Good theory. Sadly, it didn't turn out that way. In February 2003 the *Independent* newspaper published a press release from the London Business School (LBS) about research they had conducted using cameras placed in homes. The opening line read "A new report from the London Business School details what television viewers do during commercial breaks. Unfortunately for marketers, they rarely seem to watch the ads."

Although it was derived from a small number of households, further research confirms that the LBS research *was* accurate, and if anything understated the real situation. As early as the 1980s it had been shown that between 20% and 40% of us were leaving the room when an ad breaks came on (Soley 1984) and by the 1990s two-thirds were doing some other activity when watching television (Clancey 1994). By 1994, half of us actively disliked TV advertising (Mittal 1994), and nowadays almost everyone fast-forwards through the ads in previously recorded material (Goetzel 2006). We may love watching TV programs, and even love watching TV programs about ads, but we much prefer chatting to the family, making tea, checking our e-mails, and petting the dog to watching the real thing.

What explains our reluctance to engage with TV advertising? While the advertising industry was still in denial about Krugman and Ehrenberg, an explanation of sorts was being advanced by academics in psychology. In 1982, two Ohio-based psychologists – Richard Petty and John Cacioppo – decided that involvement in the product field was responsible for the way in which people processed advertising. This led to the development of what has been called advertising academia's "most influential theoretical contribution" (Beard 2002: 72): the Elaboration Likelihood Model (ELM).

The Elaboration Likelihood Model

The ELM acknowledged that there might be two different routes by which advertising could achieve a change in behavior, and that these routes would differ according to "the extent to which the attitude change that results . . . is due to active thinking" (Petty & Cacioppo 1996: 256). In essence, what Petty and Cacioppo suggested was that people who were involved or motivated by a product field would think more deeply about (i.e., "elaborate") the arguments presented by the advertising, whilst those not motivated would process the ads in a shallow inattentive manner. These two routes were known as the Central Route and the Peripheral Route. The Central Route was what one might regard as the traditional method of persuasion, in which processing is "controlled, deep, systematic, and effortful." The authors described this as follows:

> When conditions foster people's motivation and ability to engage in issue-relevant thinking, the "elaboration likelihood" is said to be high. This means that people are likely to attend to the appeal; attempt to access relevant associations, images, and experiences from memory. (Petty & Cacioppo 1986: 128)

In contrast, they described the Peripheral Processing Route as "automatic, shallow, heuristic, and mindless" and "based on affective associations or simple inferences tied to peripheral cues" (Petty & Cacioppo 1986: 191). In other words, a weak non-persuasive route somewhat similar to those described by Krugman and Ehrenberg.

Petty and Cacioppo lent weight to their theory by conducting three experiments with college students. They devised a discussion topic about a new exam stage that they knew would polarize interest and involvement amongst the students. In the first experiment they found that the involved students were influenced most by the merits of the argument itself, and that the uninvolved group was influenced more by the status of the person who was communicating the argument. In the second experiment they found that the influence on the involved group occurred with a single exposure to the argument, but the uninvolved group needed repetition of the argument before they could make their minds up. Finally, they found that attitude changes resulting from exposure to the communication amongst the involved group tended to be permanent and long term, whereas attitude changes amongst the uninvolved group were comparatively transitory and short term.

It is no great surprise that Petty and Cacioppo saw the high involvement active thinking Central Route as being more effective than the low involvement Peripheral Route. They assumed that attitude change was necessary for advertising to be effective, and what they found, in their own words, was that "Attitude changes via the Central Route appear to be more persistent, resistant, and predictive of behaviour than changes induced via the Peripheral Route" (Petty & Cacioppo 1986: 191). But this finding is entirely in line with the thinking of Krugman and Ehrenberg, both of whose theories suggested that advertising isn't able to induce long-term attitudes shifts. The difference of course is that Krugman and Ehrenberg saw Peripheral Processing as the way in which *most* advertising is processed, and regarded it as a perfectly good way for advertising to influence behavior.

At a fundamental level, the ELM does seem to make sense. Generally, we believe we pay more attention to those things we find motivating and involving, and less attention to those things we are frankly not interested in. But the evidence we have from the LBS study quoted earlier suggests market involvement doesn't actually explain our behavior towards advertising. If we paid more attention to ads about things we were interested in, our TV viewing behavior would be characterized by fluctuating levels of attention. Put simply, we would be forever attending to or ignoring ads as they came on, depending on whether or not they were for things that interested us.

And that wasn't what the researchers at LBS found. They found that people mostly avoided the ads, especially if more than one person was in the room. The only time people did tend consistently to watch the ads was late at night when they were too tired to get up and leave the room. And in my own research I have found that product involvement actually makes no difference to the level of attention paid to TV ads. Under conditions carefully designed to replicate normal viewing, the attention levels paid to ads for products and brands that were used by the subjects (and so should have been more involving) were exactly the same as those paid to products and brands that were not used by them (Heath *et al.* 2009).

Partly, this is a function of the way that ad agencies make TV ads. Often it just isn't possible to tell what brand, or even what product field, is being advertised until the end of the ad. The idea is that if you don't know what the ad is for you will watch it more carefully in order to find out. But if people are not that interested in ads in the first place then this approach backfires: they either tune out before the ad finishes, or simply don't bother to watch the ad at all.

But there is a more fundamental reason for not watching ads, and that has to do with our expectation of what we might learn from them. The subject matter of the discussion in Petty and Cacioppo's experiments was some news about a new exam, which they knew would be of great interest to those students likely to have to take it. Sadly, modern marketers rarely have the chance of putting anything half as interesting in their ads. Such is the sophistication of modern technology that brands can usually match any new ideas in less time than it takes to make a TV ad. Most TV advertising is telling people what they know already: so what motive have they for paying attention to it?

Of course, the better marketers become at matching competitors and improving products, the more choice is available. You might expect this to encourage us to be *more* alert towards advertising, not less. In practice it does the reverse.

The Tyranny of Choice

David Mick, an ethical business researcher in Virginia, has coined the term "Hyperchoice" to describe the state of mind that this produces in consumers. He writes:

> Consumption ideology now spans the world, including an imperative of consumer choice. But in today's developed economies this ever-increasing amount of buying occurs amidst an ever-increasing amount of new products, brands, and brand extensions, in the midst of an ever-increasing amount of daily demands and an ever-decreasing amount of discretionary time. (Mick *et al.* 2004: 207)

Mick and his team find that Hyperchoice confuses people, and although initially attractive it is "ultimately unsatisfying . . . and psychologically draining" (Mick *et al.* 2004: 207). But more important is the effect this has on people's willingness to make choices. Basically, with so much choice available, rather than examining the options more closely, we tend to examine them *less* closely.

You might find that hard to accept. We all like to think we are diligent in how we select what we buy, especially when we are talking about expensive items. And some of us are. I had some friends who spent weeks debating at length what to replace their ancient second car with. Should they get a saloon so they could use it as a back-up for the family car, or a hatchback they could use for transporting stuff from the store? Whilst this was going on their washing machine broke down, and within an hour they had gone straight round to a store and bought a brand new Bosch (why will become clear later). But the plain fact is that although they saw themselves as people who checked out all the options and worked logically towards the most sensible purchase, in this case they just used their intuition and bought the first acceptable brand they encountered.

Most of us, faced with having to make a "distress" purchase like this, would do the same. But the fact is, when brands are involved, we shortcut our decision-making even when we have plenty of time to think about what to buy. A research study by Van Osselaer and Alba, which I describe in more detail in Chapter 15, showed that those exposed to product attributes and brand cues together don't bother to examine the product attributes in depth; they simply look at as many as are necessary to reinforce the brand they favor, then pretend the rest don't exist.

An example makes this clearer. Suppose you are buying a laptop computer. In the absence of any brand information you have at least 26 characteristic (product cues) to examine: price, screen size, screen color quality, screen proportions, screen density, hard disk memory, processor memory, processor make, battery life, battery recharge time, weight, thickness, number of USB ports, built-in or external CD drive, built-in or external wi-fi, fire-wire connection, fan noise, sound system, built-in microphone, built-in mouse type, price, color, guarantee length, reliability, and a couple of other functional benefits. Looking through these you might quickly decide that nine product cues (price, screen size, screen color quality, hard disk memory, processor memory, processor make, weight, built-in microphone, and number of USB ports) will be sufficient to enable you to make a decision on which laptop you want, so you don't even bother to think about the other 17.

But in real life what is more likely to happen is that you go to your friendly local PC store, which stocks Sony, Samsung, Toshiba, Hewlett Packard, Packard Bell, and a few other makes, and you see a Toshiba laptop that has adequate memory and is as light as the Sony but is half the price because it is on offer. And you buy it, even though you have only used three of your chosen nine product cues to make the decision. Why? Well, Toshiba is a make you feel is reputable, reliable, and technically reasonably up-to-date, and hey, you are saving yourself some money and that can't be bad. That's the way our minds work when it comes to choosing brands.

What you probably never ask yourself at any time during this process is whether or not there is anything you might have seen by way of advertising that might have helped you in this decision process. There are a number of reasons for this. First, like all of us, you don't pay much attention to ads because you assume they are not going to tell you much. Second, because you don't pay ads any attention you can't actually recall any for Toshiba. Third, you didn't need any additional information to make your choice, so that entirely justifies you not bothering to pay any attention to advertising.

Of course, what you have conveniently forgotten is that when you made your choice of a Toshiba, you did so because you felt that it was reputable and reliable. And the reason you felt it was reputable and reliable was that you have over the months and years seen *many* advertisements for Toshiba on TV and in magazines, and you have seen hundreds of placards in shops advertising Toshiba, and you have forgotten every one of them. Exactly like Walter Dill Scott with his visit to the tailor, if someone pestered you for the reason why you chose Toshiba you would probably eventually tell them that you have a friend who bought one. But the truth is much more likely to be that you were influenced by these ads at a subconscious level, even though you are not even aware that you were ever exposed to them.

Of course, had you paid attention to the Toshiba ads and the Sony Vaio ads and the Apple ads and the Samsung ads and the Hewlett Packard ads and the Dell ads, you might have been in a better position to make an unbiased and logical brand selection. But my view is that you would probably only have done that if you worked in marketing or advertising, or in a shop like PC World. The rest of us "normal" people have better things to do with our time.

Just to illustrate how easily advertising can influence us even when we pay no attention to it, here is another interesting case study to conclude this chapter.

Orange Case Study

In January 2001, around the time of the O2 launch, the UK Orange Telecom brand ran a black and white TV ad for their WAP services. The ad featured a variety of people looking at camera with their thoughts related by a voice-over, and these thoughts told us in turn that they could do things like tell when the rain would fall and where the traffic jams were, all through their Orange network. I say the ad was black and white, but what distinguished it was that everyone featured in it had an orange square in the palm of their hands, signifying that with Orange all this information was right there in the palm of your hand. The ad was supported by a poster campaign also showing someone with an orange square in their hand, and by all accounts was a pretty visible campaign. Research showed that over two-thirds of people claimed they had seen advertising for Orange on TV recently, about twice what was claimed when it wasn't being advertised.

Six months later Orange ran another ad to publicize the news that they had again been ranked No.1 for customer service in the annual J.D. Power survey. This ad was really quite strange. It featured various catastrophic vignettes, like a huge vase rolling down some stairs and breaking, and a landlady smiling while water poured down her walls. The idea was that all the people who had suffered these catastrophes were happy because Orange was their mobile phone network provider.

Now, one has to admit that the idea that your mobile phone account is so well administered that it enables you to forgive your house being flooded is pretty far-fetched. But, on the other hand, the fact that Orange had won the coveted J.D. Power survey 2 years in a row certainly is an impressive claim. The problem with this ad was not so much that the message wasn't credible, it was that the ad itself seemed to be invisible. The number of people who claimed Orange had been advertising on TV recently didn't move at all. What is more, no one seemed to be able to recall anything about the ad, nor was there any increase in Orange's overall perceived image. All-in-all you would be forgiven for concluding that the ad was a complete waste of money.

It so happened at the time I was working with another research company, and we decided we would do some research on this Orange J.D. Power ad. What we wanted to know was not how many people could recall if Orange had been advertising on TV at the time, but how many people had actually seen the ad. We found this out simply by showing people the ad and asking them if they had seen it before. As we will see later, recognition is a very powerful memory system, so if people said they had seen an ad we knew they would be likely to be telling the truth.

We were surprised to discover that over half the people we spoke to recognized the ad when it was shown to them, so getting the ad exposed wasn't the problem. The bad news was that less than one-quarter of those who recognized the ad knew it was for Orange.

But did that mean the ad had not influenced their attitudes towards Orange? In order to find this out, we asked them some image questions about the various brands in the mobile phone market before we showed anyone the ad. This enabled us to compare the ratings of Orange amongst those who recognized the ad with the ratings amongst those who did not recognize it (and had therefore almost certainly not seen it). To be on the safe side we only looked at the results amongst those who were *not* existing customers of Orange.

And here was our second surprise. Remember, three-quarters of those who recognized the ad had no idea who it was for. Yet what we found was that although most of them were not aware of the brand being advertised, they consistently rated Orange higher than those who had not recognized the ad. And not just by a little bit: the recognizers rated Orange over 50% better than the non-recognizers on "Cares about customers" and "Easy to use," and twice as high on "Helpful" and "A brand you would recommend."

In other words, despite few being able to recall anything about the ad, and despite the great majority of those who had seen it on TV not knowing what brand it was for, this advertisement seemed to have been able to positively influence the opinions of those who had been exposed to it. It seems the ad worked not just without the message being remembered, but without the brand or anything in the ad being remembered either.

Sounds pretty unlikely. But two further published studies – one on the UK pet food brand Butcher's Dog, and another on the UK life insurance brand Standard Life – showed almost exactly the same results (Heath & Hyder 2005). In both cases the ads managed to increase favorability towards the brand amongst those who did not recall them. Indeed, the results suggested that the favorability increase might be greater amongst those who did *not* recall the ads than amongst those who did. I'm proud to say that the paper in which I and Pam Hyder of Standard Life published these results was awarded the two highest UK Market Research Society prizes, and is the only paper ever to have achieved this.

So I hope I've convinced you there is more to advertising than persuasion. If ads can influence us without any message, without us attending to or recalling the message, without us attending to or recalling the ad, and regardless of whether we like or hate the ad, then something more has to be going on. But to get to the bottom of this mystery we have first to understand a lot more about the psychology of communication: in particular how we learn, where we store what we learn, and how attention is connected with this whole process. That is the subject of the next section of the book.

Taking Advertising Apart: Summary

So far we have established four different models of advertising: Persuasion, Low Involvement, Reinforcement, and the Elaboration Likelihood Model. These are depicted on the summary chart shown in Figure 3.1.

The traditional Persuasion Model is one in which advertising is attended to and delivers one or more persuasive messages. These messages change brand-linked beliefs, which in turn create brand-linked attitudes, which result in a rational behavior response such as purchase of a brand. This model is represented by the solid line in Figure 3.1.

Krugman's Low Involvement Model suggests that advertising is mainly processed at low levels of attention and is unlikely to be able to work by communicating a persuasive message. This is represented by the dashed line in Figure 3.1. The problem with this model is that if no message is being processed then it doesn't really explain *how* advertising can change either beliefs or attitudes. Also, any attitude change that occurs is likely to be fairly modest.

Ehrenberg's Reinforcement Model asserts that any fundamental attitude change occurs after usage of the brand or product. His model would not be expected to show any great change in brand-linked beliefs, so advertising is able to work at relatively low levels of attention. But his model would show advertising acting to *reinforce* existing brand-linked attitudes, and the dotted line in Figure 3.1 represents this.

Petty and Cacioppo's Elaboration Likelihood Model is a combination of the Persuasion and Low Involvement Models. The Central Route operates much the same as Persuasion (the solid line), causing significant changes in attitudes and beliefs. The Peripheral Route operates much the same as Krugman's Low Involvement Model (the dashed line), causing only modest and short-term changes in attitudes.

The problem this chart highlights is that the Persuasion (i.e., Central Processing) Model, although most powerful at changing attitudes, appears to be unsustainable. We simply don't pay enough attention to advertising to be able to interpret and memorize persuasive messages effectively. However, neither the Low Involvement (Peripheral Processing) nor Ehrenberg's Reinforcement Models are intrinsically *more* effective than the traditional Persuasion Model, which is why advertisers and marketers have made no real attempt to adopt them. Instead they have focused their efforts on the increasingly hopeless task of using creativity to try to encourage us to pay more attention. Why I think this task is hopeless is the subject of the next chapter.

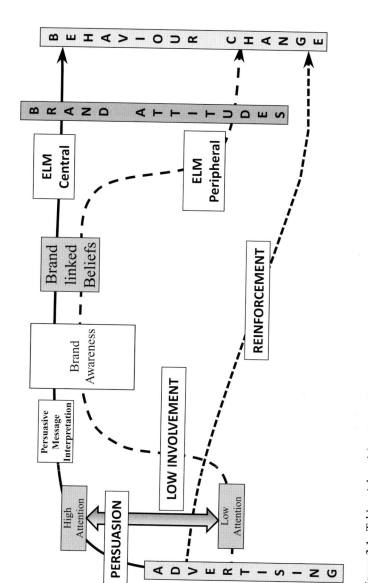

Figure 3.1 Taking Advertising Apart Summary Chart.

2
The Psychology of Communication

4

Learning and Attention

"Reason may not be as pure as most of us think it is and wish it were"

Antonio Damasio
Descartes' Error (1994)

In the same way that we all think we know how advertising works, we also all think we know how we learn. This is partly because in our western education system the very first thing we are told at school is to pay attention. Thus, we are conditioned to believe that if we don't pay attention we will not learn anything. As I pointed out earlier, we instinctively assume that if we don't pay much attention to advertising we will not learn anything; and if we don't learn anything from an advertisement then we can't be affected by that advertisement.

We have Hermann Ebbinghaus, whose seminal book *Uber das Gedachtnis (On Memory)* was published in 1885, to thank for this view of learning. Ebbinghaus is best known for his work on forgetting, having developed the famous "forgetting curve" which showed that retention is a function of strength of memory and time. But Ebbinghaus also found that strength of memory is dependent upon attention and interest. In his own words: "Very great is the dependence of retention and reproduction upon the intensity of the attention and interest which were attached to the mental states the first time they were present" (Ebbinghaus 1885). So, according to Ebbinghaus, if you want to retain something in memory that you are not especially interested in, the best way you can do this is to pay attention.

Seducing the Subconscious: The Psychology of Emotional Influence in Advertising, First Edition. Robert Heath.
© 2012 Robert Heath. Published 2012 by John Wiley & Sons, Ltd.

The problem we encounter here is that advertising does not seem to be a respecter of Ebbinghaus's rules. In Chapter 2 you may remember I referenced the experiment by Festinger and Macoby (1964) in which they found that showing an *irrelevant* video in a TV advertisement actually enhanced the learning of the message when compared to showing a *relevant* video. And at the end of the last chapter we found that people who did not recall ads (and therefore had probably not paid much attention to them) seemed to have been influenced more by them than those who *did* recall them (and so probably *had* paid attention to them). It rather sounds like we might learn advertising messages and slogans better when we are being distracted than when our attention is enhanced. How can this be?

One reason is that learning about brands is not the same as learning information in school. The simple-sounding term "Brand Learning" needs to encapsulate a lot more than slogans, product claims, and rational brand benefits. It needs, for example, to include a whole raft of varied ideas and signals, from the unique smell or taste of a particular brand, to the shape and colors of its particular pack or logo. All these are examples of information we receive which help us to learn about brands. For example, the predominant color red used by Coke and the predominant color blue used by Pepsi on their respective cans are in their own way "messages" which increase our learning about these brands, even if their meaning is not evident.

Using this definition, it is clear that every day we are exposed to thousands of messages which tell us something about brands. For example, when we go into the bathroom in the morning and pick up our tube of toothpaste, we receive messages about that toothpaste. Even if we are bleary-eyed we will be reminded of the brand logo, the colors on the pack, perhaps one or two design elements. Add to that the rest of the packs that might be visible in the bathroom, and those we might see in the kitchen when we have breakfast, and those we might see in the shop windows on our way to work or out shopping, and you can see that we are constantly deluged by information about brands, most of which simply isn't seen as being of any importance to us. I mean, does it really matter what color a can of cola is?

Krugman, in his 1965 paper, offered the view that advertising communication, set against this cacophony of communication, is likewise seen as unimportant. The result is that our learning is more like Ebbinghaus' learning of nonsense material. Ebbinghaus found that when trying to learn things that made no sense to us we tend to remember the first and last things we are exposed to much better than the stuff in the middle (Ebbinghaus 1902). But in reality the way we learn things from advertising is a lot more complicated even than that.

But before embarking on an explanation I think it is important for me to define clearly the various terms that I am going to be using. Starting with Attention.

Attention

The primary definition of Attention in the *Oxford Compact Dictionary* (1996: 57) is "The act or faculty of applying one's mind". But "mind" by definition includes our entire conscious, subconscious, and unconscious mental faculty, and it can therefore be argued that attention potentially encompasses everything we are *capable* of perceiving. To avoid confusion, the psychologist William James defined attention as: "the taking possession by the mind, in clear and vivid form, of one out of what seem several simultaneously possible objects or trains of thought" (James 1890: 403). Using this definition, if something is capable of being perceived (i.e., it is within hearing or within at least peripheral sight), but you are in no way *conscious* that you are perceiving it, you are regarded as *not* paying any attention to it. In simple terms, attention equates to *conscious* perception.

There are two different ways of defining attention. The first is what I call a "directional" definition: it is concerned with *what* you are looking at or listening to. For example, if you are looking away from something you might be said to *not* be paying attention.

This directional definition of attention is not very helpful with advertising, because it doesn't relate to how much we are learning. The second way of defining attention is what I call a "level of attention" definition, and this is much more useful. Level of attention is concerned with *how much* attention you are paying to something. Our level of attention is dictated by the amount of thinking we are doing. If you are doing a lot of thinking about an ad then you are using a high level of attention, and if you are doing very little thinking about it you are using a very low level of attention. For this reason level of attention equates to the amount of conscious learning we are doing.

Level of Attention

James defined two boundary levels of attention: active and passive. Active attention is when the level of attention is high and the application is wilful, deliberate, and controlled by the individual. Nowadays it is more fashionable to use the term "top-down processing" to denote an activity like this which is driven by specific goals (Eysenck & Keane 2000: 2). A good example of active attention is when you concentrate on what your teacher or lecturer says in class, because you are responding to the goal of wanting to learn enough to pass your exams.

Because active attention is "conative" (i.e., has to be applied wilfully) it is hard for us to maintain it for long periods. James characterized active attention not as a continuous process, but more like a wave in which there are repeated phases of high attention being applied to a situation.

The opposite of active attention is passive attention. This is when the level of attention is low, and the application is inadvertent and not under the control of the individual. This corresponds to what is known as "bottom-up processing," an activity that tends to be driven by external stimuli (Eysenck & Keane 2000: 119). A good example of this is when your attention wanders to a fly which keeps buzzing around the classroom and suddenly you find you have no idea what the teacher was telling you.

Another way of looking at these two boundaries is to use Craik and Lockhart's (1972) idea of Depth of Processing. Depth of Processing refers to the amount of attention and cognitive resource being deployed. Deep processing occurs when maximum active attention is being applied and maximum cognitive resource is being deployed. Shallow processing, on the other hand, refers to situations where limited cognitive resource is applied (Eysenck & Keane 2000: 165). Shallow processing is what Petty and Cacioppo are referring to when they talk about Peripheral Processing. So level of attention can be defined as being the amount of active thinking you are doing, or the amount of cognitive resource you are deploying at any one time.

The two definitions of attention take on greater importance when we start to think about how advertising is processed. Imagine, for example, you are sitting in front of the TV watching a football match with your computer on your lap. One minute you are paying high directional attention to the TV and deploying high levels of cognitive resource; the next minute an ad break comes on and you look away and check your e-mails. Your level of attention to the TV immediately goes from high to zero.

Now imagine you haven't got your computer. When the ad break comes on you continue looking at the TV screen, but your mind is elsewhere, perhaps thinking about the last goal that was scored, or where you are going on holiday. In this situation your directional attention is high but the amount of cognitive resource you are deploying in regard to the ad is very low. So the level of attention the ads receives is low.

Now let's take a third situation. You have your laptop this time, and you look away from the screen when the ad break comes on. But this time you keep listening to and perhaps even glancing at the ads, so you don't miss the start of the game. In this situation your directional attention is fluctuating and the level of cognitive resource is moderate. It might sound very complicated, but this is the reality we have to deal with when we think about advertising processing.

It should be pointed out that Craik and Lockhart, in similar vein to Ebbinghaus, originally asserted that deep processing would always result in more elaborate and durable memories being produced. They cited amongst others a 1964 experiment by Treisman in which "if the message was attended, more meaningful material could be processed further, and, thus, was retained longer" (Craik & Lockhart 1972: 679). However, this assertion was challenged some 6 years later by Eysenck (1978) and they were forced to accept that "the notion of depth of processing by itself is insufficient to give an adequate characterisation of memory processes" (Lockhart & Craik 1978: 174). Later, Lockhart and Craik revised their view that shallow processing leads to rapid forgetting, accepting that shallow processing of sensory information could persist "for hours, minutes, and even months" (Lockhart & Craik 1990: 98). I mention this because psychology by definition deals with assertions about the mind that make common sense but are hard to prove, and it is not infrequently the case that what seems to be common sense turns out to be wrong.

Learning from Communication

Attention is not, however, an on–off mechanism, and at any one time we may be paying attention to something at a level somewhere between active and passive, and processing it somewhere between deep and shallow. As Ebbinghaus found, the amount or level of attention we are applying at any one time will influence the type of learning that takes place.

Learning that happens when deep attentive processing is being applied actively and lots of cognitive resource is being used can be defined as Active Learning. This is Ebbinghaus's "strong" learning, and corresponds with top-down goal-driven processing. The objective behind it is not just to record information but to "understand," categorize, and relate it somehow to other ideas we have learned in the past. Rita Carter eloquently describes this as "The nuts and bolts of thinking … holding ideas in mind and manipulating them …" (Carter 1998: 195) and elsewhere it is described as Cognitive Elaboration (Greenwald & Leavitt 1984). Petty and Cacioppo summarize elaboration as follows:

> The message recipient attends to the message arguments, attempts to understand them and then evaluates them … The person then integrates all of the information into a coherent and reasoned position. (Petty & Cacioppo 1996: 256)

At the other end of the scale, learning that happens when shallow inattentive processing is being applied and little cognitive resource is being deployed can be defined as Passive Learning. This is a generally regarded as a relatively weak form of learning and corresponds with bottom-up stimulus-driven processing. We can assume that this is what Petty and Cacioppo are referring to when they use the term "Peripheral Processing."

What is learned during Passive Learning is available to the consciousness, but at a relatively low level. To clarify how this works in practice here is a fairly commonplace example.

Imagine you are driving down a busy street in a car, having a serious conversation with your passenger. You come across a bus indicating that it is pulling out, or perhaps it starts to rain. Do you stop talking when each of these things happens? Not necessarily. Yet each of them demands a judgment of some sort, which we have to perform cognitively; a bus pulling out requires you to judge whether you can carry on driving past, or if it is pulling out so fast that you should stop and let it go. Rain requires you to judge whether or not it is heavy enough to switch on the wipers. Likewise, you can follow your route, stop at traffic lights and pedestrian crossings, skip gears when you change up or down, and perform almost any number of cognitive tasks, all without taking your mind off the conversation.

The important thing to bear in mind is that when you have finished the journey you will in all probability have little if any recall of all these relatively trivial decisions you made. You will almost certainly be able to recall the conversation you had, or at the very least the key points that were made during it, but whether or not you overtook the bus, switched the windscreen wipers on, or stopped to let someone cross the road are all things you don't really need to remember, so in all likelihood you will forget them. Just the same way as we forget most of the advertising we are exposed to.

Passive Learning has generally been sidelined by the advertising industry, because, as we learned in Chapter 3, it is mostly regarded as not being able to change attitudes in the long term. According to Petty and Cacioppo, Active Learning (central processing) leads to a considered change of attitude, which might result in one of two outcomes. Either the person may be persuaded of the argument and change their attitudes in favor of the brand; or they may reject the argument – what they call a "boomerang response." But with Passive Learning (Peripheral Processing) attention levels are low and the amount of reasoning that takes place is limited. Petty and Cacioppo assert that changes in attitude can arise, but only under certain circumstances:

> The picture that these peripheral approaches paint of the persuasion process is not a very thoughtful one. If a message is associated with . . . an attractive source, it is accepted. If the message takes a position that is too discrepant, it is rejected regardless of the cogency of the arguments presented. (Petty & Cacioppo 1996: 256)

In effect, what they are saying is that Passive Learning can only effect a change in attitudes if that change is in some way already favored. What is more, they claimed that attitude changes that do take place are nothing like as enduring as those that result from Active Learning.

> If we don't have much prior information . . . or don't perceive the issues to have very much personal relevance, then the peripheral approach will probably have some success. The success will be short-lived, however, so it will be necessary for the person who is trying to persuade us to constantly remind us of the persuasion cue. (Petty & Cacioppo 1996: 267)

Active and Passive Learning both occur when some sort of attention is being paid and you are *aware* that learning is taking place. However, you may be surprised to discover that it is also possible to learn *without paying any attention at all* to the task. As Eysenck and Keane put it, "meaning may be processed without awareness" (Eysenck & Keane 2000: 122). Learning that takes place when you are not aware that you are learning is known as Implicit Learning (Eysenck & Keane 2000: 532).

Implicit Learning

Here's a simple example of Implicit Learning. Let's go back to the story of driving along having a conversation with a passenger in your car. Suppose, as you are doing this, a pedestrian starts to walk out in front of you. You would almost certainly react immediately, slam on the brakes, perhaps swerve to avoid them, and maybe even shout out something rather impolite at them for not being more alert. But given that you are engaged in a conversation, watching for buses pulling out, and monitoring the weather to see if it rains, etc., how is it that you are able to see the pedestrian in time to stop?

The fact is that all the time you are driving, or indeed doing anything, your mind is constantly processing every single detail of everything that is going on around you, without you knowing it. You have no idea your mind is doing this because this sort of processing is fully automatic and takes place subconsciously. The importance of this sort of automatic processing is self-evident by our existence as human beings; if our ancestors hadn't had some sort of system that allowed them to distinguish the footfall of a sabre-toothed tiger from the rustle of grass in the wind, they would probably all have been eaten before they got out of the Stone Age.

Psychologists used to call this sort of non-attentive automatic processing *pre-attentive processing* (Broadbent 1958), because they believed nothing was recorded in memory from it and its only function was to alert us to pay attention. Giep Franzen, for example, describes pre-attentive processing as follows:

> We are constantly scanning our surroundings, unconsciously and automatically, to determine whether there is something deserving of our focused attention ... The only mental action we perform is to determine the relevance of what we perceive ... We do not do much else with the data, because every word and image contains more information than we are inclined to use or process further at this stage. (Franzen 1999: 41)

Modern psychological theories now accept that we do learn at low and zero attention levels, but often they include this learning in other processing categories. For example, Norman and Shallice's theory (1986, in Eysenck & Keane 2000) intersperses something called "partial automatic processing" between fully automatic and fully attentive processing. The purpose of this partial automatic processing is contention scheduling: that is, resolving conflicts such as that which arises when a bus pulls out in front of you.

Eysenck and Keane provide the best analysis of the automatic processes involved in Implicit Learning:

a) They are very fast
b) They are unavoidable (i.e., they operate whether or not the stimulus is within the field of attention)
c) They do not impinge on other tasks (i.e., they demand no attention)
d) They are unavailable to consciousness

But we can add a fifth attribute to Eysenck and Keane's, which is that automatic processing is *continuous*. It is never switched off. How otherwise would a sleeping parent be able to wake up when they hear their child crying in the night?

Most of us can accept that processing goes on at what we might loosely describe as *semi-conscious* levels of awareness. This sort of processing happens when the circumstances are not important enough to warrant *full* attention, nor so completely unimportant as to warrant *no* attention. This is the same as Passive Learning, and is precisely the situation we encounter with brand communication such as advertising. We don't want to entirely ignore it, because, like it or not, we have to make decisions between brands. But our experience has led us to realise that it rarely tells us anything of real importance, so we don't want to give our full attention to it.

In psychology, the idea of shallow processing (i.e., Passive and Implicit Learning) is well accepted. In the advertising industry it is a matter for serious dissent. For example, Max Sutherland and Alice Sylvester, in their book *Advertising and the Mind of the Consumer* stated that:

> Advertising that receives only shallow processing, far from being frighteningly powerful, is likely to be very inefficient and almost certainly has less impact than advertising which is processed at a more conscious level. (Sutherland & Sylvester 2000, in Heath 2001: 49)

A similar but more dogmatic opinion was expressed by Max Blackston of Research International in response to one of my own articles: "Inducing active processing is necessary for advertising to be effective" (Blackston 2000: 31).

Many marketers would endorse the above views. It seems, after all, to be the safest option. If advertising is actively processed then surely it should stand a better chance of persuading the viewer or listener than if it is not?

But Blackston's assertion is almost the categorical opposite to the views of Alan Hedges, who said:

> It is arrogant and unrealistic to suppose that more than a tiny fraction of the available advertising messages are likely to have been selected for conscious attention and processing ... Advertising may and probably generally does "work" without ever having been processed by our higher-level rational faculties. (Hedges 1998: 24)

I fully accept that it is hard to see how processing that takes place subconsciously can contribute anything to our learning about brands. And many people assume that if Implicit Learning doesn't contribute anything to memory that we can recall, then it cannot have much of a role in influencing us. But this thinking is wrong on two counts. First, as I have already shown, advertising *does* seem to be able to influence us even when we don't recall it. Second, Implicit Learning does contribute to long-term memory in a very important way. To understand how it does this we need first to review the role memory has in storing what we learn from communication.

5

The Role of Memory

"The brain clearly has multiple memory systems, each devoted to different kinds of learning and memory functions."

Joseph LeDoux
The Emotional Brain (1998)

I should start this chapter with two apologies. First, for those who have studied psychology I apologize if I repeat ideas that you are already familiar with. Second, for those who have *not* studied psychology, I apologize for the seemingly ridiculous number of different technical terms I will be using. The unavoidable fact is that the psychology of memory, like the psychology of advertising, is extremely complex.

What are memories? It used to be thought that they were complete and perfect pictures we kept in our minds of all the things and events we had experienced. However, if that were the case the 10 billion neurons that make up our brain would have run out of memory capacity long before we reached adulthood. Memories are imperfect, and are a function not just of what is stored, but how they are retrieved. Joseph LeDoux writes:

> Even though a memory . . . is strong and vivid, it is not necessarily accurate. Explicit memories, regardless of their emotional implications, are not carbon copies of the experiences that created them. (LeDoux 1998: 202)

Psychology has long ago abandoned the idea that memories are stored together, in neat, discrete parcels located in particular areas of the brain. It

---

Seducing the Subconscious: The Psychology of Emotional Influence in Advertising, First Edition. Robert Heath.
© 2012 Robert Heath. Published 2012 by John Wiley & Sons, Ltd.

is now believed that memories are distributed all over the brain and linked together by networks of connections. Schacter described this network system as follows:

> Connectionist or neural network models are based on the principle that the brain stores (memory networks) by increasing the strength of connections between different neurones that participate in encoding an experience. (Schacter 1996: 71)

Schacter uses the term "engram" to describe these memory networks. The importance of this theory is that memories, other than those we create when we are young, are not created from scratch each time, but connect with and adapt existing networks. So the engram of a brand would connect not only with the engram of its advertising, but with the engram of many other brands and other advertisements, to produce a vast network of interlinked memories.

The brand engram also contains our beliefs and attitudes towards the brand. As I made clear in Chapter 2, these are not the same thing. Beliefs are those attributes we believe a brand possesses, attitudes are how *we ourselves* feel about the brand. The distinction is very important, because although beliefs can influence attitudes, they *cannot* influence behavior; only attitudes are able to do that.

Brand engrams are accessed by electrical connections known as pathways. Because of the connection system there can be any number of pathways that lead you into a single brand engram. You may get to it via another product in the same market, or via another product made by the same company, or via a strong need which is linked especially to this product, or via recall of advertising, or via some elements within the advertising. The pathways to a familiar brand are not infinite, but when you try to count them they turn out to be *very* large in number.

An important fact about pathways is that each time you use them they become better defined and more likely to be used in the future. This is known as *consolidation*. It is rather like walking across a field of grass. The more people use a particular route, the more they wear away the grass, the more clearly defined that route becomes, the more other people use it and so on. Eventually, what was just a faint mark in the grass ends up as a clearly defined strip of earth, which everyone then uses as the path in the future.

For example, most of us will have a very strong connection between the engram of Coke and the engram of Pepsi, because both are colas and both are almost always stacked on the shelves next to each other. So each time we buy one we see the other and the pathway between them is reinforced. By contrast, we might have a less strong pathway between Coke and Sprite, or Coke and Tango, because these brands are not so often placed on the shelves together.

Networks and pathways are created by a process known as encoding. If we learn about a brand through advertising, then the pathway into that brand's engram will be encoded via advertising. Once in place the pathway can then work both ways: a memory of the ad can trigger a memory of the brand, and a memory of the brand can likewise trigger a memory of the ad.

Encoding is different for different types of memory system. The sort of encoding that takes place in Active Learning requires ideas to be manipulated, evaluated, and often completely reinterpreted. This is done by what is known as working memory.

Working Memory

Memory is commonly divided into long-term memory – things we "keep" for later – and short-term memory – things we recall as we go along, but do not store. It may be tempting to think that we use short-term memory to perform the manipulation in Active Learning. But it was established by George Miller (1956) that true short-term memory only has a capacity of between five and nine items of information, so in order to overcome this limitation we use an additional system of temporary memory caches known as working memory.

The concept of working memory was first developed by Alan Baddeley in the early 1970s (Baddeley & Hitch 1974). Baddeley defined working memory as consisting of a "central executive" system which does the thinking, backed up by two specialized temporary storage systems, one to hold speech-based information and one for visual coding. Working memory shares the fragility of short-term memory. Schacter describes this as follows:

> Everyone is familiar with the operation of working memory from experiences in day-to-day life. Imagine that you need to look up a friend's number in the phone book. You find the number, then walk across the room to make the call, all the while madly repeating the digits to yourself as rapidly as you can. If you are distracted for even a moment during your walk to the phone, you will need to consult the book again; if you punch in the number successfully, you will probably forget it almost immediately. (Schacter 1996: 43)

Transferring memories from working to long-term memory is also done by encoding. In order to deliberately remember something, we use a technique known as "elaborative encoding." Schacter again:

> If we want to improve our chances of remembering an incident or learning a fact, we need to make sure we carry out elaborative encoding by reflecting on the information and relating it to things we already know. Laboratory studies have shown that simply intending to remember something is unlikely to be helpful. (Schacter 1996: 45)

One common example of elaborative encoding is writing things down. This has been shown to increase our learning by anything up to four times, even if we never again read what we have written. The reason is thought to be because writing increases the connections to other engrams, and improves the accessibility of the memory.

This process of encoding is, of course, the elaboration that is referred to by Petty and Cacioppo in their Elaboration Likelihood Model, and one can see why the advertising industry finds it so attractive. If advertising can persuade someone to elaborate and encode the rational message it delivers, then that message will be learned more efficiently and will inevitably be more easily recalled. The problem with this way of looking at things is that it assumes that other learning systems, because they are less efficient, are also less effective.

To understand how a less efficient learning system can actually be more effective than a more efficient one, I need to explain how long-term memory is divided up.

Long-Term Memory Systems

At its simplest, our mental knowledge can be divided into two basic types: *procedural memory* and *declarative memory*.

Procedural memory covers all the myriad tasks we learn to perform, from boiling an egg to riding a bike. It is thought by some to reside in its own system, which is able to automatically provide us with the knowledge to enable these tasks to be performed, without us having to "demand" it or indeed think about it at all. Procedural memory is what we use to manage the physical task of driving a car (changing gear, depressing the clutch, braking, accelerating, etc.) whilst paying attention to the conversation we are having with our passenger and watching for buses to pull out.

So procedural memory covers "doing" things, and can be acquired explicitly or implicitly. Declarative memory in contrast covers "knowing" things and is therefore by definition explicit. Cohen defines it as being:

> A system . . . in which information is . . . first processed and encoded, then stored in some explicitly accessible form for later use and then ultimately retrieved upon demand. (Cohen 1984: 96)

Declarative knowledge arises from two different memory systems known as semantic and episodic. Episodic memory is memory that is linked to subjective experience; semantic memory is the storage of rules, references, and meanings without the knowledge of how or when these rules were acquired. So, for example, "knowing" about skidding and nearly running someone over is likely to be an episodic memory, because it will be indelibly linked to a time and place in your mind. "Knowing" that the car drives better if you change gear frequently is likely to be a semantic memory, because it is unlikely you will recall when or even how you found that out.

Episodic memory requires much more thorough encoding than semantic memory, and I think this explains why we find advertisements hard to remember. An advertisement seen for the first time is unlikely to be anything we are familiar with, so it is a new memory. In order to recall it we have to have encoded it sufficiently thoroughly for there to be a "picture" in our mind of part of it and possibly an idea of when we saw or heard it. We also need well-established pathways to the engram of the brand that was being advertised. Ad memories are therefore the equivalent of highly complex new episodic memories and, like any episodic memory, the pathways can quite easily become obscured or lost altogether. That is why we often find we can recall an element from an ad, but not the ad itself; or we can recall the ad, but not the brand it was advertising.

That isn't necessarily true of the *influence* that an ad might have on us. An ad can influence our beliefs about a brand, which in turn can influence our attitudes towards that brand. These beliefs and attitudes are the equivalent of "rules and meanings," so they will be relatively simple concepts that are stored in semantic memory. Of course, they still require pathways to link them to the brand, but compared with ads they are quite easy to encode.

But here again we find an important distinction between beliefs and attitudes. Going back to the sports car in Chapter 2, it is very likely that that hardly any other cars can do 163 mph, so that belief will be a new memory. That means we have to encode not only the pathway linking the belief to the

Ferrari, but we also have to encode the belief itself. However, most attitudes generally already exist as concepts in our memory – we will already know what is meant by something being thrilling or exciting – so all we have to do is encode a link between the existing attitude and the Ferrari brand. That is an altogether much less onerous task for our brain to perform.

By lumping memory systems such as episodic and semantic memory together under the banner of declarative memory it is implied that these are all able to be "declared," (i.e., recalled and described). I think this is a major error, because it implies that these important memories can *only* be formed explicitly; that is, when we are *conscious* that we are learning something. This turns out not to be the case, as we will see when we consider the converse to explicit memory – implicit memory.

Implicit Memory

Implicit memory is where we store implicit (i.e. automatic) learning. Eysenck and Keane explain implicit memory as follows:

> Implicit memory differs from explicit memory in that there is an absence of conscious recollection . . . Traditional measures of memory (e.g. free and cued recall and recognition) involve use of direct instructions to retrieve information about specific experiences. Thus they can all be regarded as measures of explicit memory . . . Implicit memory is revealed when performance on a task is facilitated in the absence of conscious recollection. (Eysenck & Keane 2000: 188)

Implicit memory differs from explicit memory in two other important ways. The first is that it is much bigger in its capacity. It has to be, because it holds all the procedural knowledge that we use to live our lives. If our implicit memory were to be filled up then we might forget how to breathe, or how to get out of bed in the morning.

The capacity of implicit memory was demonstrated in the 1970s in a famous experiment by Lionel Standing (1973). Standing's experiment used recognition, which is an automatic memory function that taps direct into implicit memory. He exposed subjects to an initial set of pictures, and 2 days later showed them a second set of pictures. The second set comprised pairs of pictures, each pair containing one picture they had seen in the first set, and one they had not. Respondents were asked to identify which picture they had seen before. If their performance in identifying the pictures they had been exposed to in the initial set was better than average, the number of pictures was increased. Standing eventually ran out of funding when the initial exposed set reached 10 000 images, and still at this level respondents performed better than average at identifying which pictures they had first been exposed to.

This contradicts a belief most of us (including marketers) hold that explicit memory is our most capacious memory store. In fact, explicit memory is extremely limited. Steven Rose (1992), quoting a recall game which tests explicit memory called Kim's game, finds that subjects exposed to a set of random objects for 2 minutes and asked to memorize them can, on average, recall only about 18 items, and can rarely exceed 25 items unless trained specifically for the task.

The second way in which implicit memory differs from explicit memory is that it is more durable and long-lasting. Allen and Reber (1980) first identified this in a test of artificial language grammar learning. It was found that, after a 2-year period, many of the rules which had been actively learned had been forgotten; but the grammatical behavior, which had been learned automatically and *implicitly*, persisted and could still be manifested after 2 years.

The role that implicit learning has in this was later confirmed by word-fragment completion tests conducted by Tulving *et al.* (1982). Daniel Schacter (1996) describes this test as follows. A list of words was shown to subjects, for example, *assassin, octopus, avocado, mystery, sheriff, and climate*. They were then invited back and shown another list, which contained some of the original words and some new words, for example, *octopus, twilight, dinosaur*, and *mystery*, and asked which they remembered. This tested conscious, explicit memory. Afterwards they were then shown fragments of words, for example : *ch- - - -nk, oc- - -us, -og-y- -n, -l-m-te*, some of which were from the list shown earlier, and some not. This enabled their implicit memory to be tested.

The results, as described by Shacter, were a complete surprise:

We tested people either one hour or one week after they had studied the list. Conscious memory was, of course, much less accurate after a week than after an hour, but there was just as much priming on the word-fragment completion test after a week as there was after an hour. The implication of this finding is fascinating: something other than a conscious memory of seeing the word is responsible for priming on the word-fragment completion test. (Schacter 1996: 166–7)

This finding was a surprise because common sense says actively "learning" something should register it more strongly in the memory than implicitly "acquiring" it. In fact, the reverse appears to be true. These findings again directly contradict the assumptions made by those who adhere to the persuasion model of advertising, which are that it is the attentively processed messages that endure, and that inattentively processed content makes little or no long-term contribution to brand decisions.

There is no accepted psychological explanation for why active learning is less durable than implicit learning, because there is as yet no general explanation of how we forget. Schacter suggests that forgetting is the result of interference from the increasing traffic:

> As time passes, we encode and store new experiences that interfere with our ability to recall previous ones. I can remember what I had for breakfast today, but not what I had for breakfast on this day a year ago because I have had many breakfasts since then that interfere with my ability to pick out any single one from the crowd . . . It seems likely that as time passes, interference from new experiences makes it progressively more difficult to find a retrieval cue that elicits an increasingly blurred engram. (Schacter 1996: 76)

Using our analogy above, what he is saying is that as a lot of other pathways are created across the grass field, it becomes increasingly difficult to see and follow the original.

This could explain why implicit memory is more durable. Saving something in explicit memory is a conscious act, so you can "remember" whatever you want – you effectively have control of the field and you can adjust and add to the pathways as often as you feel is necessary. But because explicit memory is smaller than implicit memory, the field is more limited, and this means that it is relatively easy to obscure existing pathways. That is why it is relatively easy to forget something like an advertisement or a belief. But implicit memory is pretty much inexhaustible and is not conscious. This means the field is much bigger and you do *not* have control of it. So the pathways will stay there until something else just happens to come along and use exactly that same bit of the field.

Schacter and Tulving's experiments took place in situations where their subjects were able to pay as much attention as they wanted, so they were not able to test how much attention was paid. However, these experiments have been repeated in both full attention and divided attention environments (Jacoby *et al.* 1993). The findings were yet another surprise, as they showed that attention at the time of learning may be of crucial importance to subsequent conscious recollection, but is irrelevant to implicit memory.

How Does Implicit Memory Work?

So what sort of system does implicit memory use? The priming done in Schacter and Tulving's original tests was what is known as perceptual priming – the subjects did not have to understand what was shown to them in order for it to prime recognition. Following on from their experiment on word priming, they started an investigation to find out if object priming also worked. To test this hypothesis they exposed students to line drawings of two different types of objects:

- Possible objects, which can exist in reality
- Impossible objects (such as those designed by M.C. Esher), which cannot exist in reality

What was revealed was that the possible objects primed recognition just as the words had, but the impossible objects did not. From this they theorized that priming depends on a perceptually based memory system that stores information about the overall "structure" of objects. The system cannot store impossible objects because there is no consistent overall structure to store.

Using these results, Schacter and Tulving were able to deduce what sort of memory system implicit memory employed. They christened this system the Perceptual Representation System (PRS):

> The PRS allows us to identify objects in our everyday environment and to recognise familiar words. [It] is specialised to deal with the form and structure of words and objects, but it does not "know" anything about what words mean or what objects are used for. Meaningful associations are handled by the semantic memory which co-operates closely with PRS. (Schacter 1996: 184)

Considering this alongside what we have learned before about implicit memory, a model starts to develop which we can apply to brands and advertising. Here we have a system that operates well at low or divided attention levels, that produces surprisingly enduring memories of structural information about words and objects, but does not necessarily know anything about what they mean. This suggests that implicit memory is a system that can create exceptionally strong associations between brands and elements perceived in advertising, but without anything much being understood about their significance.

The problem with all this is that if anything it reinforces the views of Sutherland, Sylvester and Blackston, which are that advertising processed at a shallow level, with low or zero levels of attention, doesn't connect with any "meaning," and so isn't able to achieve anything very important in influencing behavior. But Shacter and Tulving did one final experiment which blows this idea right out of the water. This was a test to see if implicit learning could connect to conceptual memory.

Conceptual Memory

Conceptual memory is part of our semantic memory. Concepts can be defined simply as ideas that attach meaning to anything we perceive. We start learning concepts right from the cradle and they form an important part of our ability to judge the value of things around us. Because they relate to storage of rules, references, and meanings, concepts are by definition included in semantic memory.

Schacter and Tulving were aware that the established view of Implicit Learning was that it was purely perceptual and could not interact with or contribute anything to semantic memory. So they decided to test this idea and establish if implicit memory could deal with *conceptual* priming. To do this they used amnesiacs, because there is evidence that amnesia damages explicit memory but not implicit memory (Schacter 1996: 189).

What they did was to show amnesiac patients sentences that made no sense, for example, "The notes were sour because the seams split" and then show them a clue word, in this case "bagpipes." They found that when the sentences were shown on their own, even several days later, the amnesiac patients were often able to supply the clue word, even though they frequently denied ever having seen either the sentence or the clue word before.

These experiments were replicated by Vaidya *et al.* (1995), showing all four permutations to amnesiacs: implicit perceptual and conceptual cues and explicit perceptual and conceptual cues. The amnesiacs did badly on both explicit cue tests and well on both implicit cue tests.

This may seem to be straying further and further away from the subject of advertising, but in fact these are probably the most important psychology experiments in this entire book. As we said earlier, conceptual priming requires access to semantic memory in order to allow us to understand the *meaning* of a cue. The implications of these experiments are that implicit memory not only operates in the *perceptual* domain of Schacter's PRS system, but also in the *conceptual* domain of semantic memory.

This has a remarkable implication for the way in which we process advertising. You see, our attitudes towards brands depend upon concepts to give them meaning. You won't buy a Ferrari for the thrill of driving it if you don't have a "feeling" for what thrilling means. But now we have identified a way in which subconscious inattentive implicit learning, which connects with implicit memory, can store not just perceptions, but also *meaning* in our brain. We have, in effect, found a mental mechanism by which advertising might be able to influence us without our having any idea that it has done so.

6

How We Process Communication

"In order to type these sentences into my computer, I must retrieve words and grammatical rules I learned long ago, yet I do not have any subjective experience of 'remembering' them"

Daniel Schacter
Searching for Memory (1996)

In Chapter 4 we identified three types of learning: Active, which requires high attention; Passive, which requires low attention; and Implicit, which requires no attention. In the last chapter we established that these interact with a variety of memory systems. We also discovered that implicit memory – the memory system that implicit learning connects with – is able to store both perceptions *and* concepts.

If we want to understand fully how communication of any sort is processed we first have to identify the different processes that make up processing. That probably sounds like nonsense, but what I am trying to say is that although it feels like we process communication holistically as a single event, in practice different types of mental activity occur, and they communicate with different parts of our memory. The first of these is Perception.

Perception

Schacter's idea of a perceptual representation system defines the first mental act in any communication processing as perceiving something. We perceive

Seducing the Subconscious: The Psychology of Emotional Influence in Advertising, First Edition. Robert Heath.
© 2012 Robert Heath. Published 2012 by John Wiley & Sons, Ltd.

the phenomena that surround us through our senses, by seeing them, hearing them, and also by touching, tasting, and smelling them. The only senses relevant to advertising perception are sight and hearing. Note that this word Perception is being used not in the sense of the adjective *perceptive* (i.e., being alert or observant or clever) but in its simplest sense, to describe the act of "perceiving" phenomena.

To illustrate Perception let me describe another car driving story. Imagine you are driving down a motorway and the brake lights on the car in front light up. Observing the lights going on is a Perception. Note I don't say that the car in front is braking, as you can't perceive the brakes operating; in fact, you can't even see the result of the brakes being operated unless you perceive the car rapidly slowing down or stopping.

The important thing to understand is that Perception like this, as a process, is fully automatic and instantaneous. It must therefore be carried out using Implicit Learning. It is the same when you hear a sound, like an aeroplane flying overhead. You don't have to tell your brain to perceive either the brake lights or the sound of the plane, it just does it.

Perception is designed to be fully automatic to prevent us from getting into trouble. If perception was not automatic, we would fall down holes we didn't see in the sidewalk, be run over by cars we didn't hear, and generally render ourselves vulnerable to all sorts of grief. Anyone who has hit their head on a low beam they have failed to perceive in an old house will know exactly what I'm talking about.

So, back to the example. The brain has perceived brake lights on the car in front. What happens next is also automatic, which is that we "conceptualize." In other words, we link various meanings to the perception.

Conceptualization

Conceptualization also occurs instantaneously, in parallel with perception. Concepts, as we discussed in the previous chapter, reside in semantic memory, and can be defined as ideas that attach meaning to anything perceived. They have to be generated instantaneously, otherwise perceptions would be pretty useless. It's no good perceiving a hole in the sidewalk if we don't, at the same time, conceptualize falling into it and injuring ourselves.

So when we perceive the brake lights lighting up on this car ahead of us on the motorway, what concepts are generated? The first is danger. It isn't for nothing that brake lights are red. The color red is conceptualized by all of us as we grow up as a warning: when we see something red we are instinctively and subconsciously alerted to possible problems.

Another concept that might be generated by perceiving the red brake lights on the car ahead is that it is "slowing down" or "stopping." Whether or not this happens depends on how much driving you do. If you are an experienced driver then slowing down might be an idea that is embedded in your semantic memory linked to the perception of red brake lights on a moving car.

What is important is that this all happens without any action on our part. Both Perception and Conceptualization are examples of Implicit Learning that occur automatically and instantaneously. We have no control over them and no way of stopping them occurring; they happen whether we want them to or not.

What happens next, however, *is* under our control.

Analysis

Analysis is the term I use to describe what we generally call thinking. The definition of the word Analysis is to "examine in detail the elements" (*Oxford Compact English Dictionary* 1996: 32). Examination, regardless of how fleetingly it takes place, always requires us to employ some sort of cognitive resource like working memory to think about what we have perceived and consider any concepts that have been generated. It is therefore an act of cognition that we initiate and control. You can't "examine" something fully automatically (although you can, as we will see below, examine something semi-automatically).

So you've perceived the red brake lights and linked them to the concept of danger or slowing down. If, at the same time, you've perceived that the car is a long way ahead, and linked that to the concept of "no immediate threat," your analysis of the situation might lead you to do nothing, or perhaps just lift your foot off the accelerator a tad. You can do this with very little thinking. Indeed, you might think you can do it with no thinking at all. But at some level you would have needed to analyze the situation and "think" what action to take.

Why do we know this involves thinking? Well, suppose the car is quite close. Or suppose the road is wet. Or suppose you can perceive a big traffic queue ahead of the car. Or suppose your brakes are not very good. In these cases your analysis would lead you to a different course of action. Quite probably you would apply the brakes yourself starting a similar mental chain reaction in the driver behind you. And if the car ahead was *very* close you might even swerve into the lane to one side of the car to avoid crashing into it. These are all judgments that need some sort of analytical thinking to be performed.

Incidentally, that's not to say that this analysis requires a lot of attention. Thinking can take place on any point on the active – passive attention spectrum. If the situation isn't threatening, then the thinking might be done with hardly any attention at all. On the other hand, if the situation is potentially dangerous then the thinking might be highly attentive, as in "Oh my goodness, I'm about to plough into the back of the car in front."

Nor is this analysis necessarily done fully consciously. This is a complicated area, and later on we will examine the whole issue of consciousness in more detail. For now you can assume that the analysis takes place at least at some sort of semi-conscious level.

An Improved Theory of Communication Processing

So we have three different *types* of mental activity – Perception, Conceptualization, and Analysis – that interact with three different types of learning – Active, Passive, and Implicit – and interact with at least two different types of memory – Explicit and Implicit. How does this all fit together? Let's start with our three different types of learning. For ease of reference I've set all this out in Table 6.1.

As you can see from Table 6.1, Implicit Learning is fully automatic and independent of attention. This means by definition it makes no use of our "conscious thinking" faculties, what we call our cognitive resource (Damasio 2003). Implicit Learning is operating all the time we are awake, and to some extent when we are asleep as well. So we are constantly perceiving things in our environment; and, in line with Tulving and Schacter's research, we are also constantly linking these perceptions with our semantic memory and generating concepts from them. What we are *not* constantly doing is analyzing anything. Analysis requires at least some sort of attention and cognitive resource to be deployed, and Implicit Learning is independent of attention and cognitive resource. This type of Implicit Learning, according to the advertising industry, contributes nothing of value to advertising processing.

Table 6.1 Attention, Memory, and Learning Summary

Consciousness	Attention	Memory Type	Capacity	Learning	Function	Durability
Explicit	Very high	Working	Small	Active	Analysis	None
Explicit	High	Episodic	Modest	Active + Passive	Analysis	Poor
Explicit	Low	Semantic	Large	Active + Passive	Analysis	Modest
Implicit	None	Semantic	Enormous	Implicit	Concepts	Very Good
Implicit	None	Procedural	Gigantic	Implicit	Concepts	Excellent

Passive Learning is attentive but the levels of attention are low. This type of learning is semi-automatic, and is the default state for when you are not engaging in active learning. In a Passive Learning mode we don't deploy much cognitive resource, which means we will be doing some analysis of the perceptions and concepts being generated by Implicit Learning, but not very much. Also, any analysis we do carry out will not be very efficient. It's perhaps a bit like listening to a lecture when you are drunk: you think you understand and are remembering what is being said, but afterwards you're really not sure if you got it all and understood it correctly.

This might explain why peripheral processing (i.e., Passive Learning) is regarded by the advertising industry as having little long-term effect on attitudes, and therefore being a poor way in which to process advertising (Petty & Cacioppo 1996). It isn't that Passive Learning *doesn't* change attitudes, because it certainly can. Much more likely is that, because it is poor at analysis, it just doesn't change the sort of overt beliefs and attitudes that are associated with message-driven persuasion.

But one thing Passive Learning *is* good at is identifying brands. In advertising it is usual for a brand to use some sort of symbol or logo to identify itself, and these are relatively easy to recognize and analyze. This, of course, is critically important for advertising processing, as an ad can only work if you are aware at least at some level of what brand is being advertised.

Active Learning is highly attentive. It is motivated by a desire to gather information, and so it deploys high levels of cognitive resource. In an Active Learning mode we will be analyzing what we perceive and the concepts that are triggered very thoroughly and very efficiently. But because Active Learning is conative (i.e., requires an act of will for it to take place) it doesn't happen all that often, and when it does happen it often doesn't last very long.

Active Learning is the type of processing that most people in the advertising industry regard as being necessary for advertising to work. But in reality the odds are stacked against this happening. Unless you work in the ad industry, Active Learning is the least frequent way we process advertisements. Passive Learning is fairly frequently used, because this will happen most times we are actually looking at or listening to an ad. And of course the most frequent type of learning used to process advertising, the one which always happens and is never switched off, is Implicit Learning.

Now I've explained what these three types of learning do, you might think the whole thing is relatively simple and straightforward. Sadly you would be wrong. There are a number of issues that make the process even more complicated. Two of the most important are Mere Exposure (occasionally known as Subliminal Mere Exposure) and Peripheral Exposure.

Mere Exposure

The term Mere Exposure was coined by Bob Zajonc (1968) to refer to the hypothesis that simply being exposed to something could change your attitudes towards it. Some years later the theory was extended to include exposure at levels below which we are able to perceive anything. These levels, typically below 40 milliseconds, are defined as subliminal.

In a well-known experiment, Kunst-Wilson and Zajonc (1980) exposed irregular polygonal shapes to subjects at time lengths below which they could be physically perceived. This meant that any processing that took place would by definition be happening at zero levels of conscious attention *and* zero levels of awareness. Astonishingly, these experiments showed that subjects could form a preference for these irregular shapes despite supposedly not being able to perceive them. This effect is known as "priming," and is the same mechanism that was used by Tulving and Schacter in the experiments we discussed in the last chapter to demonstrate the power of implicit memory.

Does this mean that Vance Packard could have been right when he warned the American public of the dangers of subliminal advertising? The answer is categorically no. Advertising that operates below the threshold of perception has been shown to be weak at best and generally ineffective (Moore 1982), a conclusion supported by a meta-analysis of 23 studies by Trappey which showed "that the effect of subliminal marketing stimuli on influencing consumers' choice behaviour or selection process is negligible" (Trappey 1996: 528). But that is not to say that subliminal exposure has no effect. Recent experiments have apparently shown that words exposed subliminally, even if not perceived, can be conceptualized, and can cause us to manifest the same feelings as would be created if they were exposed at normal levels. So, for example, if we are shown the word "rapist" at a subliminal level then apparently it can be shown that we generate the same type of emotional responses as we would experience if the word were visible. The difference, however, is that the responses are very weak, as has been found to be the response to subliminally exposed advertising.

What this does illustrate is that we can be influenced quite easily by what might be termed "incidental" exposure. For example, in a series of experiments discussed in more detail in Chapter 15, Berger and Fitzsimons were able to show that attitudes to orange colored products such as orange soda drinks were enhanced during Halloween, when orange pumpkins are commonplace, and participants who used an orange or green pen to complete a survey chose more orange or green products (Berger & Fitzsimons 2007).

The psychologist Robert Bornstein was able to explain findings like these, and the Mere Exposure results, by using what he called a Perceptual Fluency Model. In his own words, "Perception which takes place without awareness leads to inexplicable familiarity, which in turn raises favourability" (Bornstein 1992: 197).

So although we can discount subliminal advertising exposure, it is worth noting that Bornstein's perceptual fluency explanation applies just as well to *subconscious* mere exposure. And one of the most common forms of subconscious exposure is peripheral exposure.

Peripheral Exposure

Peripheral exposure is a function of the way in which our eyes operate. During moments of fixation the eye has access to three regions of viewing. The *foveal* region is defined as the area in which detail is visible, and is a circle around the point of fixation subtending approximately 2° of angle at the eye. This area is usually capable of discerning roughly 6–8 letters. The *parafoveal* region is an area that subtends an angle of approximately 5°, equivalent to 15–20 letters. Objects and words within the parafovea can be easily recognized and attended to. The area outside the parafoveal region is defined as the peripheral region.

Recognition is possible within the peripheral region, but it is difficult if not impossible to pay active attention to anything seen peripherally. You can test this for yourself by holding a newspaper in front of your face, then moving it a few centimeters to the side without moving your eyes. You'll find that if you move it by about 5 cm you can still recognize shapes on it, but much more than 10 cm movement and you really can't distinguish anything. Yet there is no doubt that perception of some kind is still going on. And how good this perception is depends very much on how our brain treats this area, as can be shown by this story.

Some years ago I performed an experiment to investigate how people read newspapers. In order to do this I asked subjects to wear a lightweight head-mounted eye camera attached to a TV screen. The cross-hairs on the screen allowed us to see exactly what part of the newspaper they were focusing on as they paged through it.

One of the respondents was a woman in her early forties, and I noticed something very strange about her reading behavior. She would focus on the headline of an article, then look about 6 inches to the left and start tracking down as if she were reading the article. The only problem was that where she was looking there was nothing to read.

She kept doing this until she had finished the newspaper, and I then asked her rather impertinently if she had any sort of problem with her eyes. She replied that she had an early onset form of macular degeneration, where the receptors in the foveal and parafoveal region (i.e., the parts of the eye that are able to see detail) had ceased to work. This meant that she could only make out large words by looking straight at them, so she had taught herself to read small words using her peripheral vision.

The implications of this are pretty amazing. Although we *think* that the processing capacity of our periphery is poor, it seems evident from what this woman was able to do that this is just something our brains tell us. In all likelihood we are able to perceive things quite well in our periphery, but our brain deludes us into thinking we cannot in order to enable us to be better at focusing on the detail in our foveal and paravoveal regions.

Incidentally, this is only one of a number of tricks and illusions our brain plays on us. For example, as we discuss later, our eyes move across our field of vision in jumps called saccades, but our brain compensates for these jumps and makes it appear we are moving them smoothly. Our eyes also project everything on our retina upside down, and the brain automatically inverts the picture so it appears the right ways up.

Anyway, the reason that peripheral exposure is so important is that it illustrates that we can process perceptions in our periphery far better than we think we can. As I mentioned in Chapter 2, Herb Krugman noted the importance of peripheral exposure when he pointed out that we are not especially conscious of those things we see in our periphery, and that much of what people call subliminal perception is actually just peripheral seeing.

To help make clear quite why this is so important, here is a description of an interesting experiment.

The Power of Peripheral Exposure

In 1997 a team led by Stewart Shapiro decided to investigate the effect of incidental exposure of advertising on product choice (Shapiro *et al.* 1997). The test advertising comprised a line-drawn picture of a carrot, accompanied by the slogan "By Nature, Organically grown for delicious safe eating." A similar ad was also produced for a can-opener. These ads were then embedded in the left-hand column of three columns of type on a computer, so as to look like a magazine.

The next step was to get a group of volunteers and ask them to perform a test. This group was asked to read the center column of the magazine and answer some questions about it. To ensure that they did this they were assisted by a cursor which scrolled through the center column at their most comfortable reading speed. A test group worked on material where the ads were present and a control group on material where the ads were absent. Both groups performed a 5-minute distraction task before answering a series of questions about how likely they were to buy a range of different products.

The results were startling. The researchers found that in the group where the ads had been present a much higher likelihood of buying carrots and a can-opener was expressed, even though the ads had only been exposed to their peripheral vision.

To ensure that these subjects had not sneaked a look at the ads, they were shown them afterwards and the level of recognition checked with the group who had not been exposed to the ads. No difference was found. The conclusions, in the words of the researchers themselves, were that:

> Our findings indicate that an advertisement has the potential to affect future buying decisions even if subjects, who are preoccupied by another task, do not process the ad attentively and, thus, do not recollect ever having seen the ad. (Shapiro *et al.* 1997: 102)

So what explains these extraordinary results? Is it that the items were perceived incidentally in the periphery, as in the mere exposure tests; and that this perception increased their familiarity, which in turn increased favorability? Or is it that the ads were focused on and processed, but the exposure was so fleeting that they were completely forgotten? Possibly it was a combination of the two. But whatever the explanation, this test shows that it isn't just those things in advertising you look *directly* at that can affect your behavior.

As a footnote to this chapter, it is worth quoting the first line of the conclusions of this paper. The researchers said: "Advertisers should be very encouraged by the results of this study" (Shapiro *et al.* 1997: 102). One might expect they would be. Yet this experiment, published in a top-ranking world journal, has never been publicized by the advertising industry, and has, to my knowledge, never been repeated. Why? Because the ad industry sticks to its belief that it is only the most attentive of our three types of communication – the one in which Active Learning takes place – that has any real importance. And one of the reasons they stick to this line is that ad agencies have built their reputations on being able to encourage us to pay the high levels of attention necessary to facilitate Active Learning. They do this using their creativity, and in the next chapter I explain why they are not as successful as they think they are.

7

Problems with Getting Attention

"We possess quite elaborate blocking or filtering devices to prevent new information from cluttering up our memories"

Steven Rose
The Making of Memory (1992)

You'll remember that in Chapter 4 we established that people don't pay much attention towards advertising, especially TV advertising. Advertising agencies see their main task as *making* people pay attention to advertising using creativity. How exactly do they achieve this, and, more importantly, why doesn't it seem to work?

Arthur Kover is possibly the only academic I know brave enough to have actually gone into an ad agency and interviewed creative teams. These are the people we mentioned in Chapter 1 who come up with the daft ideas which often don't seem to have anything much to do with the message the company wants to get over. There are generally two people in a creative team: the copywriter, who dreams up the words, and the art director, who takes care of the visuals. Kover interviewed copywriters, because they are usually seen as the more influential members of the team (also, in my experience they tend to be more lucid and communicative than art directors!).

What Kover wanted to know was what the creative team thought creativity was for. The results of his research, again published in one of the world's leading academic journals, weren't much of a surprise to anyone who worked in advertising. The copywriters confirmed that the primary role of creativity was to get attention and the secondary role to get the message over.

Seducing the Subconscious: The Psychology of Emotional Influence in Advertising, First Edition. Robert Heath.
© 2012 Robert Heath. Published 2012 by John Wiley & Sons, Ltd.

Copywriters' implicit theories of advertising were that these two steps were sequential: first they had to break through and attract interest; second they had to deliver the message (Kover 1995: 599). More interesting was *how* they thought they could get attention, especially attention towards TV advertising, which was the dominant medium at the time. Kover reports that there were two ways copywriters believed they could do this.

> Two general ways to break through emerged: subverting and forcing. Subverting means presenting something that is disconcerting or charming, something unexpected enough that it slips past the guard of indifference. Forcing means jolting the viewer into paying some initial attention ... so that the viewer does not see or hear the unexpected. (Kover 1995: 599)

Of these, the more commonplace approach nowadays is subverting. Advertisers use words such as "ingratiating," "charming," and "seductive" to describe subverting creativity, reinforcing the connection to emotive content. Examples of subverting advertising include the Michelin Tyre "Baby" and the Cottonelle Puppy campaigns in the USA, and the Marks & Spencer "Food Porn" campaign in the UK. But the more successful approach in getting attention is probably Forcing, in that some sort of shock almost always increases the attention we pay, regardless of whether we wish it to or not. An example of Forcing is the famous Apple 1984 advertisement. In a cinema filled with zombie-like men, a women athlete runs in chased by guards and hurls a hammer through a vast cinema screen, releasing them from the grip of the people who are evidently controlling them. Another example is our old friend Gio Compario.

But although Forcing creativity gets attention, it is recognized by copywriters as something of a dead end: the more you use it, the more people get used to it, and the less well it works. As Kover writes:

> The copywriters realized that forcing gets increasingly harder. Each instance that a commercial (or any other media message) forces attention makes it infinitesimally more difficult for the next advertising message, whether for this brand or another. (Kover 1995: 600)

Of course, once the TV viewer has been "subverted" or "forced" to be attentive to the advertising, the message has to be delivered. Copywriters believed the best way to get the message over was to start some sort of a dialogue with the consumer.

To connect, the message needs to mesh with viewers' lives and needs. To make this connection, copywriters work out the message with an internalized target person. The message is hammered out in a dialogue until that person . . . can accept the message. (Kover 1995: 600)

I think the language being used here is very revealing. Note how the consumer (you and me) is characterized as a powerless target, to be made to pay attention, and then to have a message "meshed" into their lives. This attitude towards the consumer suggests copywriters see us very much as John Philip Jones described, as being apathetic and rather stupid and having information insinuated into us by the use of psychological techniques that destroy the consumer's defences.

But we consumers, like all human beings, are not as vulnerable as advertisers think we are. We have highly developed defense mechanisms to protect us against being exploited by these psychological techniques. One defense mechanism that was known about many years before Kover's research is contradiction; or, as it is called in psychology, counter-argument.

Counter-Argument

In 1984, Brock and Shavitt developed what they called their Cognitive Response Model of persuasion. In this they postulated that the ability of communication to persuade the individual lay not with them simply recalling the message, but in interpreting it into their own words, rehearsing it, then remembering what they had rehearsed. In their view:

[The] impact of [communication] on persuasion . . . depends on the extent to which individuals articulate and rehearse their own . . . thoughts." (Brock & Shavitt 1983: 91)

In other words, rehearsal of one's own thoughts is a more important determinant of persistence of persuasion than simply rehearsing the message arguments. This, of course, requires a lot of attention to be paid toward the advertising and the message to be fully understood and "elaborated." So where, you might ask, is the defense mechanism in this?

The answer is surprisingly simple. The problem that Brock and Shavitt found with this level of over-elaborated attention is that it can very easily lead to counter-argument. Put simply, the more you think about the claim an advertisement makes for a brand, the easier you find it to contradict that claim.

For example, take the claim that skin creams alleviate wrinkles and make you look young. A few minutes' consideration leads you to realize that if this was true, then it would have been plastered all over the news as a spectacular scientific breakthrough. On the other hand, putting any old cream on your face and rubbing it in probably makes your skin more flexible and pliant, and temporarily makes wrinkles seem to vanish. So, true or not, there are two perfectly valid reasons to disbelieve what the advertiser is claiming.

However, this gives scant comfort to us, the beleaguered consumer, as in order to counter-argue a claim we not only have to allow ourselves to elaborate and interpret all the messages presented to us in advertising, but we then have to spend further time studying them and rejecting them. Frankly, few people, other than those who work in the ad industry, want to spend their time thinking about advertising in that much detail.

Fortunately, our brains have conveniently given us another defense mechanism which allows us to avoid doing this. This defense mechanism is perceptual filtering.

Perceptual Filtering

As we learned earlier, our eyes and ears (and noses, for that matter) perceive *everything* that is going on around us. If all of this information were to be fed into our conscious brains at once then our mental faculties would very quickly be overwhelmed and cease to work properly. So to prevent this happening the mind automatically filters out what it considers to be the irrelevant perceptions and allows through just a few for further consideration. Everything else gets ignored by the conscious mind.

This is perfectly illustrated by what is known as Cocktail Party syndrome. Stephen Rose describes this very well:

> Perceptual filtering . . . ensures that, of all the information arriving at one's eyes or ears at any given time, only a small proportion is actually registered and even briefly remembered . . . An example is, of course, the well-known cocktail party phenomenon by which in a room full of babble one can concentrate – more or less! – on the voice of the person talking to one, yet can switch almost completely at will to listen to other conversation going on around. But it is not as if we have closed our ears to the other conversations – they can easily

intrude unasked, as for example if one hears one's own name mentioned elsewhere in the room. So the incoming information, in sound and vision, is entering our brains and is there being filtered for relevance by processes of which we are largely consciously unaware. (Rose 1992: 104)

What does this prove? First, although you were concentrating on the conversation you were having, you must at the same time have been continuously perceiving *all* the other conversations in the room. Second, because you were not aware you were monitoring these other conversations, you must have been doing this implicitly (learning without knowing you are learning is, after all, the definition of implicit learning).

Incidentally, because implicit learning links to concepts in semantic memory, the tone-of-voice of what was being said in all these other conversations might well have been perceived and conceptualized by you. So even though you didn't understand any of the conversations going on around you, you might have been able to tell if your name was being mentioned in a nice context or in a nasty context.

What has all this got to do with processing advertising? In order to understand this, let me first remind you what I said at the start of the last chapter: although it seems that we process advertising as a single holistic experience, it actually comprises a number of different components all being run at the same time. For example, there is always a brand, and usually a message about of some sort about that brand which may be spoken or written. Then there may be some sort of narrative story which accompanies the message, perhaps some characters in the ad playing out the narrative, and some sort of setting or scenery in the ad. And, of course, playing in the background there may well be some music.

Each of these different components of the ad may be processed at a different level of attention, using a different type of learning. You may, for example, process the narrative and characters actively, and the background scene passively; you may process the background music implicitly, and perceptually filter out the message. This often happens if the ad has an interesting plot, as in the Renault Clio campaign we discussed earlier. Of course, you may, if you are young and into pop songs, process the music actively and the characters passively, which is what might have happened with the Telma Noodles advertising. You may process the whole ad passively and perceptually filter out the brand, as in the Orange J.D. Power case study mentioned in Chapter 3. There are endless combinations. But the important thing to bear in mind is this: the more effective one component of the ad is in getting attention, the more attention it is likely to steal away from other less interesting bits of the ad (like the brand or the message).

Of course, if you work in advertising or marketing, you will probably actively process the whole ad – brand, message, narrative and characters, and music. Why? Because that's how you earn your living. This is one reason why people in the advertising industry find the idea of perceptual filtering rather hard to accept. Not only does it threaten their model of how advertising works (as described by Kover), it simply isn't something they do themselves when they are processing advertising.

That's not to say that some intelligent advertisers don't recognize the risks posed by trying to "manufacture" attention towards their ads. As early as the 1960s a visual device that created attention at the expense of understanding the message was known as a *"video vampire."* John Caples is famously reported to have said: "Instead of showing a big picture of the car, you show a big picture of Marilyn Monroe and a little picture of the car. If that doesn't work, you take some clothes off her."

And David Ogilvy similarly quoted a comment made by his art director David Scott that "When I want a good recall score all I have to do is to show a gorilla in a jock strap" (Ogilvy 1983: 161). What both of them knew but didn't say is that if you do include a gorgeous scantily clad actress or gorilla in a jockstrap in your ad, you'll get a lot of attention and recall for them, but no one will remember much else.

A very good case study that illustrates this is the launch advertising for the Citroën Xsara.

Citroën Xsara Case Study

The Citroën Xsara launch advertising first ran on TV in the UK in 2001. The advertisement featured the supermodel Claudia Schiffer in an elegant gold dress walking sexily down an equally elegant spiral staircase in a grand mansion, accompanied by some quite strident music. As she descended the stairs she slipped off her shawl, casually kicked off her shoes, loosened her hair, unzipped her dress, and stepped out revealing herself in her lacy bra and panties. The scene then cut to her emerging from the front door of the mansion and walking over to the car, as a man's voice said "The new Citroën Xsara coupé. It's the only thing to be seen in." As he said this she stroked the car, started to loosen her bra, and we cut to her discarding her panties out of the window. We then cut to her sitting in the car, apparently naked, as she said to the camera in a German accent "So, why wear anything else?"

As I'm sure you can imagine, this ad created a lot of interest, and perhaps not surprisingly got very high levels of recall. By recall I mean if you asked anyone at the time if they had seen advertising for the Citroën Xsara, a very high proportion of them would say that they had. The more interesting question is what exactly they were recalling? I had the opportunity to test this out when I delivered a paper at a conference shortly after the ad started being aired in the UK.

The conference was on market research, so the 600 or so people there were all quite interested in advertising. During my paper I asked the audience to raise their hands if they had seen any advertising recently for the Citroën Xsara. Some 550 hands went up. I then asked them if they could recall that the ad featured Claudia Schiffer walking down stairs taking her clothes off. Around 550 hands went up again. I then asked if any of them knew *why* she was taking her clothes off. Only six hands went up.

What had happened here is obvious in hindsight. Just as in the Renault Clio campaign, the narrative was connected with sex, and that made it extremely interesting. This was especially the case for men, who studied the ad carefully in order to see if Claudia Schiffer revealed anything. When questioned, men freely admitted that in the penultimate scene, when she is sitting in the car apparently naked, they ought to have been able to see her bare breasts, and, despite the fact that these were carefully hidden by the door and her arm, many men swore that they had. So, I think we can assume they were paying extremely high levels of attention.

Women, on the other hand, found the concept of Claudia Schiffer taking her clothes off to sell a car mildly offensive. They paid attention to the ad because they found it hard to believe such a dated approach was still being used in the twenty-first century.

But none of this attention was directed towards the car itself, and certainly none of it was directed towards the message that the advertisers were trying to get over, which was that the car was so elegant that it outshone even the clothes worn by a famous fashion model.

It is probably no surprise to you that the launch of the car was not the success that Citroën expected it to be. One Danish creative director confided to me that Citroën couldn't understand why using sex to sell the Renault Clio had been such a huge success, yet using sex to sell the Xsara had been such a flop. It's a sad condemnation of marketers that they can't see the difference in audience reaction between seeing a fictional tale of sophisticated flirting, and seeing a real-life celebrity doing a corny striptease.

The Citroën Xsara ad is perhaps something of an exception, in that women taking their clothes off aren't that common in UK TV ads and are unheard of in the USA. An even interesting example is that of the British Airways ad campaign that ran from 1992 all the way through to 2006. And in this case, in stark contrast to Citroën Xsara, they used perceptual filtering to their advantage.

British Airways Case Study

In 1984, British Airways (BA) introduced a new TV advertising campaign to launch their Super Club Class service. The launch TV ad, devised by Saatchi & Saatchi and directed by the ad director Tony Scott, featured the inside of a BA Jumbo Jet into which was to be fitted the new Super Club Class seat, the widest in the world.

The action for the ad all took place inside the cabin of the jumbo. As we watched, the roof of the jumbo mysteriously lifted off and a series of double seats started to descend into the cabin. While this happens a male voice told us: "This is the BA Super Club Class seat, the widest seat in the air. But being the widest seat in the air, it isn't the easiest to fit through the door. From May 1st on all our long haul routes, the world's widest seat."

At this point the roof closed and we saw that a small bird has flown into the cabin. The roof opened again to allow the bird to fly out, and the voice continued: "From the airline that cares about everyone who flies. BA, the world's favourite airline."

This ad might have been processed in a number of different ways. The roof of the cabin lifting off might have attracted some attention, but if active attention were deployed then this might lead to a counter-argument that if the roof were able to be removed this would almost certainly seriously compromise the structural integrity of the aircraft leading to it breaking up in the air. Amongst regular long-haul Club Class travelers the seats themselves might be subject to active attentive scrutiny, but they would probably have received no more than a cursory envious glance from the majority of the audience who could only dream of traveling Club Class. The claim by the voice-over that they were the "widest in the air" might have received some attention, but would doubtless have been counter-argued as being "the sort of thing they would say, whether it is true or not." The highest levels of attention would almost certainly have been reserved for the little bird, even though a moment's consideration would lead one to realize it could easily have been shooed out through the door.

All in all, it seems pretty unlikely that this narrative could have been perceived as evidence that BA was an airline that "cares about everyone who flies." The most logical take-out might be that BA cares about the businessmen who pay a fortune to fly in Club Class. Yet the ad seemed to have been very successful at increasingly BA's reputation amongst everyone.

I believe the secret of this success might be due to a feature that I haven't mentioned yet, one we all tend to perceptually filter out when we watch TV ads. That feature is the background music. Somewhat as an afterthought – in fact, just 3 weeks before the ad went on air – the ad agency added in a music track. The music they chose was the beautiful lilting duet from the Delibes opera, *Lakme*. No one watching the ad would have paid much active attention to this music, because the ad was all about the new seats. But it would have almost certainly been processed implicitly and subconsciously, like all the conversations in the Cocktail Party syndrome.

Now it so happens I've evidence that this music has a dramatic effect on the way people feel about flying on BA. This evidence has been derived from one hundred or more classes and seminars where I have played the soundtrack of this ad on its own, and asked those present to tell me how it makes them feel. In every case people tell me they feel relaxed, extremely comfortable, and as though they are floating in the air and being wonderfully looked after.

When we watch the ad, none of these feelings are consciously registered, because the music generates them automatically from concepts stored in our semantic memory. That of course means they cannot be counter-argued. Instead, after several exposures to the ad the perception of the music will subconsciously become linked by association to BA, and the conceptual values it triggers will be transferred to BA by a process called "conditioning." Conditioning will be dealt with in more detail in the next chapter, but for now let's just accept that people would have found themselves with a feeling that BA was a wonderfully comfortable way to fly, but with no idea why they had that feeling.

BA ran their advertising with this music for some 20 years, even playing it in their cabins as people boarded the plane. After a while everyone associated the duet from *Lakme* with BA, and in this way it became an excellent example of what we will later call an "emotionally competent brand association." Yet the ad agency never admitted the power of this music in shaping opinion towards the airline, and indeed in their two highly praised prize winning entries for the UK IPA Effectiveness Awards, the word "music" is never mentioned once (MacGill & Gnoddle 1995; Day *et al.* 2005). As far as they are concerned we must assume they didn't think it really had much effect.

Why should this be? One reason is because the music received hardly any active attention. This meant almost no one spontaneously recalled it in research, so it was nigh on impossible to *prove* that it had changed opinions, and easy to dismiss it altogether. But I'd say there is a better reason. After all, should anyone admit how effective an element that no one recalled had been in changing attitudes towards the airline, they would lay themselves open to the charge of influencing people's emotions without them knowing it. And that, of course, is the very last thing the advertising industry wants anyone to think they are doing.

So, as far as the ad industry is concerned, the role this captivating music had in making BA a success remains nothing more than speculation. Yet when they stopped using this music in 2007, after 15 years of being the only national carrier to remain in profit and successfully fend off the budget airlines, their reputation started to nosedive. It does make one wonder if this was purely a coincidence.

But the only way a convincing case can be built for the music having had a role in the rise and fall of BA is to establish how emotive elements like music are processed, and then show how they are able to exert an influence on us. This is the next part of the story.

Psychology of Communication: Summary

As we can see from the summary chart in Figure 7.1, the model has become a great deal more complex.

The top half of the chart is the zone of conscious attentive processing, and the bottom half is the zone of automatic inattentive processing. Within these zones there are three different ways in which we learn.

The top end of attentive processing is Active Learning. This operates at high attention levels, deploys high levels of cognitive resource, and is very good at analyzing and interpreting things. However, it requires an act of will to make it happen, so it isn't used to process ads very often.

At the other end of the attentive learning spectrum, in the middle of Figure 7.1, is Passive Learning. This operates at low attention levels, and deploys low levels of cognitive resource. It isn't much good at analysis, which is why it appears not to be very good at changing attitudes in the long term. In reality it just isn't very good at analyzing the sort of beliefs and attitudes that are associated with message-based persuasion.

Passive Learning is the default state for when we are conscious, so it is very often the way in which we process ads. But we can also learn when paying *no attention at all*. Implicit Learning operates regardless of attention, and is never switched off. Its weakness is that it doesn't connect to working memory, so it can't interpret or analyze anything.

There are also three different types of mental activity that take place when we are learning. Perception, which records all phenomena we perceive; Conceptualization, which links these phenomena to values we have stored in our mind during our lifetime; and Analysis, where we interpret and analyze these phenomena. Implicit Learning does perception and conceptualization, but doesn't do any analysis.

In order for advertising to work persuasively the analysis needs to be pretty thorough. That requires a lot of cognitive resource, which means the message part of the advertising must be processed using at least some Active Learning. Persuasion is represented by the solid line at the top.

On the other hand, working out which brand is being advertised is a relatively simple mental task, so this might well be able to be done using Passive Learning only. This is represented by the dashed line in the middle.

These activities – message interpretation and brand identification – are both vulnerable to perceptual filtering. When perceptual filtering occurs it

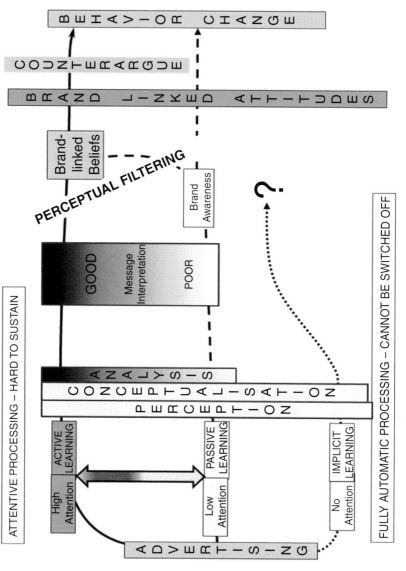

Figure 7.1 Psychology of Communication Summary Chart

can render persuasion ineffective or cause the brand being advertised not to be recorded. It often does both.

Assuming perceptual filtering does not occur, the advertising is now able to influence beliefs about the brand, which in turn influence attitudes about the brand. However, advertising can also influence attitudes directly, as in the dashed line.

But, even if the communication has overcome all these obstacles, there is one last defense mechanism we can use, which is to counter-argue it. Counter-argument, like perceptual filtering, renders persuasion ineffective. However, it requires relatively high attention to counter-argue a message and so counter-argument is less likely to impede the effects of low attention attitude change.

Implicit Learning is represented by the dotted line. It cannot be switched off, so cannot suffer from perceptual filtering; and because it is subconscious, we can't counter-argue it either. But as yet we have not been able to work out how it can influence attitudes and behavior. Nor, for that matter, have we defined how this processing interacts with consciousness. These are two of the subjects I will address in Part Three.

3

Emotion and Consciousness

8

Emotional Processing

> *"All the devices which produce emotion can be engaged automatically, without conscious deliberation."*
>
> Antonio Damasio
> *The Feeling of What Happens* (2000: 51)

Everyone in the ad industry agrees that emotion is important to advertising. Quite *why* it is important is the subject of considerable debate.

Emotion is seen by creatives as being an important component of creativity, and getting an emotional response to advertising seems to be a critical part of successful communication (Kover 1995: 605). Thinking about Kover's two different methods of getting attention – forcing and subverting – it is clear that both routes are reliant on emotion for their success. So how exactly do we process emotive content in advertising?

Up until about 35 years ago it was thought by psychologists that we process our feelings using our thoughts, and that feeling and emotion are therefore post-cognitive (e.g., Schachter & Singer 1962). In many ways that seems to make a lot of sense: after all, it is our thoughts that make us aware of what we are feeling at any one time, so surely our thoughts must come first?

But it turns out this isn't what happens at all. The belief that emotion is post-cognitive was first challenged by Zajonc (1980) in 1980. In a seminal paper he argued that there were a number of reasons why emotion could not be post-cognitive.

First, Zajonc demonstrated that affective (i.e., emotional) reactions are primary, that is, they are the first to emerge in any consideration: "when we

---

Seducing the Subconscious: The Psychology of Emotional Influence in Advertising, First Edition. Robert Heath.
© 2012 Robert Heath. Published 2012 by John Wiley & Sons, Ltd.

try to recall, recognize, or retrieve an episode, a person, a piece of music, a story, a name, in fact, anything at all, the affective quality of the original input is the first element to emerge" (Zajonc 1980: 154). For example, I remember some 60 years ago that I was scolded for being rude to the man who used to work in my parents' garden: I have no idea what I said, but the shame and humiliation of the incident is still clear in my mind.

A second point Zajonc made was that affective reactions are unavoidable: "One might be able to control the expression of emotion but not the experience of it" (Zajonc 1980: 156) A moment's consideration again shows this to be true. For example, when you go to a friend's funeral and hear a moving oration about the deceased, you can't stop yourself feeling sad even though you may be able to prevent yourself actually crying. Likewise, when you hear an amusing but slightly off-color joke, you may be able to stop yourself laughing at it, and you may even be able to tell yourself afterwards that it was not really funny, but you can't prevent yourself from finding it funny when you first heard it.

Third, he showed that affective reactions are hard to verbalize, and generally rely on nonverbal means of communication (Zajonc 1980: 158). For example, when we meet someone, we know immediately whether or not we like them, but it is almost impossible to understand cognitively *why* we like them. If someone asks us we probably just say they are "nice" or "pleasant" or "interesting." But, according to Zajonc, "these adjectives describe our reactions to the person, not the person. There simply aren't very effective verbal means to communicate why we like people and objects or what it is that we like about them" (Zajonc 1980: 157).

Zajonc also had some observations about communication. He suggested, for example: "The dismal failure in achieving substantial attitude change through various forms of communication or persuasion is another indication that affect is fairly independent and often impervious to cognition" (Zajonc 1980: 158).

Zajonc concluded that cognition and affect may depend on separate psychological and biological systems. Joseph LeDoux (1998) later refined this idea, hypothesizing that there are two different emotion circuits operating in a state of anxiety. The first of these is a fast-acting response which bypasses the "cognitive" cortex, and allows us to respond rapidly in threatening situations. The second is a slow-acting circuit which passes through the cortex, and produces a detailed evaluation of the emotional significance of the situation, and allows us to respond to situations in the most appropriate fashion.

LeDoux illustrates the two systems by describing the response of someone who comes across a snake-like stick on the path in a jungle. The initial shock triggers the fast-acting response, causing the person to jump back and break out into a sweat. The slow-acting cognitively moderated response then identifies the object as a stick, and the person relaxes. Note that both these responses might be termed "arousal," but one is instinctive, and the other is driven by cognition. LeDoux's ideas are widely quoted by advertising practitioners, but it should be noted that his model is developed specifically to describe anxiety-related responses. These responses to extreme emotion may occasionally be present in certain types of advertising (e.g., public service advertising) but it is rare that such extreme emotional content is found in brand advertising.

Emotion and Feelings

The words emotion and feeling tend to be regarded by most of us as meaning the same thing. If pressed people often say that it is our feelings that make us emotional. In psychology it is generally believed that it happens the other way round; that emotional reactions are what drive our feelings.

The person who has done more than anyone to understand the difference between emotions and feelings is Antonio Damasio. Portuguese by birth, Damasio moved to the USA to work at the Aphasia Research Center in Boston, and then spent 29 years at the University of Iowa. It was here that he developed a comprehensive understanding of how emotions are processed, and the role they have in our lives.

Damasio views emotion as a neurobiological reaction. His ideas are especially well described in a lecture he gave in 2003 at the Simpson Center at the University of Washington.[1] He sees emotion as a critically important component, not only to the way we humans behave, but to the way in which all life behaves (Damasio 1994). Emotional reactions can be detected in every life form: you can even observe emotion-like behavior in a single-celled organism, which if threatened will run away or contract into itself exactly the same way that an animal with a brain does. It therefore seems likely that the basic components that make up emotion existed in life long before the brain itself was developed.

---

[1]   http://depts.washington.edu/uwch/katz/20022003/antonio_damasio.html

So why do we have emotions? For a start they play a pretty important part in our survival. Without emotions you would have no mechanism that could register threat, and nothing to trigger a desire to run away. Without emotion, you could not register hunger and seek nourishment, and you would have no means of recognizing a member of the opposite sex and procreating. Put simply, without emotions we could not exist.

Damasio sees emotion as being important not only for the regulation of our bodies but also for the well-being of our society. We are especially sensitive to observing emotion in others, and we can sometimes tell from a facial expression how a person is feeling before they know themselves. This observational ability plays a key part in regulating our behavior. If, for example, you perceive pain on the face of someone then you know at once that they are suffering some sort of injury; and if you perceive fear you know they are feeling threatened or are in danger. If you perceive irritation or anger, you know perhaps to stop doing what you are doing, and if you perceive happiness or ecstasy then you know perhaps to continue.

Emotional reactions always manifest some sort of biological change in our behavioral state. Even when you can't observe an emotion in a person's face you can easily observe their biological reactions with laboratory tools. But we cannot see our own faces, and so we cannot observe our own emotional state. This is where feelings come in. Damasio defines feeling as simply a mental perception of the change in behavior that has resulted from our "emoting."

Which leads us back to the question "which comes first?" Again, Damasio's answer is unequivocal: although we might think that we feel before we register emotion, the opposite is true. Feelings are a response to emotion, and emotion always comes first.

How is Emotion Caused?

Emotion can be caused by a number of different stimuli. It can be a response to a physiological stimulus like a drug or a pill, or to a mental stimulus such as a joke or a story. It doesn't even have to have an external cause: we can easily become emotional by just remembering something, and we can even become emotional by imagining something that might happen. So something like a dream or a daydream, which is completely fictional and has been created by yourself, can cause you to have an emotional reaction.

Damasio uses the phrase emotionally competent stimulus (ECS) to describe anything external that causes an emotional response. He finds there are two types of ECS. The first are stimuli like loud noises, the shaking that happens during an earthquake, or the growl of a leopard, which create fear regardless of whether or not you have heard them before. We are born with sensitivity to these types of ECS because the emotional reaction has been embedded in us during evolution. The second type of ECS are stimuli like music and art, where we become conditioned to have an emotional reaction by observing the reaction of others. Sometimes an ECS can be a combination of both innate and learned responses. Damasio gives the example of infant monkeys, who respond with fear if they see a snake, but also respond with fear if they see their mother see a snake. Interestingly, if they never see their mother respond with fear to a snake in infancy then this latter conditioned response will never be learned.

It is important to bear in mind that emotionally competent stimuli do not have to be present in order to create an emotion. They can occur in real time or can be recalled from episodic memory.

> The...near accident that frightened you years ago can be recalled from memory, and cause you to be frightened anew. Whether actually present as a freshly minted image, or as a reconstructed image recalled from memory, the effect is the same. (Damasio 2003: 57)

So exposure to an ECS can have a delayed time effect. This is important when we come to discuss advertising.

How are emotions turned into feelings? Damasio finds that our response to an ECS goes through a number of quite complex stages. The first stage is evaluation and appraisal. That *sounds* like a pretty rational cognitive sort of response that will take place on a conscious level, and is probably one of the reasons why we have so much difficulty with the idea that emotion is pre-cognitive. But the fact is that although evaluation and appraisal of an ECS *can* be conscious, in many cases this first stage takes place automatically and subconsciously.

> Somehow the notion of appraisal has been taken too literally to signify conscious evaluation, as if the splendid job of assessing a situation and responding to it automatically would be a minor biological achievement. (Damasio 2003: 55)

The reason is obvious, which is if we wait until our mind is able to consciously evaluate an ECS that is threatening then we have that much less time to run away, or hit out in defense, and so on. Commenting on this appraisal stage, Damasio writes: "In order for emotions to occur there is no need to analyze the causative object consciously let alone evaluate the situation in which it appears" (Damasio 2003: 55).

The best way to think of this evaluation and appraisal is as a series of filtering processes in which the ECS is compared with the innate and acquired reactions stored in our semantic memory. The significance of this process is that it confirms that you may at any one time be in a state of emotion as a result of being exposed to an ECS, but *not* be aware that you are emoting.

Damasio's second stage of response is what he calls the "triggering" process. It is at this point that the various parts of our brain respond and create an emotion. Again, this is a fully automatic process and is the equivalent of the conceptual generation from semantic memory that we discussed in the last section. Emotion, like semantic memory, is not located in just one part of the brain; different emotions may be triggered by different locations, and lots of filtering and transformation between different parts of the brain goes on. Of course, if these various automatic filtering processes determine that the ECS isn't important, threatening, or attractive, then you may remain unaware that you have "emoted," just as when a car's brake lights go on and you do nothing.

The third stage is when the emotion itself is finally executed (i.e., brought into existence by the hypothalamus or brainstem). According to Damasio, when this happens we start to experience feelings.

Why Have Feelings?

Emotional reactions and behavior can save your life and help you take advantage of opportunities. But they cannot give you the opportunity to reflect upon the fact that certain things cause states of sorrow or joy and so on, and they cannot give you the opportunity to create from this reflection a mental "concern" for a particular object or situation. That can only be done by turning your emotion into a feeling.

Feelings, like emotions, are an essential part of our humanity. It is only by manifesting our emotion into a feeling that we can begin to construct a world in which we are mindful of the fact that there are certain things that cause us and others states of joy or sorrow, etc. This in turn is a critical step towards being mindful of others and developing models and conventions that avoid you and others suffering.

So feelings allow one to be concerned enough to produce joy for others and prevent pain for others. They also produce compassion, a feeling of empathy with the joy and pain being suffered by others. Damasio finds that feelings like concern and compassion are not necessarily learned, because they are in many cases manifested automatically. In other words we have evolved to have certain types of reaction like compassion at suffering, and moral indignation at cheating. Indeed, if we did not have access to feelings like joy, sorrow, indignation, and fear we would lead a very "neutral" existence.

We are often aware of our feelings, and when this awareness occurs then they are able to exert their maximum impact on us. But this is something of a balancing act. Research by Robert Bornstein (1992) has shown that if we are *too* aware of our feelings being influenced, the influence is diminished. The reason is that if we know that our feelings are being influenced we can rationally counter-argue that influence and weaken our response (Kihlstrom 1987). So, for example, if you know that someone is trying to schmooze you, you are prepared and can defend yourself if you want to. This is very relevant to advertising, as we will find later.

So we are more vulnerable when we are only vaguely aware that our emotions are being influenced, and most vulnerable when we have no idea at all that our emotions are being influenced. Damasio notes that most people assume that if feelings exist we must be aware of them, but this is not always the case.

> Doesn't the state of feeling imply, of necessity, that the feeler organism is fully conscious of the emotion and feeling that are unfolding? I am suggesting it does not. There is no evidence that we are conscious of all our feelings, and much to suggest we are not. For example, we often realise quite suddenly . . . that we feel anxious or uncomfortable, pleased or relaxed, and it is apparent that the particular state of feeling . . . has not begun on the moment of knowing but sometime before. Neither the feeling state nor the emotion that led to it have been "in consciousness." (Damasio 2000: 36)

This again has very important implications for advertising, which I can illustrate by going back to the example of the British Airways music. I established that this is an extremely potent emotionally competent stimulus, creating feelings of relaxation, contentment, and comfort. I also established that people who watched the TV advertising were generally unaware of the music playing in the background, and at best processed it very low levels of attention. Using Damasio's model of emotional processing, it is pretty certain that their emotions were stimulated by the music, and it is also highly likely that feelings were triggered. But, because their attention is elsewhere, it is highly unlikely that these feelings were experienced at anything other than a semi-conscious level.

So what happens to these "semi-conscious" feelings? Judging by the large proportion of people who, when played the music, recognize it as the British Airways music, it is evident that it remains in memory. And it is probable that the feelings the music evoked remain stored at some implicit level in our semantic memory as well. But do these feelings in any way attach themselves to British Airways?

The first time you see the ad and hear the music it is likely that nothing much happens at all. But the average frequency of viewing a TV commercial varies between three and thirty exposures. So the more important question is what happens after you have seen the British Airways ad, say, fifteen times? The answer is that you become conditioned.

Emotional Conditioning

Conditioning is a well-known phenomenon. Most of us have heard of Pavlov's famous experiment, where he would ring a bell before squirting meat powder into dogs' mouths. The meat powder was known to cause salivation, and what he found was that after a number of repetitions the dogs would salivate when the bell was rung, even if no meat powder was squirted into their mouths (Solomon 2006: 86).

Conditioning is in essence the transfer of a response from an unconditioned stimulus to a conditioned stimulus. The meat powder is unconditioned, because it is naturally able to make the dog respond by salivating. The bell becomes the conditioned stimulus by being associated with the meat powder and hence salivation.

The mechanism that underlies classic conditioning, or associative learning as it is sometime called, is thought to involve mirror neurons (Rizzolatti & Craighero 2004). When an animal "does" something, various neurons fire in its brain to enable it to perform that action. It has been shown in primates that if a primate observes another primate doing something, then the same neurons fire in the "observer" primate's brain as do in the "acting" primate's brain. In other words, the observer's neurons "mirror" those of the actor.

It is believed that this also happens in humans. To give a common example, when we see someone crying, our mirror neurons mimic the activity in their brain and we ourselves experience sadness. And when we observe Papa and Nicole behaving sexily in the Renault Clio ad, our mirror neurons fire and allow us to imagine the "experience" they are having.

Repetition is critically important for conditioning to take place, because, as Soloman says, "repeated exposures increase the strength of the stimulus–response associations and prevent the decay of these associations in memory" (Solomon 2006: 86). But because mirror neurons fire instinctively and subconsciously, we are not often aware that conditioning has taken place. Damasio predicts that conditioning can occur between feelings and objects, and one may have no idea why:

> As they develop and interact, organisms gain factual and emotional experience with differing objects and situations and have an opportunity to associate many objects which would have been emotionally neutral with objects and situations that are naturally prescribed to cause emotion. A form of learning known as conditioning is one way of achieving this association. [Thus] the face of a wonderful unknown person that resembles that of someone associated with some horrible event may cause you discomfort or irritation. You may never come to know why. (Damasio 2000: 57)

And this, you can see, might be exactly what happens with the music in the British Airways ad. The emotions triggered subconsciously by listening to the music become feelings, and these feelings are linked semi-consciously with British Airways. So eventually we are conditioned to associate flying on a British Airways plane with comfort and relaxation and happiness, but, as Damasio says, we may never come to know why.

Andrex Case Study

Another very good example of emotional conditioning is the Andrex Puppy campaign in the UK. Andrex Toilet Tissue is one of the UK's most successful brands, and at one point used to outsell its nearest rival, Kleenex, by a factor of nearly 3 to 1, even though it was more expensive. And even nowadays it totally dominates UK supermarket fixtures.

A number of IPA Case Studies have shown that the secret of Andrex' success was its long-running advertising campaign, which claimed the brand is "soft, strong, and very long." Note incidentally they never claimed it was "softer, stronger and very much longer," because it wasn't. It had the same number of sheets as Kleenex, and tests apparently showed that if anything it was Kleenex that was softer and stronger. So how was it that the advertising had such a dramatic influence on the brand's success?

The secret ingredient, which featured in Andrex advertising for well over 20 years, was a Golden Labrador puppy. He would do all sorts of cute things like falling asleep in the toilet tissue, or stealing the paper from a little boy sitting on the toilet. But I don't think this cute behavior was the only way it worked. Using what we have learned about emotion, I think I can build a strong case for the campaign's most potent influence being emotional conditioning.

Here's my thinking. Anyone who has stroked a Labrador puppy (and they are the most popular breed of dog in the UK) knows its fur is exceptionally soft. Also, puppies are frequently bought as presents for children when they are young, and are arguably the epitome of happy family values. So by associating the puppy with Andrex I think the advertising was able to condition us to feel that Andrex was not just incredibly soft, but also a very happy-family oriented company.

Everyone in the UK is aware of the Andrex Puppy, especially now that it appears on the packaging which, as I mentioned earlier, dominates UK supermarket shelves. But the interesting thing is if you ask anyone if they buy Andrex because of the puppy they strenuously deny it. Not surprising, you might say, because you would have to be pretty gullible to buy your toilet tissue just because the advertising has a puppy in it. No, instead people claim that Andrex is a better quality product, or better value, or the one their husband or children prefer, or some other rational reason.

Of course, once you are asked if you buy your brand of toilet tissue because it has a puppy in the advertising, you might well think more rationally about what you do. You might look more closely at the prices, or even try out another brand to see if it is softer and stronger. But up until the influence of the puppy is questioned, the conditioning effect will probably have been subconscious and unknown. In other words, you buy the product, assuming that in some way it is the best, wholly unaware that "behind the scenes" the decision is being influenced by the values that are associated with the puppy. So if the question is never asked, you would carry on buying the product, and as Damasio says, "might never come to know why."

9

Our Adaptive Subconscious

"Freud's view that consciousness is the tip of the mental iceberg, was short of the mark . . . it may be more the size of a snowball on top of that iceberg"

Timothy Wilson
Strangers to Ourselves (2002: 6)

In the last chapter I explained that Damasio's description of emotion has it being processed unconsciously. As we are seeking an explanation of how Implicit Learning from advertising can influence us, and implicit learning also operates automatically and unconsciously, it becomes important to get a clear idea of how our conscious and unconscious minds work together.

Damasio adopts the revolutionary idea that there is a representation of our body inside our brains. This representation he calls the Proto-Self. He characterizes it as a collection of maps that portray our bodies in a somewhat disengaged way. We are not fully aware of these "maps," because we attend only to the composite picture – our sense of well-being, comfort, malaise, despair, or whatever else our overall emotional state might be.

What this means is that we act as if we have two bodies: one that we are not fully aware of (the proto-self), and another that we *are* aware of, which Damasio calls Core Consciousness. Damasio provides evidence that emotions and feelings are formed in the proto-self, whereas thoughts are formed in core consciousness. And since activity in the proto-self always precedes activity in core consciousness this therefore means that emotions and feelings are always formed pre-cognitively and unconsciously (Damasio 2000: 281).

Seducing the Subconscious: The Psychology of Emotional Influence in Advertising, First Edition. Robert Heath.
© 2012 Robert Heath. Published 2012 by John Wiley & Sons, Ltd.

Psychologists generally use the term "unconscious" to describe mental activity below the conscious level. Unconscious processing can occur both when we are awake (conscious) or asleep (unconscious), all of which sounds a bit contradictory. I prefer to use the term subconscious. By subconscious processing I am referring to processing that occurs below the level of consciousness but when we are awake. The reason I use this word is that I really don't think advertising can affect us when we are asleep.

We've already established that certain aspects of processing take place automatically and below the level of consciousness. According to Harvard professor Timothy Wilson it was observed as early as 1865 by Carpenter and Laycock that the human perceptual system operates largely outside our conscious awareness. And only 9 years later Carpenter asserted that:

> Our feelings towards persons and objects may undergo most important changes without our being the least degree aware, until we have our attention directed to . . . the alteration which has taken place in them. (Wilson 2002: 10)

In other words, Damasio's discoveries about how emotional processing occurs subconsciously were predicted by Carpenter as long as 150 years ago.

The fact that perception and emotional conceptualization are independent of consciousness doesn't really threaten the established view of how we make decisions: Damasio himself accepts that emotions don't make decisions on their own (Damasio 2000: 42). The established view is that perceptions and concepts simply contribute towards our higher mental faculties, and it is these higher mental faculties that then make the decision. This view assumes that our minds operate rather like a court of law: perceptions and concepts and analysis are presented to the court, and the judge and jury (i.e., some sort of senior conscious "executive" function) decides what happens next.

Except, as we shall see, this established view probably isn't how our minds work at all.

Defining Conscious Thinking

Part of the problem is defining what consciousness is and what it isn't. The first and most basic step is to realize that, unlike in a courtroom, our most complex thinking does not take place using words. The great Einstein himself once said that words and language, as they are written or spoken, did not seem to have any role in the mechanism of his thought (Hademan 1945).

A moment's consideration makes one realize that we cannot possibly "think" in words, for the simple reason that they are too limited and too ambiguous. As Steven Pinker argues:

> [Thoughts] cannot be English words and sentences, notwithstanding the popular misconception that we think in our mother tongue . . . [Sentences] achieve brevity by leaving out any information which the listener can mentally fill in from the context. In contrast, the "language of thought" in which knowledge is couched can leave nothing to the imagination, because it is the imagination. (Pinker 1997: 70)

The second problem we face trying to understand consciousness is that as soon as you ask someone what they are thinking, you *change* what they are thinking. As in the Andrex Puppy case study, the question itself causes people to adapt their thinking, to "think" more and to think differently.

To illustrate this, consider the following: when you make a cup of tea you add milk, you need to make sure you add the right amount of milk to get the right strength or "color" for the tea. So both judgment and decision are involved, but they are judgments and decisions you make every time you make tea.

So imagine if at the point of pouring the milk I ask you what you are thinking. You will tell me that you are thinking about how much to add to get the right color, from which we might deduce this is a fully conscious, focused, deliberate act, using active processing. And this is true, because by asking the question I have *turned* it into a fully conscious, focused, deliberate act, using active processing. Had I not asked this question, you would probably have poured the milk automatically without any active thinking at all, and any judgment you would have made about the color would have been made in a state which at the very most could only be regarded as semi-conscious.

Multiple Drafts Theory

Daniel Dennett, in his book *Consciousness Explained* (1993), describes the problem. Dennett's theory is that our mind continually operates what he calls multiple drafts. These are trains of thought, only some of which "make it" to what we refer to as consciousness. So, in the case above, if no one asks us what we are thinking, there is every likelihood that the action of adding milk would be carried out without anything appearing to be communicated to our conscious mind.

Of course, if you were to perceive that the color of the tea was very dark, a perception that links to a concept of the tea tasting very strong and bitter, then you might well elevate this train of thought to a higher level of consciousness, pay more attention, and carefully add a little more milk. So what is it that decides what trains of thought achieve consciousness, and what level of conscious attention they receive?

As described earlier, the established view is that there is some sort of executive function operating in our minds which directs whether or not we bring something into consciousness or leave it in our subconscious. Dennett defines this supposed "place where (thinking) 'all comes together' and consciousness happens" (Dennett 1993: 39) as the Cartesian Theatre (after Descartes, who regarded thinking as the defining activity of humanity). In Dennett's opinion this Cartesian theater simply doesn't exist. As he puts it: "The idea of a special center in the brain is the most tenacious bad idea bedevilling our attempts to think about consciousness" (Dennett 1993: 108) and later, "There is no Cartesian theater" (Dennett 1993: 113).

What Dennett believes happens is that our subconscious mind operates all our mental activity and enacts all our decisions, and that a few of these only are then subsequently presented for our conscious consideration. This is how he describes it:

> There is no single, definitive "stream of consciousness," because there is no central Headquarters, no Cartesian Theater where "it all comes together" . . . Instead of a single stream . . . there are multiple channels in which special circuits try, in parallel pandemonium, to do their various things, creating Multiple Drafts as they go. Most of these fragmentary drafts play short-lived roles in the modulation of current activity, but some get promoted to further functional roles. (Dennett 1993: 253)

So what Dennett is postulating is that it is *not* our consciousness that drives what we think and do, but our subconscious mind. Our consciousness is probably no more than a "symptom" of a higher level of processing going on in our minds. You could analogize it to a computer with a monitor. The computer does all the thinking and calculating and processing, and some of what it does is displayed on the monitor. But the monitor doesn't actually make any decisions or execute any functions.

Dennett's ideas are not entirely new. Some years earlier, Benjamin Libet conducted a series of experiments on patients that investigated the whole idea of how our minds work (Libet *et al.* 1979). Libet found that by stimulating a certain part of the brain you could produce a "tingle" in the hand. He found you could also produce a similar tingle by electrically stimulating the hand directly, and so this enabled him to compare the response to the directly stimulated hand with that caused by stimulating the brain. He calculated that since the stimulus to the hand needed time to travel to the brain and report, the hand stimulus should take a little longer (about 500 milliseconds) than the direct brain stimulus.

But that isn't what happened. The results showed that both stimuli were perceived to happen at the time the hand would have been stimulated. Not surprisingly, these findings were seen by the science community as an anomaly. As Dennett describes it, it's a bit like a commuter from the suburbs arriving in town at exactly the same time as one who already lives there. The mind somehow referred the direct brain stimulus back in time to the point at which the hand would have been stimulated had it been stimulated. Which of course, it never was.

Libet suggested that the tingle was created subconsciously and then subsequently fed into consciousness along with a corrective time frame that made it appear to relate to a supposed stimulus of the hand. In Libet's own words: "The initiation of the freely voluntary act appears to begin in the brain unconsciously, well before the person consciously knows he wants to act" (Libet 1999: 51).

This isn't as bizarre as it perhaps sounds, as we know our minds are able to apply all sorts of corrective functions. You'll perhaps remember from Chapter 6 what our brains do to our sight, smoothing out the jumps our eyes make and turning everything the right way up? Nevertheless, Libet's experiment caused all sorts of controversy, with some commentators even claiming it challenged the whole concept of free will. In Dennett's view, however, his findings are perfectly in keeping with the multiple drafts model: all the brain does is code the stimulus in accordance with logic before it presents it to consciousness.

Dennett regarded Libet's experiment as flawed, because the subjects had to make a difficult judgment about when the signal occurred. They also did not actually do anything, simply responded to a stimulus that someone else caused. Dennett cites a much more interesting and important experiment, known as the Grey Walter Pre-Cognitive Carousel.

The Grey Walter Precognitive Carousel

William Grey Walter was a Kansas-born neurophysiologist who studied at Cambridge and worked all his life in the UK (Grey Walter 1963). He was an early user of electroencephalography to locate brain tumors. At one point he was working with patients on whom he had exposed sections of the brain – not as gruesome as you might think, as the brain has no nerves and feels no pain.

Whilst doing his work he decided, like Libet, to try an experiment. What he did was give patients a slide projector with a carousel of slides, and ask them to page through the slides at their leisure. They were free to move the slides whenever they wanted, using a simple push-button.

But there was an important catch: although the carousel had an apparently normal button for them to press in order to advance the slides, what they were *not* told was that the button was a dummy. The carousel was actually wired up to be advanced by the amplified signal from the motor cortex within their brains (Grey Walter 1963, in Dennett 1993).

If conscious thought within the Cartesian theater is what initiates action, then the patients should have noticed nothing other than the slides perhaps advancing fractionally before their thumbs actually pressed the button. In fact that was not what Grey Walter observed. What happened was that the slides appeared to move before the subjects had *made the decision* to move them. In Dennett's words:

> One might suppose the patients would notice nothing out of the ordinary, but in fact they were startled by the effect, because it seemed to them as if the slide projector was anticipating their decisions. They reported that just as they were "about to" push the button, but before they had actually decided to do so, the projector would advance the slide – and they would find themselves pressing the button with the worry that it was going to advance the slide twice. (Dennett 1993: 167)

To help clarify this, consider what happens with tennis players. Anyone who has played top class tennis will tell you that you cannot play well if you try to think about every shot. You simply do not have either the time to work out how you are going to hit the ball, nor the mental capacity to consider all the complex movements of your head, arms, and feet that are required. Professional tennis players accept that it is only when playing a shot becomes an instinct that you are able to play well.

But there is no doubt that playing tennis is a cognitive activity. You have to observe and compute the position, speed, and trajectory of the ball from your opponent's movements, and direct your arms, feet, and torso to react accordingly. Of course, at some level you are aware – or, rather, you are made aware – of what you have done. Not enough to enable you to "think" what to do next, but enough to enable you to store a mental "picture" of your movements for later consideration, perhaps when the point has been concluded.

In effect, what is going on is that your mind is playing the game for you and feeding back to you selected excerpts of what has happened. It is acting just like a computer, performing complex calculations and feeding back snippets of information about what it is doing via the monitor screen.

So consciousness, as I said earlier, is perhaps best regarded as a report of higher level mental activity, just as a change on a monitor is a report of activity within the computer. In a game of tennis there isn't time to observe whether or not the feedback of your play comes during or after the play itself, because your mind is too occupied. However, the minds of the patients in Grey Walter's experiment were not occupied, so they were able to observe the difference between their actual actions and the mental report of their actions. What they observed was that the mental *report* to their consciousness of their preparedness to press the button actually seemed to be occurring after their minds had already made the decision to press the button.

It's rather like a monitor taking a time to display what the computer has already done. The difference is that we accept that the monitor is driven by the workings of the computer; but we assume that our own actions work the other way round, and are driven by conscious thinking. What Grey Walter's experiment confirms is that consciousness merely monitors analytical processing that has already taken place subconsciously.

You might at this point be wondering what relevance has this to advertising processing. The important point is this that although conscious memory indicates the presence of analytical activity, Dennett's multiple drafts model suggests that a *lack of conscious memory does not necessarily mean no analytical activity has taken place.* In other words, we may be able to process far more from advertising than we are able to remember and report back.

Another example might help make more sense of this. Dennett describes, as I did earlier, the process of driving a car.

> You've probably experienced the phenomenon of driving for miles while engrossed in conversation (or in silent soliloquy) and then discovering you have utterly no memory of the road, the traffic, your car-driving activities ... but were you really unconscious of all those passing cars, stop lights, bends in the road...? The "unconscious driving" phenomenon is better seen as a case of rolling consciousness with swift memory loss. (Dennett 1993: 137)

In other words, Dennett's Multiple Draft theory supports the notion that various forms of cognitive processing can take place at what you might call a "rolling conscious" level without our realizing they have taken place. So the fact that we do not pay high levels of attention to advertising, and are not aware of being exposed to advertising, does not mean that we have not processed that advertising and have not extracted any message or meaning from that advertising.

So Dennett's model is adding in a different way that advertising can work at low attention. Not only can we process the emotive elements in advertising subconsciously, but we can perform analytical tasks on it at a rolling consciousness level, leaving us with no active memory and unaware that we might have paid any attention at all.

Dennett's Multiple Draft theory sits perfectly well alongside Damasio's view of the Proto-self and Core Consciousness. It explains why implicit learning and implicit memory can operate both perceptually and conceptually at a subconscious level. It explains how implicit learning can interact with semantic memory at a subconscious level. It explains how subconsciously perceived elements, like the British Airways music, can be consciously linked to British Airways without any memory of that link having taken place, and can then subconsciously trigger emotions which are transferred via conditioning to the British Airways brand, with no memory of any conditioning having taken place. In summary, it explains how we can *know* and *feel* things, even though we have never consciously been aware of learning them.

You might have observed that in the paragraph above processing seems to slip between conscious and subconscious in a rather random way. The reason is that it is really difficult to be sure which of these two levels of consciousness is being used at any one time. So does that mean that processing has now become chaotic?

Not at all. If we take on board Dennett's Multiple Draft theory, the distinction between "rolling consciousness" processing and "subconscious" processing becomes to all intents and purposes irrelevant. In Dennett's model, all processing takes place subconsciously and the only difference is that some is subsequently fed into consciousness. But even if it is fed into consciousness it is quite possible that it will be almost immediately forgotten, as in "rolling consciousness with swift memory loss." In which case, when all is said and done, it will effectively be no different to communication that was processed subconsciously.

What is happening here is that the distinction between rolling consciousness processing and unconscious processing is becoming irrelevant. For some psychologists this may be seen as heresy, because they are wedded to the notion that anything processed subconsciously cannot enter long-term memory. But we know that isn't so. Schacter's experimental work showed quite clearly that implicit (therefore, by definition, subconscious) processing communicates with semantic memory. In Dennett's model that has to be the case, as *all* processing is done subconsciously.

So the debate really revolves around whether communication processed subconsciously or with rolling consciousness is in some way inferior or ineffective when compared with communication processed with a higher level of consciousness and more attention. It is tempting to dismiss this question by pointing out that in Chapter 3 we established that, outside the industry itself, hardly anyone can be bothered to pay more than minimal attention to advertising. But I will address the issue more formally in Chapter 11 when I look at decision-making.

Hamlet Cigars Case Study

To bring this all together I have an example. Once again it is a campaign that was astonishingly effective.

Between 1966 and 1997, when cigars were still allowed to be advertised on TV in the UK, a brand called Hamlet became hugely successful. It was a small cigar, not as long as panatelas like Castella or Panama, and not as short as cigarillos like Picador or Cafe Creme. The odd thing about Hamlet is that it totally dominated this small cigar category, and other brands struggled to get a foothold in this sector.

Hamlet achieved this dominant position using a TV advertising campaign with the slogan "Happiness is a cigar called Hamlet." Their ads typically showed someone experiencing a crisis of some sort and then consoling themselves with a Hamlet cigar. One of the best of these ads ran in 1979, and took place on a golf course.

What I would like to do is to take you through the ad, describing the different processes that I think are going to be taking place. I'd like you to assume that like most people you are not paying much attention, and that you have a rudimentary knowledge of golf. So as the ad opens you perceive a flat piece of grass and your semantic memory conceptualizes this as a green on a golf course with a bunker at the side. This almost certainly happens automatically and subconsciously, but if you play golf you may get additional concepts triggered, such as pleasure, frustration, or even anger at the memory of the last game you played, and some of these trains of thought might succeed in surfacing in your consciousness.

The camera focuses in on the bunker and you perceive there is someone in it. You can tell this because, although you can't actually see the person, you can see his golf club as he raises it to take a shot. You also perceive the sound of the club repeatedly striking the sand, and you perceive showers of sand flying into the air. But you *don't* perceive a ball appearing on the green. Conceptually, it is clear that the bunker is very deep (you can't see the golfer's head) and that the golfer is having a lot of difficulty getting the ball out and must be becoming very frustrated. This might well register in your consciousness, and for a few people it might be interesting enough to get a little bit of active processing.

You perceive on the next stroke the head of the golf club waggling around in the air prior to the shot. This waggling motion conceptualizes anger, the golfer threatening his ball if you like. Your mirror neurons fire and you subconsciously experience the extreme frustration that the golfer is feeling. This frustration might again surface in your consciousness. You might become aware that this is the final desperate swipe: the continued nonappearance of the ball is instantly and consciously analyzed by you as representing that the golfer has finally realized there is no way he can get his ball out.

The next thing you perceive is silence, the sound of the striking of a match, and the start of the beautiful melody of Bach's *Air on a G String*. A puff of smoke rises from the bunker and you consciously realize this is a Hamlet cigar ad. You know this because Hamlet ads always use this music. Because the music is so distinctive you don't need much attention to make this link. Your mirror neurons fire and you feel the momentary peace the golfer might be experiencing, and the consolation that his cigar is bringing him. You might consciously and momentarily conjure up a vision of him as seen from the other side of the bunker, sitting disconsolately on the sand smoking his cigar. At the same time, your emotions are being influenced by the perception of the calming mellow Bach melody, and you personally experience a great sense of peace and tranquillity.

The next thing you perceive is the ball appearing over the side of the green. You analyze this as the golfer having given up and thrown his ball out. This conceptualizes as the person having reach such a level of frustration that he has crossed the rigid boundary of good behavior that constitutes the game of golf and cheated. But at the same time two other concepts are triggered. One is amusement, which associates with Hamlet a feeling that the brand has a clever and witty personality that you quite like; the other is that you momentarily analyze that the sand trap must be so steep and impossible to get out of that any normal person should be entitled to behave the same way. Morally, you now empathize with the golfer and feel a sense of approval of his action. Your mirror neurons fire up and you subconsciously experience a sense of relief and happiness that his (and in to some extent, your) ordeal is over. At this moment you hear and see captioned the words "Happiness is a cigar called Hamlet," and Hamlet is linked or associated with the physical sense of relief and happiness you are experiencing. This might happen consciously, and if it does then you might be able to counter-argue the claim and weaken it. More likely it happens subconsciously and thus a conditioning process either begins, or if you have seen Hamlet ads before, continues.

The ad has now finished and another ad comes on. Just as in Dennett's unconscious driving example, most conscious memories that have been created will most likely be swiftly forgotten. What is left is a subconscious feeling that Hamlet is a clever and witty brand, and an embryonic conditioning of Hamlet, associating it with calm, and peace, and tranquillity, and consolation, and relief and happiness.

How does this encourage you to buy Hamlet? This will be dealt with in more depth in Part Four. But for the time being let's assume you are an occasional cigar smoker, or at least not averse to smoking cigars. After having seen this ad a few times you would start to be conditioned to associate smoking a cigar with calm and peace and tranquillity and consolation and happiness. So next time you go through a period of anger and frustration, might this advertising not make you feel that the best way to console yourself is by smoking a cigar?

As to your choice of brand, being exposed to this ad a few times will also condition you to associate these feelings with one brand in particular: Hamlet. And since Hamlet is also by now conditioned with a witty and clever personality that you find attractive, you might also find it easy to accept the common fallacy that cigars are nothing like as bad for you as cigarettes, and are not addictive.

So you buy yourself a beer and Hamlet cigar, light it and sit down; and lo and behold, as the nicotine hits your lungs, you feel a wonderful sense of calm and peace and . . . happiness. And all this happens without you needing to be aware of or have any recall of the Hamlet advertisement.

The sting in the tail is that you have no rational reason now not to cheer yourself up by smoking a Hamlet cigar, and considerable emotional encouragement to do this whenever you want some consolation. Regardless of the addictive nature of cigars versus cigarettes, it is easy in these circumstances for cigar smoking to become a habit. And 15 or 20 years later you might find, like a Hamlet smoking friend of mine, you have contracted throat cancer. If you're lucky, like he was, you might survive.

10

Emotion and Attention

"All the evidence about 'emotional appeals in advertising' shows that their main role is to attract attention"

Erik Du Plessis
The Advertised Mind (2005: 141)

I hope that so far I have managed to build a pretty convincing case for advertising being able to exert an effect on our emotions at low levels of attention, and link this effect to brands. Well, here we encounter a bit of a problem. Some research has shown that a high levels of emotional appeal in communication *increases* the amount of attention we pay to it.

If this is true of advertising, and many people believe it is, then the case for advertising affecting us emotionally at low levels of attention starts to look shaky. Quite simply, if emotion in communication increases level of attention, then advertisements that incorporate a lot of emotive content are likely to be paid a lot more attention. If this happens, the emotive content will be processed actively and not passively. That punctures the idea that emotion is able to work subconsciously: emotive content would never have the opportunity to influence us at low levels of attention, because it would never be paid low levels of attention.

You'll recall from Kover's research in Chapter 7 that those who work in advertising believe emotive content increases attention. Their reasoning is that creativity is what enables advertising to get attention, and creativity is essentially made up of emotive content, therefore emotive content gets attention. As is often the case, they are right in a way, but wrong in another

Seducing the Subconscious: The Psychology of Emotional Influence in Advertising, First Edition. Robert Heath.
© 2012 Robert Heath. Published 2012 by John Wiley & Sons, Ltd.

more important way, and in this chapter I am going to try to get to the bottom of this apparent contradiction.

Arousal and Attention

It makes sense to start by looking at the research on which this conclusion is based. To find this we have to go back to the 1960s and the work of Daniel Ellis Berlyne. Berlyne's field of research was the role of emotion, motivation, and learning, and he theorized that learning was initiated by curiosity, which itself was driven by learning conflicts. Essentially, if something is obvious we don't spend much time thinking about it; it is only when it isn't obvious that our curiosity is stimulated and we pay attention.

The relevance of Berlyne's work lies in arousal. Arousal was defined by Berlyne as measuring "how wide awake" and "how ready to react" someone is (Berlyne 1960: 48). Using verbal study experiments Berlyne found that learning and arousal operate on an inverted U basis. He theorized that:

> [Some] degree of arousal is presumably crucial, since low arousal would presumably exclude learning [but] these verbal learning studies certainly indicate that high arousal can impede recall during the early stages of learning. (Berlyne 1964: 131)

So up to what you might call the "optimal" level of arousal our attention increases, our cognitive faculties become sharper, and our learning and recall improves. Beyond that optimal level our ability to concentrate and learn and recall anything deteriorates.

Put another way, up to a certain point arousal drives us to be more stimulated, excited, and alert, and to perceive and learn more; but if we become too aroused (i.e., too excited or over-stimulated) our perception and learning start to fall. An example of this is when you are driving a car fast; as you go faster you get more aroused and excited, pay more attention, and become more perceptive. But if you go too fast, you can become over-stimulated. Your learning capacity starts to deteriorate, and might even lose control and crash. And after the crash you find yourself unable to recall any detail of what happened.

Berlyne's theory encompassed the idea that arousal was not only driven by negative affective variables (fear, shock, etc.) but that pleasant emotional excitement and rewarding stimuli also heightened arousal. This conclusion was fixed upon by Werner Kroeber-Riel, an eminent marketing professor at the University of Saarland. Working from Berlyne's idea that the arousal potential of stimuli determined the attention given to them, Kroeber-Riel hypothesized that emotional content in advertising was a driver of attention. His "activation theory" held that "The emotional content of a stimulus induces 'phasic' activation (i.e. arousal) and activation promotes information processing" (Kroeber-Riel 1980: 151).

To test this theory, Kroeber-Riel quoted eye camera research which assessed the level of attention given to print advertising that had been manipulated to have different levels of emotive content. According to Kroeber-Riel, "Eye fixations . . . serve as a behavioural measure of information processing" (Kroeber-Riel 1980: 147). As I said in Chapter 6, our eyes do not move smoothly across the field of vision but instead fix their gaze on successive points in a series of "jumps" known as saccades (Huey 1968). During moments of fixation we can see full detail in only our foveal region, so if the brain wishes to gather more information it subconsciously orders the eye to make the jumps more rapid and the time of fixation shorter. Thus, the number of fixations per second (fps) is an accurate indicator of the amount of cognitive resource being deployed in our brains, which means it is also an accurate indicator of the level of attention we are paying at any one time. Increased numbers of (shorter) fixations indicate increased attention, and reduced numbers of (longer) fixations denote lower attention (Rayner 1998).

Kroeber-Riel's experiments confirmed that print advertisements embellished with a higher emotive content received more attention and were better recalled than those that had no emotive embellishment (Kroeber-Riel 1979). As I said earlier, his results support the view which prevails amongst most advertisers, that consumers don't want to watch ads, and it is only the emotive appeal of creativity that encourages them to pay attention and allows the message to be communicated.

Because this idea of "emotion causing arousal" and "arousal causing attention" appears to be common sense, it has become a very popular idea. For example, Ray and Batra speculate that "People may pay more attention to affective advertising" and later "Affect may enhance the degree of processing" (Ray & Batra 1983: 543), and Biel asserts that emotion is a driver of repeat viewing: "primary affective response to the commercial per se governs the decision to process further" (Biel 1990: 27). Peter Doyle adopts a similar view to Biel, stating that "If it generates negative or neutral feelings, customers are likely to avoid looking at it" (Doyle 1994: 258). Perhaps chief amongst those who hold this view is Erik Du Plessis, who proposes that "emotion . . . governs all our behaviour . . . determining what becomes conscious" and that "emotion plays a key role in directing our attention" (Du Plessis 2005: 4).

So are all these people right? Does emotion increase attention and recall in advertising. I believe the answer is no, because the research upon which they are basing their conclusions doesn't apply to advertising.

Flaws in Attention Research

Establishing levels of attention in real time is a challenging task. Not only do attention levels vary with extraordinary rapidity, but people do not actively monitor what they are paying attention to – indeed, there is evidence that in most cases people are not actually aware of what they are attending to or how much attention they are paying at any particular moment of time (Dennett 1993). For this reason many studies use inaccurate proxies to assess attention levels. For instance, one eminent textbook quotes research showing "an attention loss of 17%" when the study actually measured recall and persuasion (Rossiter & Percy 1998: 282); and another study confidently asserted that "Attention . . . contributes directly to increased purchase intention" when in fact it measured whether or not people *thought* the ads would get attention (Cramphorn 2006: 268).

A more important flaw is the assumption that the relationship between attention and one type of emotion applies to all types of emotion. Psychology experiments have shown that shocking emotional events have higher recall, fearful faces increase perception, and angry faces capture directional attention better than happy faces (Christiansen 1992; Hansen & Hansen 1994; Phelps *et al.* 2005). But negative emotions like these are rarely found other than in public service advertising. Brand advertising generally uses only positive emotive content.

A third, similar flaw is the assumption that the relationship between emotion and attention is the same regardless of how extreme the emotive content is. Kroeber-Riel, whose experiment used highly reliable fixation tracking to measure attention, embellished his stimuli using semi-nude erotic pictures, something almost guaranteed to cause arousal. But US and UK brand advertising, aside from being banned from using nudes, tends to avoid extremes of emotive content. Contemporary creativity tends to feature elements such as characters expressing mild emotion (affection, irritation, excitement, boredom, curiosity, amusement, etc.), situations that are humorous, poignant or dramatic, visual footage that is beautifully shot with high production values, and music that is uplifting or just nice to listen to. All very tame, and certainly not likely to promote the sort of response that erotic pictures cause.

A fourth flaw is the assumption that the emotion–attention response will be the same regardless of the context that it is presented in. Experiments have shown that the presence of "top-down" processing goals increases attention, yet some of the emotion–attention experiments are based on people's reactions to events in news footage or documentaries, which are likely to receive much higher levels of attention than advertising.

Indeed, practically all experimental psychology research takes place in laboratory conditions, which are known to encourage a high incidence of active attention and top-down processing. It's a fact that people will pay more attention if they are being incentivized to take part in an experiment.

In contrast, TV watching in your own home is done primarily for relaxation and entertainment (Barwise & Ehrenberg 1998). No one is paying you to pay attention, and certainly no one is paying you to pay attention to the advertising. This raises the question: are TV viewers going to be paying enough attention to be aroused by even the most emotive advertising? Indeed, recent research finds that "it is not at all evident that there should be systematic effects of processing goals on attention to advertising under natural exposure conditions" (Pieters & Wedel 2007: 224).

When processing lacks any motivation or goal it becomes free (i.e., stimulus-driven) viewing. This has been shown to be associated with *lower* levels of attention than goal-directed viewing. So, unless you work in the ad industry, the way you process advertising – particularly TV advertising – is quite likely to lack motivation and be stimulus-driven "free" processing. But none of the psychology experiments had investigated how people react to real-life TV advertising being exposed to them in real-life TV programs in real-life viewing conditions. Therefore, the theory that emotive advertising content increases attention had never ever been empirically tested.

So in 2003 I decided to carry out this experiment myself, as part of my PhD research.

Measuring How Emotive Content Influences Attention

Step 1 was to work out how to measure real-time attention accurately. This was solved by Kroeber-Riel's approach using fixation measurement.

Modern eye tracking cameras are very unobtrusive and almost weightless, and enable fixations per second to be measured with high levels of accuracy.

The next question I had to ask was if there was any theoretical background suggesting what the relationship between level of attention and emotion in TV advertising was likely to be. As we've already discussed, Damasio has shown that emotions are processed pre-cognitively, subconsciously, and independent of working memory. These conclusions are widely supported by others. For example, a paper by 12 eminent psychologists headed by Gavan Fitzsimons identifies three types of affective response: evaluations, moods, and emotions, and claims that "There is considerable evidence of non-conscious processes within each of these main categories of affective responses" (Fitzsimons *et al.* 2002: 274).

Damasio's findings are also in line with models of cognitive resource deployment, which predict that evaluation of emotion in advertising can take place when only low to moderate cognitive capacity is available (MacInnes & Jaworski 1989; Meyers-Levy & Peracchio 1992). This suggested to me that emotional content in branded TV advertising, exposed in normal relaxed low-involvement TV viewing conditions, should be able to be processed without the deployment of much cognitive resource; that is, at quite low levels of attention.

This allowed an alternative interpretation to be advanced, based on resource-matching theory (Peracchio & Meyers-Levy 1997; Zhu & Meyers-Levy 2005). This interpretation predicted that, unless motivation determined otherwise (e.g., you worked in advertising!), TV advertising would be processed as a stimulus, and without the presence of higher level goal direction. In these circumstances, advertising that had a lot of emotive content in it would be judged by the brain to require little in the way of cognitive resource in order to process it, and thus relatively low levels of cognitive resource (attention) would be likely to be deployed. The converse would be that advertising that lacked emotive content would be judged by the brain to be trying to communicate some sort of rational message, and thus relatively more cognitive resource (attention) might well be deployed.

So the two hypotheses I tested were:

- If the conventional view is right, TV advertising processing will be systematic and goal-directed, and viewers will give less attention to advertising that is lower in emotive content and more attention to ads that are higher in emotive content, the latter being more creative and more "watchable."

- But if the psychology-based view – that TV advertising processing is predominantly automatic and stimulus-driven – is correct, attention levels will be dictated by the cognitive resource required to process the stimulus presented. In this case ads with higher emotive content will be paid less attention than ads that are lower in emotive content and are therefore seen to focus more on rational communication.

To make the experiment a reliable as possible I had to replicate real-life viewing conditions as closely as possible. I therefore chose an episode of the popular sitcom *Frasier*, and had 12 TV ads professionally edited into it in the three commercial breaks. The level of emotive content in these ads was measured in a separate test, in which 26 currently on-air ads were exposed to a sample of college students, and their emotive content measured using a range of scales derived from a large-scale US study (Holbrook & Batra 1987). The six highest and six lowest emotive content ads were then chosen for our research.

It was important that none of the subjects in the main research study realized that we were interested in advertising. Participants in other research had been primed to know that advertising was of interest to the researcher, and this form of priming tends to artificially increase attention levels toward advertisements (Schmitt 1994). In order to eliminate any priming, participants were recruited via an e-mail originating from the Department of Pharmacology and asked to participate in a study to test the effect of TV watching on the eyes.

Each person was fitted with the lightweight head-mounted eye-camera, calibrated, and asked to seat themselves at what they felt was a comfortable distance from the TV. No other instructions were given, and they were free to move their heads and bodies as much as they wanted. In fact, aside from being asked to wear a lightweight skull-cap, and having a small transparent reflector visible in the lower periphery of their left eye, they might have been at home.

Aside from emotive content, a number of other factors are believed to influence the level of attention paid to an advertisement:

- Prior exposure to advertising, which was expected to decrease attention levels on subsequent exposure (Krugman 1972; Peracchio & Meyers-Levy & 1997).
- Usage of a product category or the specific brand being advertised, which was expected to increase involvement and therefore levels of attention (Petty & Cacioppo 1986; MacInnis & Jaworski 1989).

- Liking of an advertisement, which is widely believed to increase levels of attention (Biel 1990; Du Plessis 2005).

I had to make sure these did not interfere with the results, so prior exposure to ads, usage of brand and product category, and liking of the ads were measured after participants had watched the TV program and had their fixations per second measured. At this point I also reassessed the subjects' opinion of the emotive content of each of the ads.

So what were the results? The experiment showed that high levels of emotive content were associated with an average *reduction* of about 20% in attention levels. In other words, the general assumption that emotive content increases attention towards TV advertising simply isn't true. If anything, as psychology theory predicts, it reduces it (Heath *et al.* 2009).

These results cast an important light on the state of mind of normal TV advertising viewing. Advertisers have for years worked on the assumption that their target audience (you and me) are motivated by our needs to watch and try to understand at least a small part of what we see when we watch TV advertisements. But it appears that under normal viewing conditions this motivation to respond to their needs deserted our research participants. As for the other variables, they paid no more attention to ads that featured brands or products they used than ads that feature brands or products they didn't use; they paid much the same level of attention to ads that they didn't like as they did to ads they did like. And when viewing advertisements they had seen before, the amount by which their attention dropped was actually pretty small. But most important of all, when ads were creative and contained emotive material, their response was to pay them less, not more, attention.

The only plausible explanation of these results seems to be that relaxed viewers exposed to TV ads tend to use stimulus-driven processing rather than goal-driven processing. And this, of course, has a particular effect on the way ads are processed. Because we pay less attention to emotive "creative" advertising, we are less able to counter-argue it. That means any part of the message that we *do* process tends to be accepted more readily. And the emotive content itself, all of which will be processed (because emotive processing happens automatically and instantaneously and without any attention being paid), will likewise enter our consciousness without any challenge. In effect, the role of creativity, far from making us more alert and more attentive, renders us *less* attentive and *more* vulnerable.

Levi's Odyssey Case Study

To conclude this chapter I'd like to tell you about another experience I had with measuring attention towards advertising. In this case I was able to make a direct link between low attention and business success.

The ad agency Bartle Bogle Hegarty (BBH) in the UK developed a reputation for highly creative advertising for Levi's Jeans. At the start of the millennium they ran an advertisement featuring two slightly scruffy people – a young man and a young woman – silently breaking through walls and floors and eventually running up trees and flying, whilst a stirring piece of classical music played in the background. Sounds bizarre, but the action paralleled the stunts in the recently released hit movie *The Matrix*. The slogan line for the ad, visible only for a few seconds at the end, was "Levi's Jeans. Engineered for freedom."

I've been told that the ad was deemed a great success, recording an identifiable lift in sales across the Levi's range. Certainly when I've shown it to my students they all say it is extremely hypnotic and very watchable. One might therefore deduce that it gets high levels of attention.

It so happened that I tested this ad with the eye fixation measurement system as a pilot for the PhD experiment I described earlier in the chapter. I anticipated that the attention levels towards it would be exceptionally high, and certainly higher than all the other ads. In fact the exact reverse turned out to be the case. Table 10.1 shows the results.

Table 10.1   Eye–Camera Test of Attention towards TV Advertisements

Media	Fixations per Second	Ratio to Programming
First Direct Bank	2.40	163%
Citroën C3	2.40	163%
LLoyd Grossman Sauces	1.96	133%
Boots Contact Lenses	1.90	129%
Lynx Deodorant Spray	1.88	128%
Guinness Volcano	1.67	114%
Volkswagen Passat	1.65	112%
Audi 100	1.65	112%
Frazier (program)	1.47	100%
Levi's Odyssey	1.12	76%

As can be seen, the fixations per second, or attention paid to the Levis ad, were the *lowest* of all the ads tested, half that of the First Direct and Citroën C3 ads, and about three-quarters of that paid to the actual TV program. What explains this? Well, as I said earlier, fixations per second are measuring the amount of cognitive resource deployed, which equates to the level of attention being paid. In the case of this ad, there was hardly any active thinking needed to watch the ad: there were no conversations, no captions or prices, not even any product claim until right at the end. Since it wasn't *necessary* to deploy much cognitive resource, no one did. In line with resource matching theory, they conserved their cognitive resource, dropped their attention, and just sat back and enjoyed the ad.

Of course, that didn't make the ad less effective; quite the reverse. By paying high *directional* attention (i.e., looking at the screen) but a low *level* of attention, the emotive content of the ad was processed more efficiently and with less counter-argument, and that made the influence of the emotive content that much more effective.

Which brings us to the next stage of our journey. We've established that emotive creativity can be and usually is processed at low attention. Assuming that these emotive values can be transferred onto and "condition" brands, how does this persuade us to buy them? That is the subject of Part Four.

Emotion and Consciousness: Summary

We have established that Emotional Processing occurs implicitly and prior to active and passive processing. This means we have now identified a role for automatic processing and implicit learning: these are responsible for processing emotion in advertising and influencing the feelings we have towards advertising. This is represented by the dotted line in the summary chart in Figure 10.1.

We are also able to show how consciousness interacts with learning. Using Dennett's Multiple Draft Theory we can now conceive of a spectrum of attention and consciousness which runs from the top of the chart to the bottom.

- At the top is fully conscious highly attentive processing, which is hard to sustain, and is rarely applied to advertising.
- At the bottom we have subconscious fully automatic processing, which operates continuously and is never switched off. This only processes perceptions and links to conceptualization.
- In the middle of the chart we now have an area that corresponds to semi-consciousness, in which we operate passive learning. We can now reinterpret this as Dennett's "rolling consciousness with swift forgetting," which logically explains passive learning's inability to analyze very effectively.

Because the processing of emotion takes place automatically it is not influenced by perceptual filtering and counter-argument. Emotional processing sometimes leads to feelings, which likewise cannot be filtered out or counter-argued (although the expression of those feelings may be suppressed). However, what we have not yet established is any link between emotions and feelings and attitude change and behavior change. This is addressed in Part Four, which looks at decision-making and relationships.

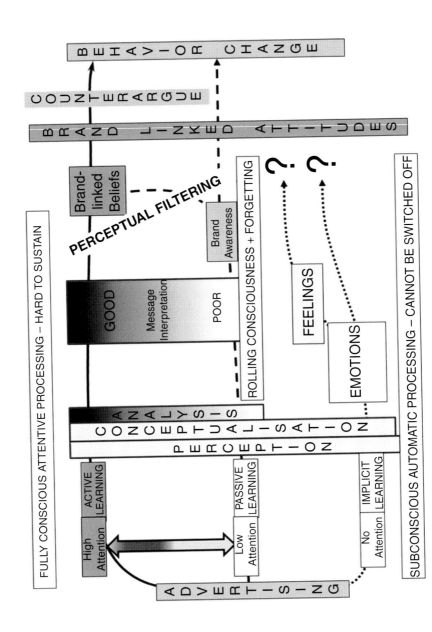

Figure 10.1 Emotion and Consciousness Summary Chart

4

Decisions and Relationships

11

Decision-Making

"The standard trap is to suppose that the relatively rare cases of conscious practical reasoning are a good model for the ... cases in which our intentional actions emerge from processes into which we have no access."

Daniel Dennett
Consciousness Explained (1993: 252)

More popular science books have been written in the last few years on the topic of decision-making than on any other. The list includes contributions from Malcolm Gladwell (*Blink*), Thaler and Sunstein (*Nudge*), Paco Underhill (*Why We Buy*), Jonah Lehrer (*The Decisive Moment*), Dan Ariely (*Predictably Irrational*), Stuart Sutherland (*Irrationality*), Robert Caldini (*Influence*), Daniel Pink (*Drive*), Ori and Ron Brafmen (*Sway*), John Kay (*Obliquity*), and several others. They are amongst the most popular of popular science books and no less than six of them claim to be bestsellers.

All these books announce gleefully that decision-making, which we always thought was a conscious rational act, turns out to be quite the reverse. Most quote the work of Amos Tversky and Daniel Kahneman, a pair of Israeli psychologists. In the 1970s, Kahneman and Tversky developed "Prospect Theory," a range of cognitive ideas surrounding decision-making, which incorporated factors such as heuristics (experiential influences) and "anchoring" (another word for conditioning). Kahneman won the Nobel Memorial Prize for Economics for his work on Prospect Theory in 2002, sadly not able to be shared by Tversky who had died 6 years earlier.

Seducing the Subconscious: The Psychology of Emotional Influence in Advertising, First Edition. Robert Heath.
© 2012 Robert Heath. Published 2012 by John Wiley & Sons, Ltd.

In the 1980s, Kahneman worked with Richard Thaler, and between them they are credited with the founding of the theory of Behavioral Economics. Behavioral Economics argues that the mind has two ways of making decisions: System 2, the reflective system, is the traditional way we think we make decisions. It is slow, controlled, conscious, and logically deductive. In contrast, System 1, the automatic system, is fast, uncontrolled, subconscious, and illogically intuitive (Thaler & Sunstein 2008). To make this a bit clearer, one of the most potent drivers of System 2 is when the brand has evidence to show that it is better than the others; one of the most potent drivers of System 1 is if someone we know uses it.

System 1 thinking is called all sorts of different names. Malcom Gladwell favors Gigerenzer's description of it as "fast and frugal" thinking (Gladwell 2006: 11). Stuart Sutherland, in a book republished in 2007, 9 years after his death, uses the term "irrationality," (Sutherland 2007) and Dan Ariely (2008: 241) talks about "irrelevant influence." Jonah Lehrer (2009: 79) refers to it as "irrational feelings" and "instincts"; John Kay (2010: 3) refers to it as making decisions obliquely. It's an interesting reflection on society that System 1 thinking has caused such a publishing feeding frenzy so many years after it was invented.

According to Thaler and Sunstein, "the activities of the automatic system (System 1) are associated with the oldest parts of our brain, the parts we share with lizards" (Kay 2010: 3). They attribute this knowledge to sources from 1998 and 2002, but in fact this notion was published by Antonio Damasio as early as 1994. Damasio also described in detail a psychological model of the two-part decision-making model in 2003, which not surprisingly incorporates a role for emotion. He evolved this using a story from a famous mining accident which took place in 1848.

The Tale of Phineas Gage (Damasio 1994: 3)

Twenty-five-year-old Phineas Gage was foreman of a work gang blasting rock from a quarry while preparing the roadbed for the Rutland and Burlington Railroad outside the town of Cavendish, Vermont. He appears to have been a well-dressed and intelligent man, and his job was a responsible one, requiring him to decide where the track should run and blast out the rock accordingly to produce as straight a line as possible. He oversaw the boring of each hole into the rock, then personally added blasting powder, a fuse, and sand, before compacting the charge into the hole using a large tamping iron. This iron was $1^1/_4$ inches in diameter and 3 feet 7 inches in length.

On September 13, 1848 around 4.30p.m., a terrible accident occurred. When he drove his tamping iron into the already prepared hole the powder charge exploded. The iron apparently flew back out of the hole, through his head behind his left eye, exited out of the top of his head, and landed some 100 feet away "covered in blood and brains."

Gage was thrown onto his back but amazingly was not killed. Damasio, quoting extracts from the *Boston Medical and Surgical Journal*, notes that he exhibited "a few convulsive motions" and "spoke in a few minutes": then having been carried by his men to the road he "rode sitting erect" in an ox-cart for three-quarters of a mile to a hotel, and "got out of the cart himself, with a little assistance from his men" (Damasio 1994: 5).

Thereafter, other than the disfigurement caused by the wound to his head, Gage's physical recovery was complete. He suffered no paralysis and no loss of physical senses other than the loss of sight in his left eye. Sadly, the same was not true of his mental recovery. His language became so foul that "women were advised not to stay long in his presence," and later he appears to have developed epilepsy. He was never able to work again, and after a chequered life, which included a spell as a circus attraction in Barnum's Museum in New York, he died after a series of convulsions in San Francisco at the age of 38.

Damasio's reason for telling this gruesome story was not to add drama to his excellent book *Descartes' Error*, but because Phineas Gage's injuries induced a particularly important change in his behavior. From being a man who was efficient, capable, and displayed keen concentration, he became "capricious and vacillating" and wholly incapable of understanding or controlling his emotions. Most important of all, having been "energetic and persistent in executing all his plans of action" (Damasio 1994: 8) he became someone who had lost his ability to plan his future as a social being. In effect, his wound deprived him of the ability to make decisions.

Using the experience of one of his own patients (Elliot), who because of a tumor likewise lost his ability to experience and control emotions and to make decisions, Damasio concluded that what happened to both Elliot and Gage was not a result of a loss of what we might refer to as cognitive function or "intelligence." In both cases very little of the brain seemed to have been destroyed, and that which was destroyed was white matter which seemed to have no special importance to our functioning as human beings. Damasio went on to identify 12 other patients with similar damage, and found in all of them "a combination of decision-making defect and flat emotion and feeling" (Damasio 1994: 54).

In developing an explanation, Damasio adopted the notion of there being a "limbic" system in the brain, a construct developed by Paul MacLean (1952) to represent the original mammalian brain. This limbic system lies beneath the more recently developed neo-cortex (i.e., "new" cortex), the part of the brain's cerebral cortex that has evolved to give us our unique reasoning powers. The limbic system, sometimes also called the "visceral" brain, was originally responsible for the processing of mammalian instinctive and survival functions (e.g., fear, sexual drive, hunger), and it is in this part of the brain that our center of emotional processing resides. As it originated as part of the body's defense system, the limbic system operates pre-cognitively and autonomically – if it didn't, we would probably have been eaten by predators and become extinct long ago.

What Damasio deduced is that the damage to the seemingly unimportant white matter severed the connection between the limbic cortex and the neo-cortex. The result was that although the patients could continue to reason with their neo-cortex and continue to express emotion through their limbic cortex, they could not *regulate* their reasoning or emotion because the two parts of the brain were unable to work together. This led Damasio to conclude that:

> The apparatus of rationality, traditionally presumed to be neocortical, does not seem to work without that of biological regulation, traditionally presumed to be sub-cortical. (Damasio 1994: 128)

This is a pretty awesome discovery. On the one hand, it suggests that the control of emotions and feelings, a critical aspect of our function as social creatures, arises from the development of our neo-cortex. But, far more importantly from our point of view, it suggests that decision-making, supposedly a rational "reasoning" activity, is largely conditioned by our feelings and emotions. In Damasio's view, our cognitive functions are effectively "hard-wired" to work via our emotions.

This isn't to say that emotions do our thinking for us or make decisions for us. In later work Damasio makes it clear that "I did not suggest . . . that emotions are a substitute for reason or that emotions decide for us" (Damasio 2000: 42). But emotions do exert a powerful "gatekeeper" influence on decisions, through a mechanism that Damasio describes as the Somatic Marker Hypothesis.

Somatic Markers

Imagine you are a small child walking down a busy street with your mother. As you go to cross the road she impresses on you the importance of looking both ways to see that no cars are coming. You hear and remember what she says, but it doesn't make much of an impression. One day when you are older you forget to look as you start to cross the road and you don't notice a car approaching. The car screeches to a halt not far from you, you jump, your emotions are galvanized, you feel a state of panic, probably break out in a sweat, and quickly step back onto the pavement. The car drives on and after a time you forget about the incident. Everything seems to go back to normal.

Except it doesn't. In future when you start to cross a road you find yourself pausing automatically and looking more closely. The previous near miss may be recalled by you, or it may briefly flash through your mind – as Dennett describes, briefly roll into consciousness and be swiftly forgotten – or you may not recall it at all. But the reason you pause and look carefully, whether you realize it or not, is because the incident has caused your "body" to create a "marker" which influences all your future road-crossing actions.

Damasio calls markers created by these sorts of heuristic experiences "somatic" markers, from the Greek word *soma*, meaning body. Note that he acknowledges that he is using the term to refer to body in its broadest sense, in other words, including "mind." Here's his description of somatic markers:

> [S]omatic markers are a special instance of feelings . . . that have been connected, by learning, to predicted future outcomes in certain scenarios. When a negative somatic marker is juxtaposed to a particular future outcome, the combination functions as an alarm bell. When a positive somatic marker is juxtaposed instead, it becomes a beacon of incentive. (Damasio 1994: 174)

Damasio believes that we go through our lives constantly creating these markers, but that we are not always aware of them or of their influence. "[O]n occasion somatic markers may operate covertly (without coming into consciousness) and may utilise an 'as if' loop" (Damasio 1994: 174). In other words, it is quite possible that, following the near miss, you will look especially carefully as you cross the road, but after a time you will have forgotten *why* you are doing this or indeed *that* you are doing it.

What relevance has the somatic marker hypothesis to brand choice and advertising? I'd say "profound." As we go through life we process perhaps hundreds of thousands of pieces of information about brands, and, if Damasio is correct, each of these will register some sort of emotional marker in our minds. Many of these will be emotionally trivial, and exert little or no influence on our behavior. But others will be emotionally significant, and leave a lasting impression.

Here are some examples. If you live in the UK you probably believe that French fashion items (clothes, perfumes, etc.) are often the best and most stylish. You probably don't know why you believe this. It may be because all the big fashion houses seem to have French names and have offices in Paris. It may be that whenever you see French people they always seem to look smart. It may be that French clothes and perfumes always seem more expensive, and therefore you think they just must be the best. It may be something your parents told you. But whatever it is, something in the past has created a "marker" in your mind which means that you expect French fashion items to be the best.

Here's another example. Have you ever asked yourself why German washing machines, cars, and power tools cost more than any others? Ask yourself now and you will almost certainly come up with the notion that somehow you believe they are better made, more reliable, and better *engineered* than others. They must be; after all, if they weren't, people wouldn't pay the extra for them. That's common sense.

But where did this idea, this "marker" that German products are better made and more reliable come from? In my case I vaguely recall my father telling me that after the war we rebuilt all the German factories for them which means they benefited from the best technology available. But that was over 50 years ago, and most people today will not have heard that story.

The same is true of Japanese electrical goods (hi-fis, TVs, etc.). Everyone thinks these are the best, but I suspect no one really knows (or, perhaps more correctly, can remember) why. Whatever markers exist to make us think that these sorts of products from these countries are superior have long been forgotten, and the markers now influence us covertly.

The extent to which these covert markers operate is illustrated by the story of the development of the Dixons–Currys Group own label brand. Dixons, a store chain which originated in photography, acquired the Currys electrical good group in December 1984. Currys' own brand was Saisho, and Dixons' own brand was Logic. The group decided to merge their own brands and conducted research to establish the best name. A variety of different brand names were developed and tested, and a Japanese sounding name – Matsui – was included, by all accounts at the last minute, just as a control.

The test result showed an overwhelming preference for Matsui, and even though most of the products being sold under the brand were made in Wales, the company had no option but to choose it. It became a hugely successful brand in its own right, and is still used by the Group for the sale of TVs and other electronic goods.

Damasio's Model of Decision-Making

Damasio incorporated this idea of markers into a model of decision-making. The model is illustrated in Figure 11.1, based on the diagram in his book *Looking for Spinosa* (Damasio 2003).

The model starts with the simple traditional reasoning model, route A. The stimulus (in our case, advertising) enters a "reasoning box," in which facts, options for decisions, and representations of future outcomes interact with one another until an option for decision is chosen. One of these options is then activated as a decision.

Damasio attaches to the "facts" box a device for organizing and sorting these out, which he calls "reasoning strategies." But this aspect of decision-making is still rational. What Damasio shows is that another route operates in parallel with our rational decision-making, which he calls route B. Route B is automatically deployed in all decision-making situations, and what it does is to covertly activate "biases related to prior emotional experiences of comparable situations" (Damasio 2003: 149). So if you have experienced a

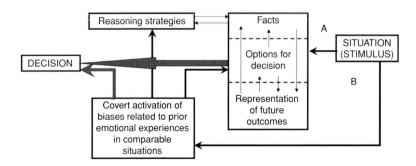

Figure 11.1 Decision-Making Model. (After Damasio 2003: 149, figure)

similar situation before, and formed some sort of somatic marker in that situation, then this will subconsciously influence your decision in this new situation.

Damasio identifies this route B as "gut feeling" or "intuition." A few moments' reflection shows this is a commonplace occurrence. How many times have you seen advertising for a product and felt instinctively that you don't trust it? The reason this happens is that sometime in the past you have had an experience of advertising over-claiming or being misleading. But the existence of route B is not the important thing. What is important is how influential it is.

Damasio is at pains to point out that an emotional signal is not a substitute for reasoning, but that it can increase "the efficiency of reasoning and make it speedier." However, he also points out that:

> On occasion (emotion) may make the reasoning process almost superfluous, as when we immediately reject an option that would lead to disaster, or jump to a good opportunity based on a high probability of success. (Damasio 2003: 148)

So what Damasio is saying is that although the decision still comes from our rational mind, it is effectively driven by our emotion. Moreover, this influence does not have to use a tangible "feeling" to be manifest, and is nearly always covert:

> First, it is possible to produce gut-feelings without actually using the body drawing instead on the as-if-body-loop [i.e., mirror neurons]. Second, and more importantly, the emotional signal can operate entirely under the radar of consciousness. It can produce alterations in working memory, attention, and reasoning so that the decision-making process is biased toward selecting the action most likely to lead to the best outcome. (Damasio 2003: 148)

This behavior occurs frequently at times when logic is compromised and finds it hard to "reason out" the decision. As he goes on to say:

> On occasions path B can lead to a decision directly, as when a gut feeling impels an immediate response. . . . The intriguing decision patterns described by Daniel Kahnemann and Amos Twersky in the 1970s are probably due to engagement of path B. (Damasio 2003: 149)

A classic situation where our rational decision-making is compromised is when we are short of time. For example, when the phone rings and someone you hardly know invites you out on a date that evening, there probably isn't time to "reason" about how much you trust them, so your intuition assesses how you feel about this person, and what past experiences you or your friends have had with accepting dates at short notice, and makes you issue an immediate acceptance or (more commonly) refusal. Of course, what you say is "Oh, sorry, I'm working/going out already this evening/washing the dog" or some other often-implausible excuse.

An experiment published in 1999 illustrates how the same route B behavior influences more mundane decisions (Shiv & Fedorikhin 1999). Shiv and Fedorikhin gave students an irrelevant task to perform, and offered them a reward of either a chocolate cake or a fruit salad. Half the sample were asked to make up their mind before the task began (time constrained) and the other half were told they could decide after the task had been completed (time unconstrained). The results showed that those in the constrained time situation were statistically far more likely to choose the emotionally more appealing chocolate cake over the rationally more appealing fruit salad, and vice versa.

The results were also reproduced when cognitive resource was constrained, by asking subjects to remember either a seven or a two-digit number. This indicates that decision-making when one's mind is "elsewhere" (e.g., shopping in a busy supermarket with your kids) is likely to results in decisions being strongly facilitated by emotion.

Two interesting caveats were found. The first is that these differences were not manifested when pictures of the two desserts were used. This suggests that intuitive behavior requires the "visceral" experience of the emotion (using our previous terminology, it requires your mirror neurons to fire off) before the emotional influence becomes effective. This may be why "production values" in advertising (i.e., the quality and care with which an advertisement is produced) can be so critically important to ad effectiveness.

The second caveat is that it was only the more impulsive subjects who reacted to their emotions, suggesting that route B does not apply equally to all people in all situations. This may account for why advertising isn't emotionally influential amongst all people, and why, in research, people find it so easy to hide their emotional vulnerability.

But, regardless of our emotional vulnerability, the presence of markers embedded in our subconscious does effectively result in us all being influenced by advertising without our knowledge. I think the Audi case study below illustrates this rather well.

Audi Case Study

In 1982, when John Bartle, Nigel Bogle, and John Hegarty started their ad agency (BBH), one of their first clients was the German car maker Audi. The story goes that their inspirational creative director, John Hegarty, was touring the Audi factory in Germany when he noticed the slogan "Vorsprung durch Technik." The literal translation of this slogan in English is "Advancement through technology," but going against everyone's advice Hegarty decided to use the slogan in its original German in UK advertising. As the *Guardian* newspaper put it in an article on January 22, 2010, "Despite scepticism … Hegarty went with his gut feeling, and the strapline is now one of the most famous and long-running in advertising."[1]

The first Audi TV advertisement came out in 1983. The tongue-in-cheek ad, laconically narrated by the UK actor Geoffrey Palmer, described three different German families driving to the Mediterranean for their summer holiday and showed that the aerodynamic and fuel efficient Audi 100 arrived long before all the others. It ended with the slogan, and Palmer intoning in his trademark laconic drawl: "Vorsprung durch Technik, as they say in Germany."

There was much comment in the advertising industry about how bizarre it was that BBH had chosen not to translate it. After a while the excitement died away and the slogan went on to become established and therefore to some extent ignored. Not so the Audi marque, which went on to become one of the most prestigious brands in the UK, ranking close in aspiration with BMW and Mercedes.

What is interesting is that, after 29 years, if you ask anyone what advertising they can recall for Audi they can hardly ever describe an ad, but many recall the slogan "Vorsprung durch Technik." If you go on to ask them what it means they look blankly at you and say "I haven't a clue, it's German." Based in this you would be forgiven for thinking the slogan has done nothing much to build Audi's aspirational reputation.

But using what we've learned about Damasio's somatic markers, it is possible to construct a case to say that this incomprehensible slogan might

[1] http://www.guardian.co.uk/media/2010/jan/22/audi-vorsprung-durch-technik-trademark

have been one of the *most* influential elements in Audi advertising. Because it triggers three very important markers.

Most of you will get the first marker at once. We already talked about the fact that Germany is rated better than almost all countries for its engineering, and clearly "Vorsprung durch Technik" is German. That means Audi is German, and therefore benefits from German engineering quality.

The second marker is almost equally easy to spot. The word "Technik" is very similar to the English word "technical" and "technology," and clearly signifies that Audi cars are technically sophisticated and developed using up-to-date technology. That positions the brand as being more interested in science than in fashion or good looks.

The third marker, I would say, is the most influential of all, yet hardly anyone spots it even though it is staring you in the face. This is the one that arises from Hegarty's decision not to translate the slogan. By leaving the slogan in the original German he enabled the brand to occupy the position of being not just German, but being *uncompromisingly* German.

Most foreign cars in the 1980s tried to play down their foreign origins. And in order to demonstrate that their cars were "anglicised," advertisers used English slogans in their advertising. BMW used the slogan "The Ultimate Driving Machine," Renault in their 1992 Clio ad used "A certain Style," and VW in their iconic Princess Diana Golf ad used "If only everything in life was as reliable as a Volkswagen." But Audi, by sticking to their original German slogan, effectively gave out a super-confident message that their cars were German and proud of it, and that they were not prepared to compromise them by changing them in any way. If people wanted a hybrid adapted to their local market then they could buy one of the other marques, but if they wanted the real thing then they should buy an Audi.

Of course, you don't *think* any of this when you see the slogan "Vorsprung durch Technik." You don't think "goodness me, that's a clever ploy by those chaps at Audi: by not translating their slogan they're telling me that they are not prepared to compromise their design for us Brits!" You don't think this because it's a slogan and in general none of us think about advertising slogans much. Indeed, if you did think too hard about the Audi slogan it would immediately lose its power, because you could quickly counter-argue that Audis are adapted to the UK market as much as any of the other German car brands.

So what does happen when you see this slogan? The answer is that you don't think about it but you do "feel" about it. You perceive the Audi name and the German slogan, and subconsciously that perception triggers the marker linked to the feeling that German engineering is the best in the world; it also triggers the marker that makes you feel that technology in a car is pretty important, and, above all, it triggers the marker that makes you feel that Audi is more German than all the rest – "German and proud of it" if you like – and that they must be pretty confident and successful to get away without translating their slogan. All these positive feelings get stored away in your subconscious, linked to the Audi name. And because they are stored subconsciously, and you are not aware that they are there, there is no way that you can erase them or stop them influencing you.

12

The Power of Metacommunication

"It is only too typical that the 'content' of any medium blinds us to the character of the medium."

Marshall McLuhan
Understanding Media (1964: 9)

In the last chapter we established that emotion acts as a gatekeeper to decisions, and that it can influence any decisions you make without you realizing it. You might be prepared to accept that emotive content in advertising might influence the day-to-day purchase of mundane goods and articles we buy in the shops. You might even be prepared to accept that emotive content in advertising could lure you into a car showroom. But I doubt if you would be prepared to accept that this same emotive content could actually play any part in the ultimate decision about what make of car you buy. Surely a decision as important as this would be driven by your rational thinking brain, would it not?

Many academics and advertisers would agree with you. For example, research has shown that although liking an advertisement is regarded by the ad industry as the single most important indicator of success in ad testing, it actually has little or no influence on our behavior (Bergkvist & Rossiter 2008). Paralleling the adage "you can take a horse to water, but you can't make it drink," this research suggests that emotive content in an ad can get people into the showroom, but it can't make them buy.

Or can it? Certainly there is no evidence that simply liking advertising can persuade you to buy the brand being advertised. But there is powerful evidence to show that feeling favorably inclined towards a company can make

Seducing the Subconscious: The Psychology of Emotional Influence in Advertising, First Edition. Robert Heath.
© 2012 Robert Heath. Published 2012 by John Wiley & Sons, Ltd.

you buy its products, and as we know that *not* liking a company can make you *not* buy its products. Also, a car company is in effect a brand, and there is evidence to show that emotive content in advertising can make you feel favorable towards a brand. This evidence comes from behavioral psychology, the psychology of relationships between people (Feldwick 2009).

Emotional Communication and Brand Relationships

Behavioral psychology is mainly concerned with psychotherapy and interpersonal behavior, and sheds some very important light on how emotional communication interacts with relationships. One of the foundation texts used by those who study interpersonal communication is the work of Paul Watzlawick. Watzlawick *et al.* (1967) established five axioms or rules for communication, and it is the first three that are most applicable to advertising.

Watzlawick's first axiom is that in an interpersonal situation communication is always taking place: "One cannot not communicate" (Watzlawick *et al.* 1967: 51). He established that even when two people are saying nothing to each other they are still engaged in communication, via their body language and the very fact that they are maintaining silence. The same can be said of a blank page in a newspaper carrying a brand name; the very fact that the page is blank is in itself is a piece of communication.

The reason that communication takes place even when you are not saying anything becomes clear with Watzlawick's second axiom: "Every communication has a content and a relationship aspect such that the latter classifies the former and is therefore a metacommunication" (Watazlawick *et al.* 1967: 54). In his view, the "communication" is what is said, but that communication is qualified and adapted by the tone and body language of the person communicating, and this is what he terms metacommunication. In exactly the same way, an advertisement can have a message or proposition that is written or spoken, but that message is qualified by the mood and tone and other elements that make up the advertisement's creativity. So in advertising it is the creativity that comprises the metacommunication.

This is very important if we want to get a clear understanding of how advertising works. It is not uncommon in the industry to hear clients saying things like "I just want an ad that communicates the facts, nothing else." What they don't realize is that one cannot "just" communicate facts. Every advertisement, however simple, has both communication and metacommunication.

Take the blank page with the brand name. The communication is the name of the brand, no question. But by putting on a blank page the brand is "metacommunicating" that "there is nothing more you need to know about me." It is also metacommunicating that "I am confident and affluent enough to buy a whole page in this newspaper and say nothing on it." As I said earlier, advertising cannot contain no metacommunication.

In his third axiom, Watzlawick draws an analogy between these two types of communication and the concept of "digital" versus "analog" content. He sees "communication" as the rational digital message, which is clear, unequivocal, easily analyzed and classified, and often lacks emotional values. In contrast, the "metacommunication" is the analog qualifier, which is highly emotional in character, and is often subtle, disguised, hard to classify, sometimes even difficult even to identify. It needs only a little imagination to see that Watzlawick's description of interpersonal communication is analogous to the terms that advertising practitioners use when describing advertising: where Watzlawick talks of "rational digital communication," the practitioner talks of the "message"; and where Watzlawick describes "emotional analogue metacommunication," the practitioner talks of "creativity."

So far so good. But what has this to do with how emotive content in advertising influences our purchase behavior? The explanation lies in the way in which relationships are created, and the way in which they break down.

Watzlawick's main area of research was on the way we form relationships. Essentially, he monitored couples who were having problems, and coached them on different ways to overcome these problems. In the course of doing this he discovered something very important. He found that when relationships between couples were on the verge of collapse, the "communication" was often perfectly reasonable and sensible, but it was the "metacommunication" that was causing the breakdown. In other words, although people were saying good things, the *way* in which they said them was causing friction and negativity. So merely improving *what* people said to one another had little effect on their relationship.

However, Watzlawick found that if you were able to correct the metacommunication, you could repair the relationship rift relatively easily. Indeed, improving the metacommunication was so successful that the relationship was able to survive even when the couples said damaging and negative things to each other.

From this Watzlawick concluded that it is this analog metacommunication aspect of communication that is the main driver of relationships. In simple terms, it isn't *what* you say that builds relationships, but *how* you say it.

The implications for advertising are pretty momentous. What Watzlawick's research indicates is that it isn't the rational message in an advertisement that builds brand relationships, but the emotive creativity that surrounds that message. This means that the communication of the message in advertising, which occupies 90% of the time and effort of advertisers and marketers, may actually have relatively little importance for the long-term health of the brand. Conversely, the creativity, which generally is left entirely up to the whim of the creative people beavering away in the depths of the ad agency, might turn out to be the one thing that is critical to the brand's long-term health. In other words, the whole process of developing advertising may have got itself turned upside down.

Marshall McLuhan, whose quote starts this chapter, had very much the same idea. His most famous quote – "it is sometimes a bit of a shock to be reminded that, in operational and practical fact, the medium is the message" (McLuhan 1964: 7) – hints at the idea that the carrier of the message is more influential than the message itself. But when he says "It is only too typical that the 'content' of any medium blinds us to the character of the medium" (McLuhan 1964: 9) it is very evident that he is talking about communication blinding us to the power of metacommunication. That is frequently what happens in advertising. We note and we counter-argue the message, but in doing so our attention is drawn away from the emotive metacommunication in the creativity. This slips unnoticed into our subconscious, and because we are not aware of it, we cannot counter-argue it, and we are unable to mitigate its influence on our relationship with the brand.

This idea of having a "relationship" with a brand might seem a little far-fetched to some of you. Companies and brands are inanimate objects. Surely we don't have the same sort of feelings for them that we have for our spouses and partners and parents and children and friends?

In fact, there is a lot of evidence to say that we *do* treat companies and brands like "part of our family." The scale of attachment we have for them may not approach the magnitude we have for people, but the feelings are there nevertheless. OK, no one is suggesting you might love your loo cleaner, but don't we feel emotionally attached to our inanimate cars and bikes? Just go onto the internet and you will find vast groups of people whose entire life is dedicated to marques such as Alfa Romeo, VW, Harley

Davidson, Ducati, etc. Indeed, they are so influential that these aficionados have become the target of considerable (and mostly unsuccessful) marketing activity. The same sort of attachment can be found in markets as diverse as skis, trainers, beer, clothing, vitamins, soft drinks, and computers. Talk to an Apple enthusiast for a few minutes and you'll often find this is someone with a real affection for their computer. And the same emotional attachment can be found amongst those who buy ecological washing powders like Ecover, even if their enthusiasm is comparatively muted. So at some level we "relate" to practically all the brands we buy regularly, although we are not always aware that these relationships exist.

But even if you accept that you might feel attached to your favorite brands, what evidence is there that Watzlawick's theories apply to them? Surely if we have an attachment it might be rational, deriving from the performance of the product, not how we feel about it? Metacommunication in human communication might influence our interpersonal relationships, but what evidence is there that metacommunication in advertising can influence our brand relationships? The short answer is that there wasn't much until I and two of my colleagues decided to test this out. This is what we found.

Testing Watzlawick's Theory

In order to test if Watzlawick's theory applies to advertising we needed to do two things. First, we had to find some way of quantifying the strength of the relationship – the attachment if you prefer – between people and brands. Second, we had to find some way of measuring communication and metacommunication.

Brand relationships are relatively easy to quantify. A simple measure of attachment is the favorability that someone expresses towards a brand. Favorability is not only a metric that can apply both to users and non-users, but it can also be quantified easily using an expanded semantic scale. We used a simple 10-point scale running from "extremely favorable" to "extremely unfavorable."

The quantification of the amount of communication and metacommunication in a piece of advertising was a little more complicated. Watzlawick *et al.* described communication as essentially rational, and metacommunication as essentially emotional in nature. So the level of communication in an advertisement is going to reflect the amount of rational "message" that is seen to be contained in it. Conversely, the level of metacommunication is going to equate to the perceived amount of emotive content, or creativity, there is in the advertisement. The only problem is that you can't really ask someone directly how much message, or how much creativity they think there is in a particular advertisement, as they would probably look at you as if you were mad.

The solution was to deduce these measures by asking a set of indirect questions about the advertising content. Fortunately, this was already being done by a proprietary advertising research system, the CEP®Test.

The CEP®Test had been developed as part of an online copy testing system to help evaluate the absolute and relative levels of emotional and rational content in advertising. Using a battery of 10 statements, the CEP®Test quantified two constructs: Cognitive Power™, which measured the potency of the message and rational information in the advertisement; and Emotive Power™, which measured the potency of the emotional content in the advertisement. These two constructs closely parallel Watzlawick's communication and metacommunication. So if Watzlawick's axioms were applicable to advertising, then it should be the Emotive Power that correlates with strong brand relationships, rather than the Cognitive Power.

Our experimental work was carried out in 2005 and published in the *Journal of Advertising Research* (Heath *et al.* 2006). The first experiment we carried out was run via two online surveys in the USA. In the first survey, we selected a group of 23 TV advertisements currently on air in the USA across a number of different product categories, and played these to a general population sample. We then asked the questions in the CEP®Test, and worked out the ratings for the Cognitive Power and Emotive Power for each advertisement.

In order to measure how well each advertisement had influenced brand relationships, a second general population internet sample was recruited. These respondents were not initially shown the ads, just asked to rate each of the brands featured on favorability, using the 10-point scale. They were then shown selected clips of each of the ads and asked whether they had seen them before on TV. That meant we could now split the brand favorability scores between those who recognized and those who did not recognize the advertisement. This produces a "shift" in favorability which indicated the extent to which the advertising had improved the brand relationship for that respondent while it was on air. Levels of usage were controlled to ensure that there was no bias introduced by having significantly more users in either the recognizer or non-recognizer samples.

Table 12.1 US Correlation Coefficients. (From Heath *et al.* 2006)

		Cognitive	*Emotive*	*Fav-Shift*
Cognitive Power[TM]	Pearson Correlation	1		
	Sig (2-tailed)			
	N	23		
Emotive Power[TM]	Pearson Correlation	0.403	1	
	Sig. (2-tailed)	0.057		
	N	23	23	
Favorability Shift	Pearson Correlation	0.291	0.532**	1
	Sig. (2-tailed)	0.178	0.009	
	N	23	23	23

** Correlation is significant at the 0.01 level (2-tailed).

These two tests enabled us to examine the relationship between the shift in brand favorability and the Emotive Power and Cognitive Power of the advertisement. What we found was that there was a modest but highly significant positive relationship between Emotive Power and favorability shift. But there was no significant relationship at all between Cognitive Power and favorability shift. The statistics are shown in Table 12.1.

These findings indicated, as we suspected, that it was only the Emotive Power in the advertisements that correlated with improvements in Brand Favorability. And, as Watzlawick's research suggested, the Cognitive Power (or message) had little or no influence.

In order to test if the results were applicable only in the USA, a second identical experiment was run in the UK, using a group of 20 TV advertisements currently on air in the UK. Results are shown in Table 12.2.

As can be seen, the UK data showed an even stronger significant positive relationship between Emotive Power and favorability shift, and in this case a non-significant *inverse* relationship was found between Cognitive Power and favorability shift. This implied that the more evident the message was in the UK advertising, the *less* it was likely to influence favorability towards the brand. So, despite differences in advertising styles between the USA and UK, the results were remarkably consistent. Emotive Power showed a significant linear relationship with the shift in favorability. Cognitive Power showed no significant relationship.

Table 12.2 UK Correlation Coefficients. (From Heath *et al.* 2006)

		Cognitive	Emotive	Fav-Shift
Cognitive Power™	Pearson Correlation	1		
	Sig (2-tailed)			
	N	20		
Emotive Power™	Pearson Correlation	−0.241	1	
	Sig. (2-tailed)	0.307		
	N	20	20	
Favorability Shift	Pearson Correlation	−0.275	0.587**	1
	Sig. (2-tailed)	0.240	0.006	
	N	20	20	20

** Correlation is significant at the 0.01 level (2-tailed).

These results show that Watzlawick's theory does appear to apply to advertising. The rational message in advertising seems to have little or no influence on brand relationships, just as the rational communication between people has little or no influence on interpersonal relationships. Conversely, the emotive "creative" metacommunication in advertising appears to be able to build strong brand relationships, just as the emotive metacommunication in interpersonal communication builds strong interpersonal relationships. So the daft creative ideas we discussed way back in Chapter 2, that often appear to have nothing whatsoever to do with what is being advertised, are suddenly revealed as possibly having a direct influence on how attached we become to brands.

Is there any evidence to say that this sort of advertising creativity has anything more than just a marginal influence on behavior? Well, consider the Telma Noodles case study which was discussed in Chapter 3. Here was an advertisement that had no message at all, yet somehow resulted in a brand achieving spectacular launch success. And here is another much more well-known case study, which happened in the UK just over 3 years ago.

Cadbury's Gorilla Advertising Case Study

On August 31, 2007, the UK chocolate company Cadbury's new ad agency launched an extraordinary TV advertisement for the Cadbury's Dairy Milk chocolate brand. It featured what appeared to be a gorilla (in reality the actor Garon Michael in an extremely expensive and lifelike custom-made gorilla suit) playing the drum sequence in Phil Collins' hit song *In The Air Tonight*. The ad was launched in a break in the highly popular TV series *Big Brother*, and was accompanied by extensive PR activity. Within a few days of its first going on air there was hardly anyone who had not heard of the Cadbury's Gorilla ad.

When you try to describe it, the ad doesn't sound that remarkable. In fact, I think most people would regard it as being little more than a bit of amusing nonsense. Some 60 of the 90 seconds are spent in close-ups of the gorilla anticipating the moment when he can start playing, and it fades out shortly after the iconic 10-beat entry riff. The only message appears in the last 5 seconds, when you see captioned on the screen the words "A glass and a half of joy." And that's it.

It's hard to understand what this is meant to be communicating about the product. If, like me, you are one of the older members of the viewing audience, you might recall that Cadbury's Dairy Milk used to claim it contained "A glass and a half of full cream milk." But how that relates to a drumming gorilla is still pretty hard to fathom. The ad agency themselves (Fallon London) apparently intended that people would see this as "a minute and a half of happiness" brought to you by Cadbury's," but since there is no reference at all to the 90-second length of the advertisement that has to be taken with a pinch of salt. To all intents and purposes, like Telma Noodles, this is an ad without a message.

Nevertheless, the effect of the ad was dramatic. According to Wikipedia:

> Despite reservations that the campaign might prove too abstract and have little effect, Cadbury reported that sales of Dairy Milk had increased 9% from the same period in 2006. Measurements of public perception of the brand carried out by market research firm YouGov showed that 20% more people looked favourably on the brand in the period after the advert's general release than in the previous period.[1]

That all sounds pretty impressive, but it actually gets better. Subsequently, it turned out that the effect of the ad on Cadbury's Dairy Milk sales was not that exceptional, given that the brand had been the subject of extensive marketing support preceding the launch of the new campaign. But what was exceptional was that Cadbury saw an increase in sales across *all* of its

---

[1] http://en.wikipedia.org/wiki/Gorilla_(advertisement)

products, an increase which they could only attribute to the Dairy Milk advertisement.

So here we have an ad that has no real message creating an uplift in sales across all the brands of a 186-year-old company. The only explanation seems to be that people's attachment to the Cadbury's brand had been influenced by the ad, and this conclusion is supported by the YouGov poll findings of a 20% increase in favorability for the Cadbury's brand.

Six months later Fallon launched a second ad in the series, this time with even more publicity. This new ad featured a group of airport trucks having a race up the runway to the music of Queen's mega-hit *Having A Good Time*. It was an almighty flop. Sales of the brand and the company showed no uplift, and the ad was quietly consigned to the dustbin.

So how exactly did the Gorilla ad work? Fallon themselves evidently were not sure, as they rang me up in 2008 to ask if I could help them understand why the second ad was such a disaster. As far as they were concerned, both ads showed unlikely events, both had iconic pop music tracks, and both were launched in a shower of publicity. Yet one succeeded beyond all their dreams, and the other didn't work at all.

Using what we have learned so far, it is possible to assemble a very plausible explanation for why one ad worked and the other did not. One must admit that not many of us cherish the desire to drive an airport truck down a runway racing with a bunch of other airport trucks; and even if we did, we can't see the actual drivers in the ad, so there are no facial expressions we can use to trigger mirror neurons and create feelings of excitement we can relate to. Effectively, these are little more than animated vehicles, and it isn't easy to feel any sort of affinity with a cartoon character truck unless you are a toddler.

On the other hand, most of us have a little part inside us that longs to act like a wild animal, and quite a few of us have another little part that longs to play the drums like Phil Collins did in *In the air. . . .* By putting these two cherished ambitions together, the Gorilla ad effectively encapsulates two of our most basic visceral desires for fulfillment. And the gorilla's facial expressions are so well directed that our mirror neurons can use these to trigger the same sense of anticipation and excitement that he is experiencing. One might expect that any company perceptive enough to realise all this is one worthy of respect and liking.

I'd say that this increased respect and liking for Cadbury, and the consequent marked improvement in people's relationship with the company, would be quite enough to drive up the sales of what are mostly impulse purchase items. And we know, it was the totality of the company that was affected, because sales went up across all Cadbury's products.

Of course, had anyone asked me if the Gorilla ad had increased my favorability towards Cadbury and made me buy more of their products, I would have laughed at them and strenuously denied it. After all, however entertaining the drumming gorilla is, I wouldn't want to be seen as being influenced by such trivial nonsense.

13

The Subconscious Seduction Model

"Advertisements ordinarily work their wonders . . . on an inattentive public."

Michael Schudson
Advertising, the Uneasy Persuasion (1984: 3)

Having now assembled a lot of new learning about how advertising works and might work, you might ask why it is necessary to go to the lengths of building a new model. Why can't we just bolt the stuff we have learned onto the existing persuasion model? The reason I think a new model is needed is that our whole buying environment has changed so much in the last few decades. We have new technology, new ways of interacting with one another, and a huge increase in the number of decisions we have to take each day.

New Technology

It's no use pretending that the world is the same as it was. Take films. Fifteen years ago these were the mainstay of TV schedules. Families would glue themselves to the TV for an afternoon or evening to watch a film. And that gave the advertisers an unrivalled opportunity to expose their ads to us as a group.

Not any more. Films most often come on DVD either from the supermarket or from companies like LoveFilm. We can watch these anywhere (e.g., bedroom, car, kitchen) and any time (e.g., lunchtime, midnight, 3 a.m.) On the rare occasions when there is a film on TV we haven't seen, most of us

Seducing the Subconscious: The Psychology of Emotional Influence in Advertising, First Edition. Robert Heath.
© 2012 Robert Heath. Published 2012 by John Wiley & Sons, Ltd.

will record it and play it back at our leisure, fast-forwarding through the ads. And we don't even have to watch it on TV with other people, because we can watch it alone on our own computer. Despite the widescreen and flat screen (and imminently 3D) TV, the era of watching the television together as a group is largely a thing of the past.

Although not entirely. Soaps and reality shows still abound, and these are still the best chance there is for an advertiser to get a good audience. But an audience watching a group of minor celebs in a jungle being bullied into eating insects probably isn't quite the same as a family relaxing together watching a quality film. The sad fact is that advertisers can no longer guarantee that their ad will be seen in a premium entertainment environment by a relaxed and compliant audience.

The New Social Environment

Alongside the change in technology, the social environment in which advertising operates has changed as well. For those of us who live in the West, TV advertising is no longer the novelty it was when it first came out. Indeed, those who were born on the day the first ever TV ad was transmitted for Bulova watches in the USA (July 1, 1941) will have celebrated their seventieth birthday in 2011. And the first TV ad transmitted in the UK was for Gibbs SR Toothpaste on September 21, 1955, so those born on that day will be 56. Only a small minority of us have ever experienced a world when there was no TV advertising, and it shows in the way we disregard it. As Michael Shudson suggests in the quote at the start of this chapter, when it comes to advertising, particularly TV advertising, the vast majority of people believe it deserves scant attention. And that, generally, is what it gets.

It is also undeniable that the marketing environment in which advertising operates has changed. The days when advertisers would trumpet details of their new products on TV are pretty much over. Mainstream TV is a hugely expensive medium to use if you want to go into detail about anything. And, aside from that, any genuinely new product idea is often matched by competitors in less time than it can take to make a TV ad. Take the example of the Dyson DC01 Vacuum Cleaner, which appeared on the market in 1993 with a transparent bagless system that allowed you to see what you were cleaning up off your floors. A revolutionary idea, yet within 6 months, about the time it takes to write, research, plan, and shoot a TV commercial, it is said there were no less than four other brands of transparent bagless vacuum cleaner on the market.

When major product innovations are able to be matched this quickly, what sense does it make to use expensive TV to announce anything but the most revolutionary new ideas? So a direct consequence of the speed with which brands match each other's performance is that TV ads nowadays are used not to "sell" the product but to build positive attitudes towards and relationships with the brand. If you want product details then you can find them on the internet.

It's perhaps worth reminding ourselves what brands are there for. They arrived in the first place as a way of distinguishing one farm's cows from another of lesser quality, and turned into a way of distinguishing one company's products from others of lesser quality. But then it became clear that, far from a simple identification device, brands could be used symbolically to extend and enhance what the company was offering. And this became a two-way benefit, because we, the consumers, found we could use brands as a way of shortcutting the onerous task of deciding what to buy.

This is very effectively illustrated by an experiment which I alluded to in Chapter 3, conducted in 2000 by Stijn Van Osselaer and Joseph Alba (2000). Van Osselaer and Alba devised a pair of imaginary brands of inflatable boat, each with a range of different product attributes. They then exposed different groups of students to these product attributes, which gave them an indication of how people behave when buying unbranded products. What they found was that the students examined the attributes until they were satisfied they had established which of them signified quality, then ignored all the others. All as you might expect.

They then looked into what happened when they exposed the subjects first to the branded boats. Their view was that brands "signal" quality but do not "prove" quality, so when product attributes that prove quality are available then people should ignore the brand and revert to studying the product attribute. But this isn't what happened. When brands were exposed first the students quickly formed a preference, and then instead of examining the product attributes to find out which signified quality, they simply examined enough to support their brand preference. Consideration of all the other product attributes was effectively "blocked."

The idea that the mere presence of branding may inhibit our learning behavior from attributes in this way seems at first to be counter-intuitive. We like to think of ourselves as logical humans who behave in a logical and deductive way. The problem is that we don't live in a world where we have enough time available to allow us to be logical and deductive. Most of those who live in developed countries lead busy lives where shopping is an activity that has to be integrated with and around activities like looking after our spouses, our children, our houses, and consuming media. And what compounds our problems is that when we do decide to buy something we find ourselves offered an ever-increasing range of items to choose from.

The Tyranny of Choice

I can still recall my first sight of the canned tuna fixture in the Sainsbury's supermarket in Greenford in 1999. The fixture was roughly 20 feet long, and contained an almost endless variety of big round tins, small round tins, small oval tins, and large oval tins. These contained anything from tuna chunks to tuna steaks to tuna slices to tuna fillets, and the type of tuna varied from ordinary tuna to skipjack tuna to "South Seas" tuna to yellow fin tuna, and these were available in anything from brine to sunflower oil to olive oil to tomato sauce to mayonnaise to mustard sauce, and so on. And all this was merchandized under four or five different brand names.

Finding this choice bewildering, I decided on a simple strategy, which was to choose a brand that claimed to be "dolphin-friendly": except I swiftly discovered that *all* the brands were dolphin-friendly. And that's the problem. Nearly all reputable brands offer exactly the same thing.

This is exactly the state of "ultimately unsatisfying and psychologically draining ... hyperchoice" which we discussed in Chapter 3. And this, of course, is why Van Osselaer and Alba found their students using brands as an excuse to "block" the study of product attributes. It has become the new human nature for us to seek for shortcuts that save us time and effort. And we don't just do this in trivial product categories. Take the onerous task of choosing a new washing machine. It is said that a broken washing machine is rated as one of the most stressful situations that can happen to us (behind divorce and house-buying), so not surprisingly the single overriding property that everyone seeks when buying a new one is reliability. But go into a store looking for a washing machine and you'll find a bewildering variety of program types, spin-speeds, green credentials, and prices, but not a single claim or shred of evidence regarding how reliable a machine is. Hardly surprising that Gerard Tellis finds that "Contrary to popular perception, many consumers do not resort to active search, even for expensive and infrequently purchased products" (Tellis 1998: 121).

So how do we go about making decisions in this confused "hyperchoice" world? The answer is that we rely on Damasio's route B, the "covert activation of biases related to prior emotional experiences in comparable situations." This, of course, is what Damasio identifies as "gut feeling," or intuition.

Intuition

The *Oxford Dictionary* defines Intuition as "the ability to understand something instinctively, without the need for conscious reasoning."[1] And that's how we feel when we use our intuition: we understand which product to buy even though we can't rationally explain why. In reality, the reason we think we understand what to buy is that over our lifetime we have laid down hosts of emotional markers that are now resident in our subconscious and capable of being covertly activated.

Here's an example of how intuition works. At some time in our life we have a friend whose washing machine breaks down on them with traumatic results, and they blame the breakdown on the fact that they bought a cheap washing machine made in Country X. Quite soon you forget this, but it creates a subconscious marker in your mind against cheap washing machines made in this particular country. So when you next need to buy a washing machine you find inexplicably that you avoid those brands made in Country X, and those brands that are especially cheap.

Indeed, as with Van Osselaer and Alba's students, you don't really look very hard at any of the other brands, because what you *feel* you want to buy is a Bosch. And why do you intuitively want a Bosch? Because another marker makes you feel that German products are the best engineered in the world, and therefore most reliable, and the word Bosch could not be more German!

Of course, it helps that the Bosch machines are a bit more expensive than all the other brands. Why? Because the marker in our minds that tells us not to trust cheap washing machines makes us especially vulnerable to slightly more expensive washing machines. And it helps even more that the Bosch is being offered at 10% off regular price, because that makes it only a *little* bit more expensive than the other brands. Mind you, it's only able to offer 10% off its regular price because countless other people are doing the same as you and intuitively choosing a Bosch washing machine.

---

[1] http://www.oxforddictionaries.com/definition/intuition?view=uk

Mostly, this sort of intuitive decision-making happens without our being aware of it. And it is commonplace, not exceptional behavior. That's not to say that the marketing establishment accepts that it goes on. John Bargh laments that:

> Although in the past decade of consumer research there has been increasing attention to the possibility that there may be automatic or nonconscious influences on choices and behavior, the field still appears dominated by purely cognitive approaches, in which decisions and actions are made deliberately. (Bargh 2002: 280)

So in many respects the sort of decisions we make regarding which washing machine we buy might have already been made for us before we set foot in the shop. This is the extent to which we are prey to external influences. Of course, advertising hasn't really played a part in this washing machine scenario, but it is easy to show how it can.

"Along comes an ad . . ."

So there you are, slumped in front of the TV watching a repeat of *Friends* or *Desperate Housewives* or some other show, when the ad break comes on. Let's assume you're too lethargic to go and make tea or change channel, so you just sit there. TV is known to induce a sort of trance-like lethargy in most of us: I recall Bruce Goerlich saying, in defense of the 30-second TV ad, that "There are a lot of consumers coming home in the evening, taking their brain out and putting it in a warm bowl of water, and watching television."[2] That is what we watch TV for, to relax and not to have to think too much.

Being in this sort of lethargic state means your attention level towards the TV is not going to be that great. And given that we don't expect to learn anything of great importance from TV advertising there isn't going to any motivation to increase it when the ads come on. Nevertheless, when an ad starts you'll either recognize it as one you've seen before or not. (Remember, Lionel Standing's picture experiment showed our recognition powers are prodigious.) If you do recognize the ad as one you have seen before, your

---

[2]   Verbatim quote by Bruce Goerlich, Executive Vice President of Zenith Optimedia, at the lunchtime panel of the Advertising Research Foundation (ARF) Conference, April 17, 2007.

attention level will almost certainly fall even more, because you will know instantly there is nothing new that you will learn from it.

So let's assume you don't recognize the ad, and that it isn't for something that you are desperate to buy. As the ad proceeds you register a stream of perceptions and these trigger a stream of concepts. All this happens automatically and subconsciously. Periodically you'll see or hear something that might get you to actually pay a little bit of attention and do some analysis. Typical amongst the things you pay a bit of attention to is the identity of the brand being advertised (note that I say "identity" because often it is a logo, not a name, that alerts us to the actual brand). Why should we want to pay attention to this? Simply because it is instinct to want to decode what is passing by our eyes and ears, and we know that no ad makes sense unless you know who it is for. But, in line with Dennett's hypothesis, the likelihood is that the period of attention will be short and the brand name will roll briefly into consciousness and then be swiftly forgotten.

I think ad agencies are rather stupid when it comes to deciding where to put the brand in an ad. They worry that if they put it in early on then you'll realize who the ad is for and mentally switch off. So they often put the brand right at the end of the ad, thinking that we will pay attention to find out who the ad is for. Sadly for them, most of us will switch off pretty quickly if we don't find out fairly soon what the ad is advertising, and by the time the brand arrives at the end we will probably have forgotten what little we absorbed about what the ad was trying to say about it.

Occasionally, our curiosity does lead us to attend sufficiently for us to understand the message the ad is trying to get over. If we do this then the message will do one of two things: it will either generate a set of beliefs, which might then change our attitudes; or it might change our attitudes directly. If there's no incentive to remember these changes (e.g., they're predictable, banal, or just plain unexciting) then we might perceptually filter them out and forget them instantly. If we pay a lot of attention to them, we might counter-argue them and decide they are rubbish.

If the ad does get an interesting message into our head and change our attitudes, there may well be an increase in likelihood that we might at some stage in the future buy the brand. But, with perceptual filtering, counter-argument, and general lethargy, most ads will fail to register any rational message for longer than a few seconds after the ad has finished.

As I said earlier, if this ad is one we have been exposed to before, the chances are that we will pay less attention than we did the first time. Our analytical faculties will therefore be even less engaged and the likelihood of us interpreting or recalling a message even smaller. Of course, should the ad mention something that is genuinely "new," and therefore of interest to us (like an especially low price for a car, sofa, or holiday, or an interesting or important website, etc.), then there is a much better chance we will remember it. But in general there is only a very small chance that a TV ad will get us to pay attention to the sort of predictable rational messages in most ads. It is too easy to dismiss as hogwash claims like "our product is the best on the market," or "it tastes good because we use only the finest natural ingredients," or "we guarantee satisfaction or your money back."

But there are other consciously processed elements that stand a better chance of sticking in our mind. If the ad consistently and repeatedly uses a slogan, or shows a well-known character, a unique drawing or design, or a particular sequence of events, you will, even in a lethargic state, associate it with the brand over time. A well-known example is the Intel jingle. It comprises four notes, the first and third the same, the second higher and the fourth higher still. Practically everyone in the world recognizes it, because it is played in the advertising of every computer that uses an Intel microprocessor.

These associations can be incredibly long-lasting: many people in the UK still recall slogans like "Keep going well, keep going Shell," "Go to work on an egg," and "Guinness is good for you," even though they are half a century old.

To demonstrate this to yourself, try filling in the brands in these US ads: "Just do it," "We try harder," and "That'll do nicely." Or if you live in the UK, try "Beanz meanz . . . ," "I bet he drinks . . . ," and "Liquid Engineering." I've no doubt you found that surprisingly easy.

What, if anything, do these slogans achieve? To understand that we have to leave the conscious and look back into the subconscious.

Subconscious Associative Conditioning

Let's go back to the stream of perceptions and concepts you get when you are exposed to an ad. As we've discussed already, these occur throughout the advertising, because we can't switch them off. So every element of an advertising campaign that gets stuck in your mind brings with it a whole raft of concepts. And this is axiomatic: as Watzlawick states, *every* "digital" communication element has a corresponding "analog" metacommunication concept riding on its back.

Sometimes these concepts are emotionally sterile. The Intel jingle, for example, is purely a branding device and conveys little in the way of conceptual values. Using Damasio's terminology, it is an example of an emotionally *incompetent* association. But most communicate rather more. For example, Papa and Nicole in the Renault Clio ad trigger the concepts of style and sexiness; the Andrex Puppy triggers the concepts of family values and softness; the British Airways music triggers the concepts of relaxation and contentment; the drum-playing Cadbury's Gorilla triggers the concept of liberation; and the Hamlet Cigar music triggers the concept of consolation. And in each case these emotionally competent associations, exposed repeatedly, condition us to feel the brand being advertised has these same emotional values.

Just occasionally we become actively aware of these conceptual emotional associations (e.g., when someone from a market research company asks us what we associate with puppies). In most cases they remain hidden away in our subconscious. There they act in the same way as Damasio's somatic markers: when we come to make a decision, they are able to covertly influence how we make that decision. They also operate as a subconscious gatekeeper if we try to make a decision that goes against them. And, if we are in a hurry to make the decision, they can drive our intuition, and effectively make the decision for us. We can illustrate the influence of these associations using the case study of the famous Michelin Baby Campaign.

Michelin Baby Campaign Case Study

In 1984, Michelin appointed the ad agency Doyle Dane Bernbach (DDB) to handle their advertising. DDB had the idea of using babies in their advertising, along with the slogan "Michelin, because so much is riding on your tires." Michelin ran advertising featuring babies for 17 years, until someone in their marketing department presumably decided either that people were getting bored with them, or (more likely) that they didn't say enough about the actual tires. Either way, the account was put up for review in February 2001 and DDB lost it. The last baby ad ran in April 2001, advertising Michelin's victory in the J.D. Power Customer Service awards.

One of the most moving of these ads featured a baby sitting in a car tire, with a large rather shaggy dog sitting next to it. In the background is playing a fake weather forecast, predicting that the unseasonably warm weather might turn into "severe thunderstorms and localized flooding" then "snow, turning to freezing rain." As we hear this, the dog goes off screen and returns wearing a yellow oilskin and carrying one of her puppies (also dressed in a yellow oilskin) by the scruff of the neck. The dog gently deposits her puppy into the tire alongside the rather confused-looking baby.

During the two decades that they ran, these ads strengthened Michelin's brand image year after year. Not just amongst women with babies, but amongst the population as a whole. How did they do this? Well, simply seeing a baby triggers the concept not only of cuteness but of extreme vulnerability, which in turn triggers the concept of safety. Thus, without the need for any rational product performance claims, the baby conditions us to associate Michelin tires with safety. In the absence of any good reason to buy another make, this marker would exert sufficient influence on our choice of tire to make us favor Michelin.

But mostly we purchase tires after we have a blowout, or when we are told that our tires are no longer legally roadworthy. It's what is called a "distress purchase," and as such means we have to make our minds up fast. In situations like this, Damasio predicts our intuition will drive the decision directly. And what drives our intuition? Why, the baby marker that has conditioned us to believe that Michelins are the safest tires. So that's what we buy.

Subconscious associative conditioning like this can be extraordinarily long-lasting, partly because it is subconscious and so is never counter-argued. In the case of Michelin, a Goodyear case study written some 6 years after the baby campaign ended stated that:

> Despite being off the air for years, Michelin's "baby" campaign firmly associated them with safety. According to Millward Brown brand tracking data, Michelin led Goodyear in 2006 in overall opinion and purchase consideration, and had significantly higher ratings on important attributes such as trusted brand and high quality.[3]

So one way that TV advertising can influence us while we sit there in our lethargic state is by subconscious associative conditioning. But there's another subtly different way that advertising can influence us subconsciously, and that's by manipulating our relationship with the brand. This is especially the case with TV advertising.

---

[3] http://s3.amazonaws.com/thearf-org-aux-assets/awards/ogilvy-cs/Ogilvy_08_Case_Study_GoodYear.pdf.

Subconscious Relationship Manipulation

Most of us don't mind TV advertisements. They are, after all, usually designed not to be too offensive. We don't necessarily find them actively entertaining any more – research shows this has nearly halved over the last 20 years – but we mostly don't find them all that annoying either. And we know that TV advertising pays for our TV channels, and is something we should therefore really not complain too much about.

Because we don't mind TV ads, and we don't expect them to tell us much that is new, we let them run by with fairly good grace. Sometimes they are beautifully made, play lovely music, tell us nice stories, or show glorious countryside. Occasionally they are quite funny and entertaining. So as long as we don't let ourselves be seduced by their message, what could possibly be wrong with watching them?

The answer is nothing, provided you don't mind your relationship with the brand being subconsciously manipulated and your attachment to it being subconsciously increased; because mostly this is what is happening. The 2006 Dove Superbowl advertising is an example.

Dove Self-Esteem Fund Case Study

Dove is well-known for its quite outspoken advertising campaigns. Their "Campaign for Real Beauty" and their "Pro-Age" campaigns are just two examples.

In 2006, as part of their Campaign for Real Beauty, Dove decided to found the Dove Self-Esteem Fund, as an "agent of change to inspire and educate girls and young women about a wider definition of beauty."[4] In support of this move they made a TV commercial and ran it at the 2006 Super Bowl. Using the Cindi Lauper hit *True Colors* as a background, the ad showed a sequence of cameos of girls of ages ranging from about 7 to 10 looking really depressed and miserable, and then the same girls looking happy, invigorated, and confident.

Of course, many people are very cynical about ads like this, and at a conscious level they would counter-argue the brand's involvement, saying things like "I bet they spent more money on getting the ad into Super Bowl than they gave to support the kids." But the ad, showing the transformation

---

[4]   http://www.dove.co.uk/cfrb/self-esteem-fund/about.html

of the young girls from miserable to happy, and playing the beautiful music track, is very moving and has a terrific feel-good factor about it. And research confirmed that, unlike the vast majority of Super Bowl ads, 92% of people liked it and 93% found it emotive.

So no matter how much you consciously reject their motives, the ad does make you feel good about Dove, and will enhance your attachment to the brand. You don't have any option, because the only defense you have against this is your rational counter-argument. It's like watching someone cry in the movies: it doesn't matter how much you tell yourself it is a film, your mirror neurons will make you feel sad.

And there are two further things worth bearing in mind. The first is that you will only consciously reject the Dove Self-Esteem Fund ad if you paid sufficient attention to it. The second is that your conscious mind is incredibly busy and not that capacious. So, as we showed in Chapter 5, it is likely that the connections to your cynical counter-arguing rejection engram will be overwritten by you and forgotten pretty swiftly. But the feelings generated about the brand are held subconsciously in your inexhaustible implicit memory, and you are unable to overwrite the connections. So the improvement in your relationship with Dove will be with you forever, or at least until some negative metacommunication comes along to give you a bad feeling about them.

What is being revealed here is that advertising can, simply by exposing us to emotive content that makes us feel good alongside a fleeting exposure to a brand, affect our attachment to that brand. And this emotive content doesn't have to be stuff that makes us laugh or cry; it can be background music that is uplifting or nice to listen, or people expressing their emotions (love, anger, excitement, boredom, curiosity, appreciation, amusement, etc.), or situations that are humorous or poignant or dramatic, or scenery that is elegant or beautiful, or even just footage that is just beautifully shot with high production values.

So how much does this matter? Well, it wouldn't matter at all if every brand on the supermarket shelf was manifestly different from all the others. If that were the case then our choices would be based on what the brand does not how we feel towards it. But, as we discussed earlier in this chapter, most brands are not that different from each other nowadays, and virtually all brands satisfy our needs perfectly well. In these circumstances how we feel about a brand can become the way we choose a brand.

And even if the brands *are* different in some important way, bear in mind Damasio's model of decision-making, which showed that our emotions act a gatekeeper in influencing our decisions. We are simply unable to make rational decisions without our emotions concurring. So if it comes to a choice between a brand that has no particular defining character, and one that we feel good about, the odds will be stacked in favor of the latter. The bottom line is that all those apparently innocuous images we see in advertising are what in many cases are driving our behavior.

The Subconscious Seduction Model

So here is my recipe for the alternative way in which TV advertising in the twenty-first century influences us:

It starts with emotive metacommunicating content. That may be emotion that is present throughout the ad itself and influences the way we feel about the brand (as in the Dove Self-Esteem Fund), or it may be emotive values that attach to a component of the ad and that become associated with the brand and so condition it to have the same emotional value (as in the Michelin Babies and the Andrex Puppy).

We generally like positive emotive content, and we generally trust what we like. We don't tend to pay much attention to ads (especially TV ads) and one of the main reasons we *do* feel the need to pay attention is when we want to counter-argue what they are telling us. The more we like and trust an ad, the less inclined we are to counter-argue its message, and the less attention we feel we have to pay towards it.

As Bornstein found, the lower level of attention we pay to an ad or to a component of an ad, the less we are able to counter-argue it, and the more the ad is able to influence our emotions.

The more the ad influences our emotions, the better it is able to condition the brand to have that emotion and create positive brand relationships. These conditioned associations and positive relationships make use feel more favorable towards the brand.

One of Watzlawick's key findings was that although the content of communication (i.e., the messages in an ad) fades and vanishes quite quickly, the subtle emotive brand attitudes generated by the emotional metacommunication are safely tucked away in implicit memory, and these will endure for a very long time.

So at some time in the future when it comes to a purchase choice in which there is very little to choose between two brands, we will intuitively choose the one we favor. And because we don't remember how we formed the attitudes and markers that created this intuitive feeling, we can't easily prevent it from influencing us.

This also explains why we all have so much difficulty remembering ads. The details of the ads themselves fade quite fast, because these are complex pseudo-episodic memories whose recall pathways can easily be blurred and overwritten. And any rational message content in TV advertising, which we've already established we don't pay much attention to anyway, will also fade as quickly as the memory of the ad itself. But the emotional metacommunication memories that influence our feelings toward the brand will endure much longer. And we may have not the slightest inkling that they are there.

Decision and Relationship: Summary

We now have a complete chart of the new Subconscious Seduction Model (Figure 13.1), and it shows a number of important additions. For example, Brand-Linked Attitudes are qualified now according to whether they are Overt (i.e., those we are aware of and able to recall) or Covert (those we are not aware of and would have difficulty recalling). Behavior Change is also now qualified by whether the behavior is Rational (i.e., based mostly on reasoning) or Intuitive (i.e., based upon feelings or markers stored in the mind from past comparable experiences).

The first thing to point out is that a dotted "emotion" lines now joins the solid "persuasion" line in driving Rational Behavior. This reflects emotion's role as a gatekeeper in decision-making. As we saw in Chapter 11, we cannot make decisions if our emotions do not concur with them.

The second thing is that overt attitude changes and rationally driven behavior are both able to be counter-argued. This means that the top half of the model depicts a state in which we have our defenses against advertising alerted. Conversely, the bottom half of the model depicts a state in which we have little or no defense against advertising. It is almost impossible for us to defend ourselves against covert attitude change and intuitively driven behavior. In the case of covert attitude change we are unlikely to be aware that our attitudes *have* changed unless someone subjects us to hypnosis; and in the case of intuitively driven behavior we are unlikely to know exactly what is driving our intuition.

So anything operating towards the bottom of the model is going to be able to exert an influence on us which we won't find very easy to resist. The first of these "lower level" influences is the box marked Emotionally Competent Brand Associations.

Three influences – Brand Awareness, Feelings, and Emotions – all converge into this box marked Emotionally Competent Brand Associations, which lies a little way up from the bottom. The reason it is positioned here is that these are entities like the Andrex Puppy and the Marlboro Cowboy that are not *themselves* covert, but are known and often well recalled as being linked to brands. What *isn't* so well known, however, is that these devices are Emotionally Competent Stimuli (ECS) which trigger potent and relevant emotional concepts, and on repeated exposure "condition" us to feel that the brand has the same emotional values as the entity. Thus, the Andrex Puppy conditions us to feel that Andrex is both soft and

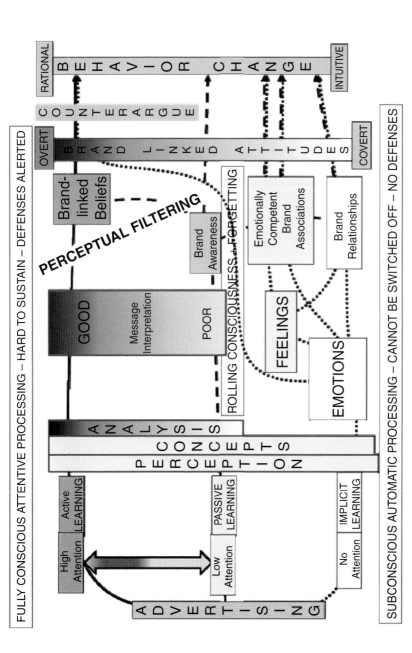

Figure 13.1 The Subconscious Seduction Model

family-oriented; and the Marlboro Cowboy, as we will see in Chapter 16, conditions us to feel that if we smoke the Marlboro brand then people will see us as being tough and independent. In this way they change our attitudes towards the brand in a covert way, without us realizing they have done so.

At the bottom of the model is the Brand Relationship box. The creativity in advertising is able to influence both our emotions and often our feelings, and these in turn can influence our brand relationships via metacommunication. This again mostly happens covertly: most of us are not really aware that we have feelings for brands, let alone that a piece of music played in an ad, for example, will be influencing them. It just isn't the sort of thing we tend to think about or talk about.

Well, a model is one thing. How much this really has an effect on us is a much more important question. And that is answered in the final part of the book.

5

Taking a Fresh Look
at Advertising

14

Under the Radar

"You've got to say it in such a way that people will feel it in their gut. Because if they don't feel it, nothing will happen"

William Bernbach
Bill Bernbach Said (1989: 01)

Some of you might feel that I've exaggerated the problem, and that advertising, although capable of influencing us subconsciously, has little real effect when processed this way. I suppose you might think it comes down to whether we are the "apathetic and rather stupid consumers vulnerable to psychological techniques that destroy our defences" that John Philip Jones (1990: 237) described us as; or the housewife "more experienced in buying her normal products than the industrial purchaser buying an atomic power station" that Ehrenberg (1974: 31) thought we are.

Doubtless the answer is a bit of both. We are certainly well informed, but we are also quite apathetic when it comes to buying many products. And occasionally, as illustrated by the experiment I'm going to describe next, we can find ourselves influenced by psychological techniques that make us seem very stupid.

How Easily We Are Influenced

This experiment was conducted by Gary Wells and Richard Petty (1980). They gathered a group of students together ostensibly to ask them to test

Seducing the Subconscious: The Psychology of Emotional Influence in Advertising, First Edition. Robert Heath.
© 2012 Robert Heath. Published 2012 by John Wiley & Sons, Ltd.

a new type of headset for use when riding a bicycle. The students were put through various tests, one of which was to sit down and listen to what sounded like a radio broadcast. One group of students was asked to vigorously move their heads up and down while they were listening, as if they were riding a bike along a bumpy track. Another group was also asked to vigorously move their heads as if they were riding a bike, this time from side to side. A third control group was asked to keep their heads still.

The broadcast the students were listening to contained some music tracks and also a debate about tuition fees. Half of each group listened to a discussion about a proposed increase to $750 and the other half to a discussion about decreasing them to $400. At the end of the test the students were asked various questions about how much they liked the music and how much they felt tuition fees should be changed by.

The results I find astonishing. Amongst the sample listening to the discussion about an increase, those who were moving their heads from side to side suggested an average fee increase of 20% *less* than the control group, and those moving their heads up and down suggested an increase of 10% *more* than the control group. Amongst those listening to the discussion about a decrease, those who were moving their heads from side to side suggested a fee decrease of 3% *more* than the control group, and those moving their heads up and down suggested a fee decrease of 18% *less* than the control group. So those who were nodding their heads consistently agreed more with the discussion, and those shaking their heads consistently agreed less with the discussion.

What this tells us is that the simple act of nodding or shaking our heads, even though for wholly unrelated reasons, can actually change our attitudes about a subject. So ask yourself this question: if moving our heads can influence our feelings this much, how much more can the calculated subconscious emotional influence of advertising affect us?

The Wells and Petty study was conducted over 30 years ago, so you might think we are all a lot smarter now. So is there any more recent evidence that these sorts of environmental cues can influence our actual purchase behavior? Well, here's another set of experiments, this time from 2007. Jonah Berger and Gráinne Fitzsimons (2008) carried out six studies into the effects that perceptually related or conceptually related environmental cues had on brand choice.

In their first experiment they tested consumers outside a local supermarket during and after Halloween. The reason for choosing this time period was that during Halloween there were a significant number of orange colored pumpkins on display, and afterwards there were none. What they found was that orange colored chocolate bars and soft drinks were mentioned by the shoppers over 50% more often *before* Halloween, when the orange pumpkin cues were all over the place, than after.

Of course, all this showed was that our attitudes can be influenced by the environment. So in a second experiment they gave people different colored pens (orange and green) to complete a survey with. Afterwards they then asked them to choose between 20 pairs of commonplace purchase items (food, drink, detergent, etc.), some of which were orange, some green, and some other colors. You've guessed it: they found that those who used the orange pens to complete the survey were more likely to choose orange products, and those who used green pens were more likely to choose green products.

OK, so maybe when it comes to trivial purchases like these we can be influenced more easily. What about more important products? In the next two experiments they studied the purchase of a digital music player. In the first study they chose two groups of students: one group that had recently traveled, and another group that had not. They showed the two groups a slogan linking the new music player to luggage. Lo and behold, they found those who had been traveling (and had therefore been in close contact with luggage) were 40% more likely to choose the new music player, and were prepared to pay 50% more for it. In the second study they displayed the slogans on trays, and found that those who ate in canteens that used trays were similarly influenced, compared with those whose canteens did not use trays.

Seems like magic, doesn't it. But all these experiments are really doing is confirming how easy it is for advertisers to influence us by targeting our subconscious.

A fifth experiment was about eating fruit and vegetables, and again used slogans either linked to trays or not linked to trays. The slogans on their own had the same effect on consumption of fruit and vegetables, but the *amount* of fruit and veg eaten in the canteen that used trays was significantly higher amongst those who saw a slogan linked to a tray, compared with those whose slogans were not linked to a tray.

Finally, in their *pièce de résistance* sixth experiment, they ran two apparently unrelated studies. In one study people were shown pictures of dogs; in the other, the same people were asked to evaluate brands of trainers. The research subjects were checked to make sure that they didn't see any connection between the two studies. Despite this, it was found that the more dogs they were exposed to in one study, the more favorably they evaluated Puma sneakers in the other study. The inference was that dogs are associated with cats, and cats are associated with pumas, so if you are exposed to dogs you are much more likely to choose Puma Trainers.

Berger and Fitzsimons are not the first to have identified how our surroundings influence our behavior. Ap Dijksterhuis has also found that "consumer behavior is strongly influenced by subtle environmental cues" (Dijksterhuis *et al.* 2005: 193). But the Berger and Fitzsimons study is perhaps the first to show hard evidence of how vulnerable our subconscious is to these external influences. In their own words: "These results support the hypothesis that conceptual priming effects can have a strong impact on real-world consumer judgments" (Berger & Fitzsimons 2008: 1).

An even more recent personal example of how easily we can be led astray arose from my fascination with the tinned tuna fixture which I touched on in Chapter 13. My strategy, being a fairly regular tinned tuna purchaser, was to go for the packs where four standard tins of tuna are banded together. These packs invariably carry an outer label announcing they are extra value in some way. That means they solve the problem of hunting through the tins deciding which to buy, because they at least save you money.

I'd noticed that these banded packs have started to take over more and more of the shelf space. One day, prompted by a friend of mine, I decided to check the price of one of these banded packs, conspicuously labeled in yellow as "special price." In the UK nothing in a supermarket actually carries a price ticket any more, so in order to check the price you have to find the label on the front edge of the shelf itself. Eventually I found it, and the price was £3.26, a little over 81 pence per tin. Then I noticed that the price of the identical individual tins was only 75 pence per tin!

Sad to say, I was not really very surprised. I've had years of first-hand experience observing how supermarkets exploit their consumers: for example, how they move frequently purchased goods like eggs and tinned tomatoes around the store in order to make experienced shoppers walk into different areas and see different things. But I must say I have never thought that they would stoop to this sort of practice. I've subsequently been told it is commonplace, and of course the reason why they can get away with it is that we consumers are quite lazy. None of us wants to spend more time shopping for groceries than we need to, and so if we can take short-cuts, then we do. And a common short-cut is to buy whatever brand is in a multipack, assuming that this means we will make a few pence saving.

So, having established how open to influence we are, let's return to the subject of advertising. Bill Bernbach, who is quoted at the start of this chapter, knew very well how advertising needs to work if it is to be successful. He, like many other highly successful creative directors, knew that unless advertising influences the target audience's emotions, it achieves nothing. However, he also said, "If an advertisement goes unnoticed, it achieves nothing" (Bernbach 1989: 01). He probably didn't know that emotional influence occurs instantaneously and automatically, and when it happens like this we have no effective defense against it.

An excellent example of how emotional content can lurk in our subconscious and influence us without our knowing is the advertising campaign that was run in the UK in the 1980s for a brand of beer called Hofmeister.

The Hofmeister Bear Case Study

Hofmeister was what we in the UK call a draught (or draft) lager. Lager is a pretty bland-tasting drink at the best of times, and because this was designed like all UK beer at the time to be served in pints and half-pints, it was very weak, around 3.2% ABV (alcohol by volume). And being served ice-cold, it was virtually impossible for anyone to tell one brand of lager from another by taste.

In order to overcome this lack of product distinction the brewers turned to advertising, and a veritable tidal wave of now famous campaigns was the result. Perhaps the most notable of these was for Heineken, which in 1974 used unashamedly Monty Python-style humor alongside a narrative in which it reinvigorated tired policemen's feet to make the claim that "Only Heineken can do this, because it refreshes the parts that other beers cannot reach." Elsewhere Carlsberg used Orson Wells to assert laconically that it was "Probably the best lager in the world," and people pronounced "I bet he drinks Carling Black Label" about a variety of characters performing unlikely humorous stunts. This led to the coining of the phrase "drinking the advertising" to denote how young people could not care less what the product tasted like, but chose their beer brand purely on how good the advertising was.

In the early 1980s, the UK brewer Courage introduced Hofmeister. Originally from Bavaria in Germany, their version of Hofmeister was brewed in the UK, and by all accounts wasn't very nice: the BBC News in 2003 described it as "weak and flavourless fizz."[1] The most distinctive part of the Hofmeister brand was the can it came in, which carried a picture of a bear, and the first advertising featured this bear along with some worthy observations about what a fine Bavarian beer it was. This had next to no effect on sales or distribution – in those days just getting onto the counter was the greatest challenge for a draught lager – so the ad agency (Boase Massimi Pollitt) came up with the idea of using a slightly more adventurous bear character in their advertising.

This was no ordinary bear. Their Hofmeister Bear was a lifesize teddy bear in a gold velour, padded-shouldered jacket that acted out the part of the ultimate "cool dude." He was unashamedly modeled on the character Fonz in the TV sitcom hit *Happy Days*, even down to copying his trademark catchphrase "aayy" (those of you old enough to remember Fonzie will know exactly what I am talking about). The Hofmeister Bear talked with a cockney accent, walked with a swagger, and (of course) was a magnet for pretty girls.

The first and most iconic of these new Hofmeister Bear advertisements ran in 1983. The Bear is bemoaning his dull life in the forest with Ronnie the Rabbit, whose greatest excitement is seeing a leaf fall to the ground. Attempting to alleviate his boredom he steals a can of Hofmeister from a picnicking couple while they are wrapped up in each other arms, and discovers: "A picture of my grandpa on it." He drinks it, enjoying "a cool cut to the back of the throat that was so good, I decided to leave the forest." (It is worth noting that the "cool cut" had absolutely nothing to do with the flavor of the beer and was caused almost entirely by it being served extremely cold.) The result is that he not only finds companionship (i.e., girls) but reveals an extraordinary aptitude for playing pool and darts. The ad is accompanied throughout by a very funky disco track, and ends with the bear exhorting viewers to imitate his behavior: "If you want poetry, stand and stare, but if you want great lager, follow the Bear."

This ad transformed Hofmeister's fortunes: in a matter of a few months it went from a failing brand to a runaway success. A number of other ads were run, featuring the bear playing pub games, in a disco, on a beach holiday, and so on, but ironically the success of the campaign was also its downfall. Once the authorities spotted the effect the advertising was having they stepped in to ban it, on the grounds that the bear had become a "hero of the young" (i.e., a celebrity amongst children), and the use of heroes of the young to advertise beer was specifically outlawed by the Code

---

[1]   BBC News, Thursday, October 16, 2003.

for Advertising Practitioners (CAP). It's interesting to note in passing that they made no attempt to ban the ads from portraying sporting or sexual prowess, both of which were likewise infringements of the CAP Code, presumably because it was argued by the ad agency that the perpetrator was only a bear.

So how did the Hofmeister Bear advertising persuade young people to buy Hofmeister Lager? An explanation is furnished by a fascinating piece of research which was conducted by Roy Langmaid and Wendy Gordon (1988). I use the term fascinating because this was one of the few research studies ever carried out in which respondents were hypnotized, a practice that the UK Market Research Society banned shortly afterwards.

The research procedure Langmaid and Gordon used was to ask respondents what they could recall about various TV advertisements (including the Hofmeister Bear ads) and then hypnotize them and ask them the same question again. One respondent, Sean, claimed in his pre-hypnosis interview that all he could recall about the Hofmeister ad was that it was "the one with the bear in the disco. He's dancing around with all the people." Even on specific prompting, he stated quite categorically all he could recall was that the bear was "Just fooling around in the disco. All I remember is the disco and the bear in the disco."

What was astounding was that when hypnotized, Sean recalled every single detail of the ad: the precise way in which George danced, what he was wearing even down to the hat and the red braces, even the way he "walked with his shoulders." Sean also understood the message of the ad, that drinking Hofmeister was about having fun and feeling good, and even admitted: "I want to try some. Feel as good as the bear."

The suggestion by Langmaid and Gordon at the time was that Sean was someone who had studied the Hofmeister ads carefully at high levels of attention, but felt too embarrassed to admit he knew anything in detail about it. Given what we now know this sounds unlikely. Much more likely is the following scenario.

Sean, like most young men at the time, would have seen the ads a few times and processed them at a relatively low level of attention. What he saw was then stored in explicit and implicit memory. The bear's way of walking and talking would have triggered a subconscious memory of the Fonz and therefore stored a concept of "coolness." The majority of the detail in the ads was retained in his implicit memory but quickly erased by his explicit memory. One detail, however, would have stuck, which was the sight of the bear dancing adeptly in a disco and being admired by the girls.

Being told that you are useless at dancing is something many young people experience at some point in their lives and would almost certainly have been present as a subconscious emotional marker in Sean's mind. The result is that this detail about the dancing would have been retained in his explicit memory, and been fed back when he was asked to recall what he remembered about the ad. Subconsciously, however, Sean would have craved the notion of being like the bear, and being able to dance in a way that impressed the girls like the bear did. This would have been stored in his implicit memory, and when hypnotized, this subconscious desire was accessed and revealed, along with the consequent subconscious desire to drink Hofmeister lager.

What is most important is that the power of the ad to motivate him to want to try Hofmeister was covert: it was not accessible to his explicit memory, but would have been present and influential in his implicit memory. So when he happened to be in a pub where Hofmeister was being dispensed he might well have decided to drink a pint, without really knowing why he wanted to.

What do we make of this story? The main thing it reveals is that practically every detail of every ad you have ever seen is going to be stored somewhere in your implicit memory, and might well at some point in the future, or even right at this minute, be subconsciously influencing you, as the bear influenced Sean, to want to try the product being advertised.

On the subject of beer advertising being able to influence you without you realizing it, here's another interesting case study.

Budweiser "Whassup?" Case Study

In 1999, Charles Stone III wrote and directed a short film, *True*. The action mostly comprised Stone and several of his friends sitting around talking on the phone. Each time they greeted each other they used the phrase "Whassup?"

The film achieved popularity in a number of film festivals, and was eventually picked up by a Chicago creative team working for DDB. The film was turned into an ad using most of the original cast, and first aired on December 20, 1999. The sight of the five guys greeting each other with the elongated "Whassup?" followed swiftly by a collapse into giggles rapidly turned it into an international hit.

The ad said next to nothing about the beer, beyond the initial and final greetings when one guy asks, "So, whassup, Beep?" the other replies, "Watching the game, having a Bud," and the original guy says, "True ... true." Aside from portraying Bud drinkers as young and "streetwise," it's hard to be sure what if any idea or message the ad was trying to get over, but within a short period people all over the world were saying "Whassup?" to each other and then laughing. The ad also won a number of awards (the Cannes Grand Prix and a Grand Clio), and in 2006 was voted into the Clio Hall of Fame.[2]

Rather like the meerkats in the UK, people regard Whassup? as having been an astonishingly successful ad. Yet no one has ever claimed it increased Budweiser sales, and with a brand the size of Budweiser it would probably have been impossible to work out if it had. It certainly gave even more awareness to the brand, but since Budweiser is already the world's best-known beer, it isn't clear what if anything that would have added. So the ad looks rather like it was just an outrageously funny and rather silly indulgence aimed at making Bud seem a little bit more in touch with the world of younger drinkers. Of course, when you're as rich as Budweiser, there's no reason not indulge yourself now and then?

Except I think it may also have been something else. Deliberately or not, I suspect it may have been a brilliantly executed piece of social engineering. You see, in my description of the ad I've omitted one small detail. In Whassup?, none of the characters was white – they were a mix of Black, Hispanic, and Chinese – and the way they spoke reinforced their urban and ethnic backgrounds. And until Whassup? ran, I would say that the picture most people had of the average Budweiser drinker was probably of an ordinary white guy tending a barbecue in his yard or necking a bottle at a ball game. So I think what this ad very cleverly did, by becoming so well known, was to subtly and covertly re-engineer the perceived user profile of Budweiser. In simple terms, Bud went from a beer for white Americans to a beer for all Americans.

Now let's imagine for a moment that this message was the overt communication objective for a piece of advertising. Imagine the controversy if ethnic origin was identified as being the subject of a TV commercial. Imagine the risk to the Budweiser brand reputation. Yet this highly controversial communication objective was accomplished by Whassup? simply by

[2] http://en.wikipedia.org/wiki/Whassup%3F

cleverly cloaking it in a more prominent overt message of having fun and being "streetwise." By doing this, the ethnic message is not processed consciously and explicitly, but subconsciously and implicitly: it is then stored in the subconscious implicit memory of every person who has seen the Whassup? ad, waiting for the moment when they ask themselves what sort of person drinks Budweiser. And when they do, the answer will be "everyone." I would say as a marketing strategy, deliberate or not, it is nothing short of brilliant.

15

The Hidden Power of New Media

"Critics of advertising usually forget that if it were eliminated or abolished, other methods would necessarily be substituted for it."

Daniel Starch
Principles of Advertising (1923)

The speed with which Whassup? crossed the globe was an early indication of the power of electronic communication. The effect new media like this have on the way we are exposed to and process advertising is the next thing we need to consider.

There's a lot of fuss made about the power of the web, especially given that companies spend relatively little on paid internet display advertising. A survey for *Marketing Magazine* in 2011 found Procter & Gamble, the UK's biggest advertiser, spent just 1.3% of its total advertising budget on the internet, and Unilever just 1.9%. The most interesting statistic was that the biggest spender was our old friend O2, the highly successful company with the invisible TV ads. Perhaps they know something we don't?

Certainly there is lots of potential for internet advertising. A survey in 2010 found that on average people in the UK spent 3.7 hours per day watching TV, 2.1 hours listening to the radio, and 1.8 hours using the internet.[1] And internet usage has increased 38% in the last 2 years, so by the time you read this it might have overtaken radio.

---

[1] Institute of Practitioners in Advertising (IPA) 2010 Touchpoints survey.

Seducing the Subconscious: The Psychology of Emotional Influence in Advertising, First Edition. Robert Heath.
© 2012 Robert Heath. Published 2012 by John Wiley & Sons, Ltd.

Viral advertising is still relatively rare. When it is a success it can be an extremely inexpensive way of communicating; after all, the cost of seeding an ad on the internet is minimal compared with the cost of traditional media. In effect all you are paying for is the production of the film. And the returns can be spectacular. John West's Tinned Salmon, for example, has become one the UK's best known brands, simply by releasing a humorous viral film.

John West Salmon Case Study

Tinned salmon, for those of you who have not tasted it, is not exactly a gourmet dish. It is rumored that the John West Tinned Salmon ad was made as a bit of a joke, and released accidentally. The company were going to withdraw it, but it was such a huge viral success that they gave up and didn't bother.

The ad opens with a group of very large bears catching salmon from a river, presumably somewhere in Canada. A voice-over tells us "At the river mouth, the bears catch only the tastiest, most tender salmon, which is exactly what we in John West want." As the voice says this, a man in orange waders runs into the scene yelling, and starts to attack a bear who has caught a huge salmon, with his fists. The bear fights back with a mixture of boxing and kicking, easily repelling the man's attack. The man, unlikely to beat the bear by fair means, then points to the sky and says "Look, an eagle." As the bear looks up, the man kicks him between his legs, and the poor bear falls to the ground groaning. The man picks up the huge salmon and marches off, as voice over says "John West endure the worst, to bring you the best."

I use this ad in my classes, to try to get my students to understand how complicated modern advertising is. The students easily identify the intended message as being that John West Tinned Salmon is made with the tastiest, most tender salmon. The problem is that none of them believe this for a moment (i.e., it is swiftly counter-argued), any more than they believe John West's employees really go around beating up bears to get their fish.

Does that mean the ad isn't effective? Not at all. I imagine the John West name lodges in the explicit memory of many people who see this ad, along with a perception of the general scene (river, bears fishing, natural unspoilt landscape, etc.) I also imagine that for most of us the perception of all this natural scenery generates a concept of natural goodness, and perhaps sustainability, which will lodge subconsciously in our implicit memory attached to the John West brand name. So this ad, if watched often enough, might well be able to condition people by association to feel that John West is a company that respects nature and supplies fresh natural produce – not to mention having a good sense of humor. Not bad for a few thousand pounds spent on making a film.

Of course, things don't often go so smoothly. Occasionally, if the public don't like a viral ad, or don't like the company being advertised, it can be hijacked and modified to make the brand owners look like idiots. This practice is also known as "subvertising," the emphasis being on the word "subvert." There are quite a few examples of ads that have been the subject of cyber attacks like this. And of course if this does happen, then *everyone* gets to see the recut version, and no one ever sees the original. An example is a famous ad for Evian Mineral Water featuring babies roller skating, of which there are a multitude of different versions now.

For this reason, and because seeding ads onto the internet can be a tricky business, viral ads are still relatively rare. The more common form of display advertising on the internet is banner ads.

Banner Advertising

We are all familiar with the small banner ads brands place around the edges of internet pages. Few of us look directly at these ads, and so they tend only to be visible in our peripheral vision as we go about searching for more important information. For this reason they generally don't bother us much. And, just as we think we are not influenced by TV or print advertising if we don't look at it, we all assume that we are not influenced by these internet ads if we don't look at them or read them.

Much the same is true of newspapers. These also comprise pages of mixed text and pictures, like the ones we find on the internet. In my experiments back in 2006 we found people tended to try to avoid the ads by just reading around them. Sometimes they would give the ad a fleeting look of between one-tenth and half a second (especially if there was an offer of some sort); occasionally they would give it a longer one or two second scan; and *one* elderly person actually looked carefully at one of the ads and even read the copy at the bottom. If my experiment is representative, that means the odds of a newspaper ad actually being read are about 1 in 4000.

The question this invites is how much information we are able to extract from an ad with this sort of reading behavior. If we study or glance directly at the ad, possibly quite a lot, but even if we read around an ad, our gaze will pass quite close to it, and it is going to be clearly visible in our periphery. And let me remind you of Shapiro *et al.*'s (1997) research study which we covered in Chapter 7. Their research found that ads placed in the outer columns of a three-column newspaper had an effect on choice of the items being advertised, even when the subjects never looked at them and didn't recollect having seen them. So this suggests that advertising exposed in our peripheral vision *might* be able to influence us, even when we don't look directly at it.

What about reading? Most of us believe we are unable to read anything placed in our periphery. However, let me again remind you of the case of the woman we also discussed in Chapter 7, who had macular degeneration. This woman was able to teach herself to read by looking about 6 inches to the left of the letters. So the capacity to read in the periphery is there, even if our conscious mind doesn't accept it. Armed as we are with more knowledge of how our brains work, we can make a little more sense of all this.

How We Read

When we read the news in a newspaper we tend to scan the headlines and read fragments of the body copy with our foveal and parafoveal regions (the high definition areas of the retina). We do this very fast, as we search for things we might want to spend more time on. We don't read by looking at the letters as a child does; we read by recognizing words and sometimes groups of several words in one go. But you might be surprised to learn that we don't always read the words in a sentence in the order they are printed: often we read a headline backwards, and quite often we read the article text like an 'S', reading one line the right way and the next backwards. We might even read one paragraph and then skip up to read an earlier one. It sounds totally random and daft.

But if you think about the way our minds work, it actually makes sense. Most of our reading is done without our remembering any of the actual words we just read: what we do is read and continuously form images and interpretations. It's a bit like Dennett's example of rolling consciousness during driving; the words enter our conscious mind and roll straight out again leaving their meaning behind.

When we are reading really fast (as is often the case with scanning newspapers) it is likely that the words themselves don't enter our conscious minds at all, but are processed and interpreted by our subconscious, and just the meaning of the sentence is passed on to our attentive consciousness "monitor." Consider, for example, that it has been shown that we can actually read a sentence of words with the letters all jumbled up, as long as the first and last letter of each word are correct. (Try it on this sentence: Ask ysoreluf waht aiserdmetnvsts you wree wtincahg on tvesoilen lsat nghit.)

So, often all we need in order to recognize a word is to be able to recognize a few of the letters. What this means is that when we scan pages on the internet, we may not only see and process pictures in our periphery, but it is quite possible we may scan and extract meaning from words in our periphery as well.

Now the full significances of Sean's subconscious recollection of the Hofmeister ad in the last chapter becomes clear. Just as with TV advertising, everything we see and hear on the internet goes into our inexhaustible implicit memory and stays there. Everything we recognize triggers concepts which we also store. Now add into that all the things we see as we go about our lives: the signs outside shops and the myriad images we process as we pass the shop window; the billboards, posters, and car cards we pass on our way to and from work; the back page ads in magazines being read by other people; even the tiny ads on the handles of gas (petrol) pumps and on the undersides of taxicab seats. All this phenomenal quantity of material is being collected and stored by us all the time. And all of it is sitting there, waiting for the moment when it can subconsciously help us by "directing" our behavior.

And this almost endless list of exposures is being added to all the time. As I write this, perhaps the most insidious form of advertising of all has just been allowed here in the UK. I refer of course to product placement in TV programs.

Product Placement

Product placement has been happening for years in films. A company would approach the film-makers and offer their products for free, provided they were shown in the film. One of the best known of these deals was the exotic Aston Martin shown in James Bond films. But the idea that no money changed hands was rather called into question when BMW apparently outbid Aston Martin, and took over the Bond movies.

Product placement also happened in TV. You can't really portray a realistic scene in a pub or coffee bar without a can of Coke being visible. Again, this was for years done without any regulation. Now it is above board and open, which means that the number of brands we see on TV is probably going to explode.

Why do I call this insidious? Well, we saw earlier that, in Kahneman and Twersky's Behavioural Economics theory, one of the most potent influences on our behavior is if we see other people we know using something. If one of our friends uses a particular brand, that apparently is one of the best reasons we can find for considering using it ourselves.

So now consider the relationship we have with the characters in the TV series we faithfully watch every week, never missing an episode. Are they not akin to friends? Certainly I would say they are. And so if in the show they use (and therefore appear to endorse) a particular brand of shampoo, coffee, or pizza, will we not feel that these brands are good and reliable and worthy of consideration? Of course we will.

Not immediately, of course. For a while the novelty of product placement will mean we will be alert to it, spotting and commenting on the brands we see scattered around every program. The danger will come after a few weeks or months or years, when we *stop* noticing these products, because when we stop noticing them, we also stop being able to think about and consider and counter-argue their presence. That's when they will start to communicate direct and unchallenged with our subconscious.

To illustrate how effective this kind of marketing is, let's consider the marketing strategy of the world's most successful brand – Coca Cola.

Coca Cola Case Study

Have you ever asked yourself why Coca Cola is the biggest and most successful soft drink in the world? Probably not, unless you are unlucky enough to work on the business of one of its competitors. Well, ask yourself now.

I expect you'll be able to come up with several explanations for its extraordinary success, but the first one will undoubtedly be its unique formula and great taste. Coke tastes great! Everyone knows that, just as everyone knows the secret formula is supposedly locked up somewhere no one can get at it. The unique taste of Coke is one of the greatest pleasures we recall from our childhood, and often one of the nicest rewards we can give ourselves even today.

But here's a thing. If you put the two leading brands of cola – Coke and Pepsi – side by side in identical glasses, and ask people to taste them, which do you think they choose? The answer, as anyone who has seen the Pepsi challenge ads of the 1980s will know, is Pepsi. Pepsi Cola's flavor is preferred by most people in blind taste testing, and that's a fact.

This was what sparked one of the greatest marketing catastrophes of all time: New Coke. Coke's marketing manager in the 1980s, Serge Zyman, decided that since Pepsi's flavor was preferred by most people he would relaunch Coke with a flavor that was similar to Pepsi, and call it New Coke.

Except Coke drinkers didn't like that one bit. They clamored for Coke to bring back the original, and eventually that's what happened. Yes, folks, people actually wanted to have back the product they liked less!

Now to anyone like me who has studied marketing for 40 years this behavior isn't actually that much of a surprise. By way of a brief diversion let me tell you about a research study conducted by Katherine Braun in 1999. Braun created samples of orange juice of varying quality by taking good quality juice and adding contaminants. She then gave the range of juices to people to taste, claiming it was a trial for a new brand. Following a distraction task, half the subjects were then exposed to advertising for the brand. It was found that the advertising confounded the subject's ability to accurately judge the quality of the juice, leading to substandard product being highly rated. She concluded that "advertising received after a direct product experience altered consumers' recollection of both objective sensory and affective components of that experience" (Braun 1999: 332).

If you think that's a one-off, consider the story of Stella Artois, the UK's most successful beer brand. In 1990 the brand owners, Interbrew, planned to introduce a major TV campaign to replace the highly successful print ads that had been running. Before they did this they had to overcome a serious problem pretty similar to the one that Coke thought it had: Stella Artois was very bitter, and when tasted blind (that is, without any packaging) many people didn't like its taste compared with other beers. So a number of preferred recipes were developed and tested. But what they found was that although the new recipes were preferred by four out of five people, once they were put into the Stella Bottle the *old* recipe was preferred by four out of five people. In other word, Stella drinkers preferred to drink a product they actually didn't like much (Heath 1993).

So let's get back to Coke and ask ourselves the question that all this invites: if Coke's taste isn't actually the best there is, how come it sells more than

Pepsi and all the other brands of Cola put together. What is it that makes it so successful?

Many people will answer that it is the advertising that is the key to Coke's success. But aside from the ad that apparently gave us our modern interpretation of Santa Claus, and the famous "I'd like to teach the world to sing in perfect harmony" campaign of 1971, how many famous Coke ads can you remember? I'll bet the answer is not many, because aside from the famous Diet Coke campaign, I'd say there haven't really been any.

The thing about Coke is that they don't care that much about media advertising. Oh, they spend loads of money on it, because they have loads of money to spend, but deep inside the marketing department in Coca Cola Headquarters in Atlanta they know perfectly well that advertising isn't what makes them the success they are. They are much more concerned with another very different idea: ubiquity.

Ubiquity is about being everywhere. It is said that the Coca Cola marketing objective is that you shouldn't be able to walk more than 100 yards in any city in the world without seeing either a Coke can or a Coke bottle or the Coke name or the Coke logo. And why is ubiquity so important? Because the more you see something, the more you assume people must be buying it, the more popular you assume it must be, and the more you feel you can rely on it being good.

But the insidious thing about this "ubiquity" strategy is that after a time none of us really *notices* Coke any more. It's just there. It's part of the wallpaper of our modern world. We take it for granted. All of which means that practically every exposure we have to Coke as we go about our busy lives is an exposure to our subconscious. And our subconscious has no moral judgment capability, because that function is taken care of by our conscious mind. So our subconscious, if it could talk, isn't going to say to the conscious mind "Hey, you, listen up, do you realize that all these exposures to Coke are conditioning you to believe that it has to be the best Cola in the world?" Much more likely it would say something like "Let's face it, if Coke wasn't the best then someone out of the millions of people all over the world that drink it would have done something about it before now." Of course, it won't say that either, because your subconscious can't reason. So it won't understand that New Coke tried exactly that and failed.

And, as I said earlier, the same will quickly become true of products placed on TV in our favorite shows. After a time we just won't notice them. But our subconscious will carry on registering them, sitting alongside our favorite characters, and sometimes even being drunk, eaten, or used by our favorite characters. And, to our subconscious, that will be the equivalent of these products being *endorsed* by our favorite characters, who we feel are our friends. So product placement will effectively be the same as personal endorsement, making it the most potent advertising media of all time.

Is this right? Should brands be allowed to influence us like this? Shouldn't there be a law against it? These are the questions we are going to address in the next chapter.

16

Legal, Decent, Honest, and Truthful

"Advertising is only evil when it advertises evil things."

David Ogilvy
Ogilvy on Advertising (1985: 207)

What we've found so far is that the way we process advertising is far from simple. It is fair to say that most advertising has a message which most of us choose either to ignore, or to process and swiftly forget. This is fine and acceptable and isn't the point in contention. The big issue is that most of these messages are delivered along with a whole raft of emotive baggage, generally called creativity.

Often this creativity is in the form of emotionally competent associations: we instinctively link these associations to the brand being advertised, not realizing that they subconsciously condition the brand with their emotive values. But I've already established in Chapter 10 that creativity doesn't necessarily increase attention, and therefore much of the rest of this creativity is processed subconsciously (or at best fleetingly, using Dennett's rolling consciousness). But being subconscious doesn't mean it ceases to influence us; it means that it influences us even better, acting as a marker that covertly directs our intuitive decision-making.

And in some respects this media advertising is only the tip of the iceberg. The commercial creative material we are exposed to on TV ads sits alongside everything we are exposed to on the internet, in newspapers and magazines, on the radio, in the cinema, not to mention all the other material we identified in the previous chapter.

Seducing the Subconscious: The Psychology of Emotional Influence in Advertising, First Edition. Robert Heath.
© 2012 Robert Heath. Published 2012 by John Wiley & Sons, Ltd.

Why does this happen? Why do we collect all this stuff in our minds? From the anthropological viewpoint, it is pretty easy to explain. Consider this situation.

Imagine that you're a mammal creeping through the jungle 20 million years ago. You don't have much of a reasoning brain, but you have some pretty smart senses. You have exceptionally good perceptive powers such as hearing and smell, possibly even quite good eyesight. But these faculties are useless unless you can attach some meaning to the various things you are hearing, smelling, and seeing. For example, you need to be able to distinguish between the quiet step of a small creature that you might be able to have for lunch, and the quiet step of a large creature that might be eyeing you up so they can have you for their lunch. It also helps if you can tell if the large creature is aggressive, or just fat and lazy.

This all requires quite a bit of conceptualization to take place. You need the ability to instantly sense the difference between anger and nervousness and fear, because this will tell you whether to run, hide, or attack. Those mammals who have refined these basic instinctive emotions and who have them linked intimately to their decision systems are going to be the ones who survive and thrive. The rest will die out.

After some millions of years you've evolved into a proto-human and you start to develop more reasoning capacity. But the instinctive emotions are all still there in your mammalian brain, linked intimately to your decision systems. Our vulnerability to emotive communication is part of how we evolved and we can't do anything about it.

Suppose we managed to mutate our genes so that we didn't have these irritating emotions. We would be like Mr Spock from *Star Trek*. Every decision would be logical, and we wouldn't be vulnerable to the subconscious influence of all the emotive baggage in advertising. OK, we wouldn't be able to cry when we see a sad movie either, but no real problem there. But we also wouldn't be able to fall in love, which means we would be less likely to have babies, and even if we did have babies we wouldn't feel the intense attachment that makes us want to nurture and protect them, and which enables them to grow up to have babies of their own. So eventually our gene mutation would die out.

So from an anthropological point of view we have to have emotions in order to be human. And that means we can't stop ourselves being influenced by creativity in advertising. All we could do is try to stop advertising having any creativity.

The obstacle to this is Watzlawick's second axiom (see Chapter 12). This states that every communication also has metacommunication. It is impossible to communicate without at the same time "qualifying" that communication with relationship-influencing elements. A plain white page with some type in the middle signifies a brand that reveres simplicity. A plain black page with some white type in the middle signifies a determined assertive brand. Even the way a sentence is constructed has metacommunication. Someone who says "Buy our brand, it's the best" has a completely different character from someone who says "We think our brand is the best." Trying to somehow expunge creativity from advertising is, frankly, a pointless exercise.

So why not ban all advertising? Aside from the commercial impact on our newspapers, TV channels, radio stations, and internet search engines, practically all of which exist because of advertising revenue, all that would happen is that something else would take its place. If you ban media advertising, do you also ban messages and designs written on packages? Do you ban people handing out leaflets in the street to anyone passing? Do you ban people going round the country, as they used to in St Elmo Lewis's era, knocking on doors and selling products direct to people on their doorsteps? And even if you ban it in your country, how do you ban it in other countries? No, much as people love to say things like "I hate advertising, they ought to ban it all," it simply isn't a practical option.

Of course we can and we do control advertising, especially for products that are damaging. The heading of this chapter – Legal, Decent, Honest, and Truthful – is the mantra that is used by the Advertising Standards Authority (ASA), the government body that oversees standards in advertising throughout the UK. But the ASA only acts when there are overwhelming breaches of decency and honesty. And when it does act, its regulatory system can be exceptionally slow in having any effect. For example, because no one complained it allowed Gallaher to advertise Hamlet Cigars on TV for 25 years. And, as we shall see in the next example, it also allowed Marlboro to become the most popular cigarette in the UK – even though cigarette advertising was completely banned.

The Marlboro Cowboy Case Study

Each year I teach two courses at the University of Bath on Advanced Advertising Theory. One of the classes is taught to final year undergraduate students, all of whom are aged between 20 and 22. This means they were born around 1989–1991, predominantly in the UK.

In one of my lectures I show them a picture of a man in a cowboy hat saddling up a horse. The man has a cigarette in his mouth. When I ask them who he is the vast majority of the class immediately recognize him as the Marlboro Cowboy.

They are surprised when I tell them that the Marlboro Cowboy only ever appeared in the UK on billboard advertising, and the ads featured a distant shot of a herd of cattle being driven by some cowboys. And they are astonished when I tell them that these ads ran in the UK for only 3 months in 1974 – roughly 15 years before they were born.

Well, that's not quite true. What actually happened was that the ASA banned any shots of cowboys, but they allowed them to continue to show open countryside and grazing herds of cows and horses, and to use the line "Welcome to Marlboro Country." They also continued to allow them to use the famous Marlboro "red rooftop" packaging symbol. They even allowed them to show fences with saddles and other cowboy accoutrements, suggesting the cowboy was there but just out of shot. This went on for at least 3 years after the ban, with tens of millions of pounds being spent. At one stage it was reckoned that Philip Morris were actually paying more in revenue to the London Underground subway system than the government of the day.

But how is it that so many young people in the UK recognize the Marlboro Cowboy, an advertising icon that has never actually run here during their lifetime? Partly because it continued to run in the USA for many years after it was banned here. Partly because it continued to run on media such as airline magazines that were unregulated and freely available to anyone flying to and from the UK. But mostly because there was so much publicity about the banning of the cowboy that it virtually *guaranteed* that everyone knew that Marlboro used a cowboy in their advertising.

Why is this a problem? Let's go back to the beginning, and the stream of perceptions and concepts that occur when you see an advertisement. Remember, these perceptions and concepts occur throughout the time you watch the advertising, because we can't switch them off. So imagine that alongside a fleeting conscious registration of the Marlboro red-rooftop pack you perceive a cowboy. You will instantly and subconsciously trigger concepts that you have in the past linked to this sort of image: the open range, herds of cattle, big country, riding horses, and a rugged outdoor life. The reverse is also to some extent true: if you perceive open ranges of countryside, herds of cattle, horses and saddles, you will very likely subconsciously conceptualize the Wild West and cowboys.

I imagine these concepts are especially influential if you are American, because the cowboy is a symbol of how the west was won and the country was founded. In the same way that the humor in the Hamlet ads legitimatized smoking cigars in the UK, I'd guess the presence of a cowboy subconsciously legitimizes the habit of smoking cigarettes in the USA: the sort of feeling he might generate is: "If the pioneers of our country smoke Marlboro, why shouldn't we?"

More importantly, when you see the cowboy or anything linked to the cowboy's lifestyle you will subconsciously conceptualize the sort of personal characteristics you link to this lifestyle (i.e. toughness, freedom, and independence). After you've been exposed to these images a few times in conjunction with the Marlboro brand then the characteristics that you associate with the cowboy will be transferred to those people who smoke Marlboro. In other words, without realizing it you will start to be conditioned to feel that Marlboro smokers are likely to exhibit the same characteristics of toughness, freedom, and independence as the cowboy. And this works whatever country you live in, because all of us are exposed in our childhood to films showing tough cowboys.

Now it is well known that the one thing young people crave more than anything else is freedom, independence, and (in the case of men) the opportunity to be seen as being tough. No surprise, therefore, that more young people smoke Marlboro than any other cigarette. It's no coincidence that they do this, it's a direct consequence of the conditioned attitudes subconsciously embedded in their minds by the Marlboro Cowboy.

This conditioning has to be subconscious in order to be effective. If everyone were aware that the advertising was trying to associate Marlboro smokers with characteristics such as toughness, freedom, and independence, this would be discussed by young people and turned into a joke: "Ha ha ha, I see you're smoking Marlboro to try to make yourself look macho, what a wimp you must be!" This mirth would nullify the effect of the conditioning by effectively counter-arguing the notion that Marlboro smokers are "real men," and replacing it with the notion that they are just ordinary people trying to make out they are tough and independent. But because the perception and conceptualization of toughness is subconscious, it is never openly discussed, and never counter-argued.

Eventually, in the early 1980s, the ASA finally banned outdoor advertising for cigarettes. By that time the clever people at Philip Morris had introduced a heavily subsidized range of macho clothing. This featured items such as denim jeans, cowboy-style shirts, belts with pictures of Marlboro Country, and many other items. These were not cigarettes, so Marlboro were able for years to continue to use the red rooftop and the line "Come up to Marlboro Country" to advertise their clothing.

And they had another, even more devious scheme going on alongside this: sponsoring motor racing.

Marlboro Grand Prix Sponsorship Case Study

In 1974, around the time the cowboy was being banned from Marlboro billboard advertising, McLaren Racing Limited struck a deal with Philip Morris to have them sponsor their Formula One Racing Team. The deal was that the cars would be painted in the red and white Marlboro Red Rooftop design, and the drivers – Emerson Fittipaldi and James Hunt – would wear Marlboro red-rooftop style racing overalls. When James Hunt was celebrating his 1976 World Championship victory, he was probably puffing away at a Marlboro cigarette.

Being a world champion racing driver is the stuff of most young boys' dreams. Almost all young men aspire to the millionaire lifestyles of racing drivers, and thirst for the sort of excitement and danger that is the lifeblood of motor racing, not to mention the evident attractions of fighting off the sort of gorgeous supermodels that hang around the necks of racing drivers. Yet if anyone were to suggest 20 years ago that Marlboro's sponsorship of Formula One racing meant that young people were being conditioned to associated smoking Marlboro with wealth, excitement, danger, and sexual success, they would have been laughed at. Why? Because the conditioning was entirely subconscious: no one could have proved it is taking place, so no one could have banned Marlboro from doing it.[1]

And no one tried, because no one in government had an interest in doing so. Formula One was one of the few sports that the British still excelled at, and cigarettes were in effect paying for it (and paying a fortune in taxes). Banning cigarette sponsorship of motor racing would have been very bad for votes and revenue.

---

[1]   They could have, of course, by hypnotizing people, but that had been banned as a form of market research.

As Formula One became more and more popular, as the coverage of races on television received greater audiences, Marlboro exposure became greater and greater. This was because although Marlboro trackside hoardings were banned in the UK, they weren't banned in other countries, so every overseas Grand Prix had a track emblazoned with red rooftop advertising. In effect, Marlboro was still on TV.

And Phillip Morris was even smarter. In 1980 they struck a deal as subsidiary sponsor of another Grand Prix team, Ferrari, and in 1993 they became Ferrari's main sponsor. Ferrari racing cars were already red, so it took little ingenuity to pop a white "house" shape with the word Marlboro in it on the red cars, and there you had the Red Rooftop. This logo and the Marlboro name remained on Ferrari Formula One cars until 2008. Thirty-four years of conditioning young people to associate Marlboro with wealth, excitement, danger, and sexual success, and no one did a thing to stop it.

The story doesn't end there, incidentally. Although they were forced to take off the Marlboro name, Ferrari came up with a new "barcode" type logo that still to this day appears on their drivers' overalls, plain to see when they are being interviewed in the paddock or when they win any race. A barcode that is "considered by a specialised F1 website as subliminal advertising for Marlboro, evocating the top-left corner design of a Marlboro cigarette pack."[2]

Now, the evidence linking cigarette smoking with health problems is so strong that most countries are happy to ban it. But where do you draw the line? Here is another rather less black-and-white case study.

McDonald's Case Study

The Golden Arches of McDonald's welcome millions of people every day. Since 1963 a jolly character called Ronald McDonald has also inhabited them, bringing fun and laughter to kids of all ages. McDonald's can see nothing wrong with this. After all, hamburgers don't kill you like cigarettes are supposed to; and they don't cause addiction, like alcohol is supposed to. If kids are allowed to eat them then why should one of their favorite icons be banned from advertising them?

2   http://en.wikipedia.org/wiki/Marlboro_(cigarette)#cite_note-6

For good reasons, according retired physician Alfred David Klinger of the Boston-based non-profit making advocacy group Corporate Accountability International. Klinger is quoted as saying:

> Ronald McDonald is a pied piper drawing youngsters all over the world to food that is high in fat, sodium and calories. On the surface, Ronald is there to give children enjoyment in all sorts of way with toys, games and food. But Ronald McDonald is dangerous, sending insidious messages to young people.[3]

Is Klinger right to insist that Ronald McDonald be "retired?" Hamburgers are consumed in such quantity now that it is said they not only contribute to heart disease and obesity, but, through the increase in cattle grazing, are a major contributor to greenhouse gas emission. Personally I think we should probably eat less of them, and if one way of encouraging this to happen is by making them less attractive to children, then maybe that's a good thing. There's no question that children like clowns, and so I'd probably agree that the clown shouldn't be used to sell the burger.

But many others – possibly half of the population of the USA for a start – might vehemently disagree with me. Kids, they might say, like hamburgers because hamburgers are delicious. And they like McDonald's hamburgers because they are amongst the most delicious. And it is better for kids to eat hamburgers, which have nourishing beef protein, lettuce, and tomato, than live off pizzas that are mostly carbohydrate. Plus, Ronald McDonald has now cleverly been repositioned to front up a charity providing 305 Ronald McDonald Houses which provide overnight accommodation for parents visiting children in chronic care hospitals.

Who is right? I've no idea. And to be honest it isn't as if every McDonald's ad has Ronald in it, or every McDonald's restaurant has a resident clown. And at least the debate is out in the open, and people can make up their own minds about whether they want their kids to eat at McDonald's and run the risk of being entertained by a clown. So ethically I'd say no one is trying to mislead anyone.

But there's another aspect of McDonald's, and indeed some other burger chains, that is not so much out in the open. Go to a McDonald's, or Wendy's, or indeed Burger King restaurant, and you'll find yourself confronted with

---

[3] http://finance.yahoo.com/news/McDonalds-says-no-way-Ronald-apf-1794463468 .html?x=0

a blaze of red and yellow, and occasionally blue (and the last time I went inside a McDonald's the tables and chairs were all these same colors as well). These are exactly the same shades of bold primary color that are found on Lego and Duplo and Mega Bloks and Fisher Price and the vast majority of baby toys. A baby or small child exposed to these colors would instinctively process them and feel that these restaurants are a friendly and safe environment, because they "look" exactly like the toys their parents buy for them and encourage them to play with. By the time that child grows into an adult, they may well be conditioned to feel that McDonald's and Wendy's and Burger King are associated with the colors of their childhood, and couldn't possibly be bad places.

And I do know one thing. Instinctively, and for no reason I can identify, I rather like McDonald's and Wendy's. It isn't just that I especially like their double-decker, I rather liked them as soon as I set foot inside one their restaurants. I felt much more at home than I did in Kentucky Fried Chicken, with its stark red and white color scheme. And I've a vague feeling the reason I like them is because their color schemes use the colors I was surrounded with at home, when I was growing up.

How much these colors influence the behavior of others I don't know. And we never will know, because no one in their right mind would try to force McDonald's or Wendy's or Burger King to change the color schemes on their logos and restaurant frontages, any more than they would get Coca Cola to take down all the millions of signs they have erected all over the world. They'd be laughed out of court before they sat down.

But in Chapter 14 I did present a case study in which chocolate bars and soft drinks were mentioned more by people during Halloween when orange colored pumpkins were around. And it is a fact that hamburger consumption in the USA in 2006 was the equivalent of two quarter-pounders per week for every person in the country. So if you strip out those who never eat hamburgers that's probably four hamburgers a week for the rest. I leave it to you to decide if there is a link.

17

How to Spot Subconscious Seduction

"Ads are carefully designed by the Madison Avenue frog-men-of-the-mind for semiconscious exposure."

Marshall McLuhan

Understanding Media: The Extensions of Man (1964: 203)

Spotting when advertising has seduced your subconscious is not easy. I've worked with advertising for 40 years, and even I miss many of the more subtle influences within advertising campaigns.

One way to detect when advertising is seducing your subconscious is to be vigilant. Watch out for when you unaccountably find yourself liking or favoring a brand, and then start looking for what might be influencing you. It's not an ideal solution, because the influence may well be something you don't recall, like some music in the background of an advertisement that your conscious mind didn't notice, but your subconscious did.

A great example from the past is the startlingly successful US advertising for the Volkswagen Beetle.

Volkswagen Case Study

Given that the Beetle (or Bug as it was known in the USA) was Hitler's "people's car," and World War 2 had ended less than 25 years before, one might have expected the launch of this model in the USA to be less than a

Seducing the Subconscious: The Psychology of Emotional Influence in Advertising, First Edition. Robert Heath.
© 2012 Robert Heath. Published 2012 by John Wiley & Sons, Ltd.

resounding success. Fortunately for VW they appointed DDB to handle the account.

DDB's initial print advertising campaign started in 1959, and was to do with the tiny size of the Beetle compared with the vast cars beloved of Americans at that time. One of the first ads to appear featured a tiny picture of the Beetle alone on a single page ad, with the headline "Think small" underneath. A later advertisement addressed the reliability of the revolutionary air-cooled three-cylinder car, showing a car with a huge clockwork winding key projecting from the rear. The headline read "It isn't so," suggesting that although the car ran like clockwork it wasn't actually powered by clockwork. The clever thing about these ads was that they were one of the first examples of a company poking fun at itself. This sort of self-deprecation subconsciously suggests to us that the company has terrific confidence in its product, otherwise how would they dare to be rude about it?

Later in the 1960s VW went onto television. One of their first ads was about a snowplow. Nearly half of the minute-long ad featured a man getting into his car in heavy snow, starting it (first time), and then driving through the snow. After 25 seconds a quizzical, slightly laconic voice-over then asks very slowly, "Have you ever wondered how the man who drives a snowplow drives to the snowplow?" The man gets out of the car and trudges through the deep snow, as the voice continues "This one drives a Volkswagon. So you can stop wondering." Finally, from the darkened shed the snowplow roars into life and drives slowly off, revealing as it passes the VW Beetle sitting there covered in snow.

Nothing wrong with that, you might say. Indeed, like many great ads, it doesn't at all appear to be seducing your subconscious. But consider this. Because nothing is said about the VW Beetle's reliability, there isn't anything you can counter-argue. No overt claim is made about how well it starts in the cold. Nothing is said about the fact that it is air-cooled, so doesn't have a cooling system that can freeze. No one mentions how the engine is in the back, over the driving wheels, which means it handles really well in slippery conditions. In fact nothing specific is claimed at all.

And another clever thing about the ad is that it is 1 minute long, even though what it says could easily have been squashed into 15 seconds. Can you guess what the effect of this is? Just this: the ad is boring. Nothing happens for half the ad, and then all that happens is a man gets out of a car and starts a snowplow. Recall what I said about resource-matching in Chapter 10, and you'll see that if there is nothing to analyze (and frankly there isn't anything much to analyze in this ad) we will reduce the level of cognitive resource we deploy and pay less attention. And by deploying less cognitive resource and paying less attention, we diminish our ability to counter-argue what claim the ad does actually imply about the car.

So by the end of the ad we have no factual ammunition which we can attack the Beetle with, and are in no real mood for counter-arguing anyway, so we just let the claim pass unchallenged. After a few exposures we will subconsciously feel convinced that the VW Beetle really is better in terrible weather conditions than other cars. And because this feeling is subconscious, there isn't any easy way to "un-feel" this conviction.

Snowplow is, in my opinion, a brilliant piece of subconscious seduction. And I suspect the judges at the 1964 Cannes Film Festival agreed with me, because they awarded Snowplow their gold medal. But if you're not convinced by the Snowplow ad, consider another VW ad which DDB made and ran in 1969. This time the subject was a funeral.

The Funeral ad opens with a shot of a cortège of large black traditional American cars driving towards and then past the camera. An organ strikes up with somber church music, and an elderly man's voice then starts to slowly read out what is obviously the text of his will. "I, Maxwell E. Stavely, being of sound mind and body, do hereby bequeath the following. To my wife, Rose, who spent money like there was no tomorrow, I leave one hundred dollars and a calendar." As this is said we see the grieving widow mopping her eyes as she sits alone on the enormous back seat of one of the cars. The voice continues with only the briefest pause "To my sons', Victor and Rodney, who spent every dime I gave them on fancy cars and fast women, I leave fifty dollars . . . in dimes." As we hear this we pan from one son to the other, also sitting on an enormous car seat, one wearing shades and the other horn-rimmed glasses and both looking decidedly sleazy. The voice continues, now with the pitch rising indicating some anger and loss of patience: "To my business partner Jules, whose only motto was spend, spend, spend, I leave nothing, nothing, nothing." As this is said we cut to Jules, smoking a huge cigar, sitting between and being consoled by two very blowzy women. And as we pan along the cortège of huge cars, the voice continues, calmly again: "And to all my other friends and relatives, who never knew the value of a dollar, I leave . . . a dollar." Finally, following on right at the end of the cortège, we find there is a tiny black VW Beetle, and we see through the window an honest looking young man mopping his eyes as he drives. The voice says "Finally, to my nephew Harold, who oft-times said, 'A penny earned is a penny saved,' and who also oft-times said, 'Gee, Uncle Max, it sure pays to own a Volkswagen,' I leave my entire fortune of one hundred billion dollars." And as this is said we finally see a satisfied smile cross the face of Harold.

What has this ad told us? Well, the only claim about the product is in the one line at the end, which says that "it sure pays to own a Volkswagen," in other words it apparently saves you a lot of money. But of course it also *suggests* that buying a Volkswagen signifies that you are a smart and decent person, one who might be worthy of benefiting from the generosity of others. OK, that last bit is certainly rather an ambitious claim, but it's hardly what we would call subconscious seduction.

So where is the seductive element in this? I'd say it is this. Throughout the ad what is being shown is a succession of greedy, thoughtless, spendthrift, irresponsible people, and all these people are shown being driven in enormous cars. So although nothing is claimed overtly, what the ad does is create an association between large cars and greedy venal people. The effect of this over time is going to be that the cars eventually become conditioned with their greed and venality. We end up subconsciously feeling that anyone who buys a traditional big American car is thoughtless, spendthrift, and irresponsible.

You may or may not have realized that this is going on from my description of the ad. Certainly I'd say few people realized it at the time. The brilliantly understated way in which the ad was made, with a total absence of hard sell, and indeed virtually no overt reference to the car at all, meant all of these negative feelings about big American cars were processed subconsciously. If it *had* been evident that the ad was knocking US cars, suggesting all those who drove big cars were nasty people, this claim could easily have been counter-argued by pointing out that the vast majority of fine upstanding and generous Americans in 1969 *did* drive large cars like these. But because the thought wasn't conscious it wasn't counter-argued and no one complained.

What was the result of this subtle and brilliant advertising campaign? Despite its German origins the VW Beetle was a spectacular success. By 1965 VW had a 67% share of the US imported car market. Even in 1969, when this market was being flooded with new entries and the Beetle was over 10 years old, they still had a 51% share.

DDB's advertising is an example of how profitable seducing the subconscious can be. Another one is the Tesco case study.

Tesco Supermarkets Case Study

If you ask anyone in the UK what advertising Tesco was running when it became the biggest UK supermarket chain, they'll tell you it was Dotty, the shopper from hell, played by UK comic actress Prunella Scales. Dotty was created in 1995 to launch a sensational new service that Tesco had just introduced. This service allowed you to take back anything you had bought, for absolutely any reason, and they would either give you your money back or replace it with something else.

The minute-long launch ad starts with Dotty creeping up and shocking her daughter who is quietly working at her desk, by presenting her with a large trout. Dotty says, "I don't like the look of this fish." The daughter asks what is wrong with it, observing that it looks perfectly fresh, and Dotty replies, "I know it's fresh, it just looks a bit ... sullen." In response to the daughter's astonishment she continues, "It's mouth goes down at the corners ... look." With this Dotty imitates someone pulling their mouth down, and we cut to the poor trout who mouth indeed does make it look very miserable. The daughter, attempting to patronize her evidently slightly mad mother says, "Mother, it's a trout, that's the way trout look, they were born like that," at which the mother says, "I think we should take it back." "Where to?" asks the harassed daughter sarcastically, "Lake Windermere?" "No, Tesco," replies her mother. By now getting to the end of her tether the daughter says assertively, "You can't take a fish back just because it looks miserable. What do you expect them to say? 'Have this cheerful sole instead, Madam'?" At which point we cut away to a calm and indulgent Tesco fishmonger, who parrots this exact phrase: "Have this cheerful sole instead, Madam!" whilst presenting Dotty with her replacement fish. The mother smiles happily: "Oh, yes, that's the one." A kindly male voice-over then tells us that if you're not happy with any of their products for any reason, Tesco will give you an exchange or refund instantly. Finally, to her daughter's evident fury, Dotty walks off with the fish observing, "He looks like my first husband. I'll enjoy cooking him!" The ad ends with the voice-over saying the slogan "Tesco. Every little helps."

There is no question that this was a brilliant promotion, and a brilliant ad to launch it with. The campaign continued for nearly 10 more years, advertising a succession of further Tesco initiatives in the same rather self-effacing way.

But this was not the campaign that helped Tesco achieve leadership in the UK. That was a different campaign, now lost in the mists of time. To understand how it worked we have to go back to the start of the Tesco story.

The Tesco brand apparently started in 1924 when the enterprising grocer Jack Cohen bought a shipment of tea from a Mr T.E. Stockwell and decided to combine his initials (TES) with the first two letters of his name (CO).

It developed a reputation as a "pile it high and sell it cheap" sort of shop, and by the 1980s it had grown to be the biggest supermarket chain in Europe. However, in the UK it remained stubbornly in second place to Sainsbury's, whose reputation for selling fresh foods dated back to the nineteenth century.

To try to rectify this, Tesco brought out a new campaign for their fresh meat in 1983. The ads featured TV celebrity restaurateur Robert Carrier, whose Islington restaurant Carrier's was one of the most highly rated in the world. The format was simple persuasion: Robert Carrier praised a piece of meat for its freshness and leanness, and then revealed it had been bought (of all places!) in Tesco.

The campaign was a total flop. One of the reasons that came out in research was that the ads just were not credible. Tesco stores at the time were mostly described by people as being old-fashioned and tawdry places, with boxes piled up in the aisles, unwashed floors, and sullen unhelpful staff. Not the sort of place that would be conducive to buying lovely fresh meat, no matter how persuasive Robert Carrier was.

To rectify this Tesco set about revolutionizing their outlets. Stores were rebuilt, aisles cleared of boxes, and everything was kept spotlessly clean. Staff were trained not only to answer any question you had about where something was, but to actually *take* you to the fixture and show it to you.

So how should they advertise their brand-new shops? Fresh food was still the main battleground, and having now refurbished their offering you might think Tesco would revert to the sort of smug self-satisfied creative style epitomized by Robert Carrier. Not a bit of it. Newly appointed agency Lowe Howard-Spink developed a campaign that was the categorical opposite. It featured the popular comedian Dudley Moore as a totally inept Tesco buyer sent on a quest for French, free range, corn-fed chickens. In the first ad run in 1990 the less-than-helpful French farmer has him wandering through the forest in search of them (calling "here, chicky chicky chicky"). Subsequent ads showed him hot-air ballooning and accidentally discovering 260-year-old Melton Mowbray Stilton, crashing his little van and coming across fine Italian grapes, and so on. Finally, he discovered the long sought-after chickens, but overcome with pity released them back to the woods.

Alongside Dudley Moore's antics, what this campaign did was cleverly showcase a whole range of new and different high quality products, all of which were regularly available in Tesco stores. I remember being a frequent purchaser of their excellent organic corn-fed French chickens, which were surprisingly good value and very delicious. But why adopt this strange self-deprecating advertising? Surely the message it gave to people was that their fine produce was only there by chance, and underneath their shiny new stores they were as shambolic and disorganized as their old stores made them seem?

The answer of course is that the Dudley Moore ads were a supreme example of advertising seducing our subconscious. What they did was to show that Tesco, far from being unbearably smug as they were in the Robert Carrier ads, were happy to poke fun at their own obsession with quality and originality in food. The result was that *subconsciously* everyone *felt* Tesco must be very successful and very good at what they were doing. After all, we know that only those who are extremely confident don't mind being the butt of people's jokes: people who lack confidence or have anything to hide are the ones who prefer to be told how wonderful they are.

The result was that over a period of 3 years Tesco's reputation grew in leaps and bounds. By 1992, the end of the Dudley Moore campaign, they achieved their aim of becoming the UK's biggest supermarket group. It was not for another 3 years that they launched the Dotty campaign. So it wasn't fussy Dotty who won them market leaderships, but shambolic Dudley Moore.

Stella Artois Case Study

Possibly the most famous campaign in the UK was another one by Lowe Howard-Spink, this time for Stella Artois.

I mentioned Stella Artois' bitter taste in the last chapter, but I didn't explain how the advertising was able to make the brand so successful. The Stella advertising story started back in 1979, when it launched using a campaign with the slogan "reassuringly expensive." The idea was that Stella spent so much money on its ingredients (the finest hops, barley, etc.) that the brewers had to charge an enormous premium for it. This was in part true, but not because the ingredients were really that much more expensive. It was because the beer had 5% alcohol, and so attracted more excise duty.

Either way, Lowe Howard-Spink cleverly turned the high price of Stella into an indicator of its quality. Of course it wasn't that expensive – only about 20% more than the ordinary 3.5% alcohol by volume "cooking" lagers – but it did make you drunk *much* more quickly. According to a head brewer I spoke to, the reason is that your body removes the equivalent of about 1.5% alcohol from what you drink, so a 3.5% lager is effectively 2%, and a 5% lager is effectively 3.5% – nearly twice as strong.

So the real reason Stella was successful probably had more to do with its potency than its taste. Of course, UK advertising regulations forbade anyone claiming their beer was stronger than others, but by cleverly saying the beer was more expensive the advertising implied that it had more alcohol, and so both tasted better and was more effective at getting you drunk.

By the early 1990s Stella was selling so well that the brewers wanted to run a TV advertising campaign. The problem they faced was that by then the UK beer market had switched to home consumption of bottled beers. There were countless bottled beer brands that were also 5% alcohol by volume, and in a lot of outlets Stella Artois was no more expensive than the other bottled brands. In fact, because it sold so well in supermarkets and off-licenses (liquor stores) it was often *less* expensive than others.

Lowe Howard-Spink decided they couldn't get rid of the very successful Reassuringly Expensive idea, because to do so would be to suggest that Stella wasn't as good quality as it used to be. I was working on the account at the time, and after I saw some work from an Italian creative group I came up with the idea that "Stella Artois tasted so good that people would give up anything for it." The creative director Adrian Holmes gave that to the creative department and waited to see what came out.

The result was a piece of seductive genius, written by the copywriter Charles Inge and his art director wife Jane. Most people at the time thought Stella Artois was French, and coincidentally Provence had become the part of France most Brits aspired to visit and live in, mainly because of a very funny book by the journalist Peter Mayall entitled *A Year in Provence*. It also happened that an art-house film set in Provence, entitled *Jean de Florette,* had recently been a minor box-office hit, and this film had some very engaging music. So the creative team came up with the idea of a mini-playlet set in Provence, using the *Jean de Florette* music.

In this playlet the dialogue is entirely in French, with no subtitles (even though the ad was for the UK market), and the music plays in the background throughout. It features a French peasant farmer taking his carnations to market on a donkey cart. The weather is exceptionally hot, and the farmer stops at an inn to buy some food. The rather tubby and unsympathetic inn-keeper demands "*dix francs*" (10 francs) for a ham roll, but it turns out the farmer hasn't any money, so the inn-keeper accepts a couple of bunches of carnations as payment.

The farmer settles down to eat his roll, but spots out of the corner of his eye the inn-keeper pouring a glass of Stella Artois. We see the farmer enduring a few moments of indecision, then cut to him taking his first drink of his ice-cold Stella. As he does this he closes his eyes in what can only be described as sheer ecstasy. We then pull back to see that the entire inn is covered in carnations. The implication is, of course, that the Stella is so expensive that he has given away his entire cart-load in order to be able to afford it. The film ends with the caption "Stella Artois – Reassuringly Expensive."

A year later a second ad was made. The location was similar, but this time the playlet featured an impoverished painter and another inn-keeper. Like the farmer, the painter has no money, and so trades his painting for a half-pint of Stella. When we pull back we see the walls of the inn are covered by priceless impressionist masterpieces that have presumably likewise been traded for Stella Artois.

The effect of these two ads, and others that followed, was to catapult Stella Artois to brand leadership of the entire lager market. So how did they do this? Rationally, the message in the ads was complete nonsense. Stella Artois wasn't expensive; it was about the same price as other beers, and in any case no sane person would risk their livelihood for a half-pint of beer. Clearly, something else must have been making people buy the brand. But when you asked people why they thought the ads were so brilliant (and they did think they were brilliant), all they could come up with was that they made Stella somehow seem "different" from all the other brands of lager.

I believe the reason people couldn't explain why the ads were so good was because drinkers were not aware of what going on. You see, all the other lager brands at the time were using humor, often quite silly and down-to-earth humor, in their advertising. This humor was designed to entertain drinkers and ingratiate them to with brand. By adopting a quite serious tone, Stella positioned itself being in a class of its own. And by mimicking *Jean de Florette*, and having the dialogue entirely in French, it subconsciously flattered the viewer into feeling that they were not only smart, but also "in tune" with sophisticated art-house entertainment. The net effect was that anyone who drank Stella Artois felt they were intellectual, intelligent, and in some way "a cut above" other beer drinkers. Of course, because this communication was subconscious, the drinker's feeling of superiority was covert, and therefore couldn't be identified and counter-argued.

But in what way was it subconscious? Surely it must have been obvious that the brand was trying to position itself as posh and upmarket? Well, no, it wasn't, for the very good reason that the ads had another perfectly valid *raison d'être*: they were ostensibly all about how *expensive* Stella Artois was. By keeping the original slogan and high-quality message, the ad agency deluded viewers into thinking the ads were just about high price, when in fact they were all about aspiration and "classiness." So the message of expense acted as a way of suppressing examination of the creativity, in exactly the same way that the message about the new club-class seats suppressed any examination of the background music in the British Airways advertising.

The Stella Artois TV campaign ran for 12 years, but in my opinion it never succeeded in improving on the two first ads. Charles Inge left to set up his own ad agency, and other creative teams in Lowe Howard-Spink started working on the account. The agency lost its understanding of how the gentle ads set in peaceful Provencal countryside worked, and the humor became darker and more extreme: a wartime inn-keeper pretended the beer had run out in order to deny the man who had saved the life of his son a Stella; a man drank the Stella his father had requested as his dying wish, and then blamed the priest; a good Samaritan found himself abandoned by those he had helped when it came to paying for the beer they had ordered for him; a prisoner on a *Papillon*-style convict ship got himself put into the unbearably harsh punishment cell just so he could enjoy his Stella undisturbed, and so on. These ads won creative awards, but perhaps as a result of its increasingly nasty humor, the potent brew became known as "wife-beater." By 2007 the brand was losing share despite almost continuous price promotion, and the campaign was discontinued.[1]

But this sort of influence isn't restricted to subconsciously processed music and style imagery. Occasionally you can be subconsciously seduced by something that is literally staring you in the face. A good example is Nike advertising.

Nike Case Study

Nike has been advertising its sports shoes and trainers on TV since 1982. Its agency Weiden + Kennedy has achieved worldwide fame through its TV and cinema ads, many of which feature celebrity sportsman. The campaign is perhaps best known for its iconic slogan "Just do it," rumored to have been coined by Dan Weiden at a meeting in 1988. My personal favorite is the 90-second football match ad first run in 2006, where a team of famous football players find themselves playing a team chosen by the Devil. They

---

[1]   http://www.dailymail.co.uk/news/article-494149/Where-did-wrong-beer-wife-beater.html

manage to win against all odds, the implication being that this is because they are wearing Nike boots.

At the end of this and every other Nike ad appears the famous "swoosh" logo. This was designed by a graphics student Carolyn Davidson in 1971 and the story is that she was paid just $35 for the rights to use it (although it is said that she has been further remunerated since).[2]

Nike are at pains to point out that their logo is a swoosh, loosely based upon the wing in the statue of the Greek Goddess of victory, Nike, who apparently was the source of inspiration for many great and courageous warriors.[3] But here's an interesting fact: when I went on the internet and typed in Nike Swoosh I got around 3.3 million results, but when I typed in Nike Tick, I got around 2.9 million results.[4]

This suggests that quite a lot of people think the Nike logo is a tick. So what? Does it really matter if it is a tick or a swoosh? Possibly not; after all, it is only a logo. But let me remind you of what we discussed in Chapter 14. Remember that Wells and Petty found people could be influenced just by nodding or shaking their own heads. And Jonah Berger found they could be influenced just by filling in a questionnaire with a particular color of pen. It doesn't take much to make us buy things.

So consider this scenario. Imagine you are a teenager, and you need a new pair of trainers. You are well-acquainted with the Nike advertising, you know all the celebrities in it, and you know the slogan and the logo. The logo links to the concept of being right and pleasing people. It's a well-embedded somatic marker, because at school you see a tick many times, even if it isn't on your own work. But there are many other more important reasons for wanting a pair of Nike trainers: they are cool, they are expensive, all your friends want to wear them, and most of all your parents will not put up the money for them. And as we know, we all want something much more if we can't have it. So when a market researcher comes and asks you what trainers you want to buy, there are plenty of things to talk about and the Nike logo simply doesn't come into the conversation.

Now imagine you are the middle-aged mother or father of this teenager. Your desire for flashy trainers is long gone. You pay scant attention to the Nike ads, which are full of noisy action and have a story line you often find incomprehensible. You make little attempt to remember anything, because

[2] http://en.wikipedia.org/wiki/Swoosh
[3] http://www.logoblog.org/nike_logo.php
[4] Test conducted October 2011.

you are not interested. However, you perceive the slogan "Just do it" and you undoubtedly perceive the "swoosh" logo.

Your son is a nice kid but lazy. You keep telling him to get on with things but he doesn't. Over and over again, you say "For Pete's sake, just do it." Subconsciously you associate the phrase "just do it" with the concept of your son doing what you tell him to.

As with your son, the swoosh logo triggers the concept of being right and pleasing people. Markers embedded like this in one's youth are very powerful, and subconsciously we all want to be associated with ticks, not crosses.

When your son shows you his worn out trainers you take him down to the store to buy some new ones. He shows you a really expensive pair of Nike trainers. You know that Nike must be reliable because you see them advertised regularly. They are really too much for you to be able to afford, but for some reason your intuition tells you that perhaps if you do make an exception and find the extra money, this will be some sort of turning point in your son's behavior and he will start to flourish.

What you don't realize is that these feelings are being subconsciously generated by the conceptual values of the tick (doing the right thing) and the slogan (my son behaving the way I want him to). Finally, your son says "Aw, mom (dad), just do it!" and you do.

The important thing about this illustration is that if you are asked why you purchased Nike trainers for your son, you probably won't really know. You'll make up something about them being on offer, or being better quality. You'll swear blind that you haven't been influenced by any Nike advertising, and probably won't even be able to recall any if you are asked. And it won't occur to you to mention the tick logo, because the feelings they triggered were subconscious. But whether you know it or not, and whether you like it or not, your subconscious mind has been very cleverly seduced.

Conclusion

"We find advertising works the way the grass grows.
You can never see it, but every week you have to mow
the lawn."

Andy Tarshis, A.C. Nielsen Company
quoted in Mayer (1991: 179–80)

To finish up I'll try to summarize what the book has covered and what subconscious seduction is.

Going back to the start of our journey, I showed that the preferred view of the advertising and marketing industry is that ads are simply there to convey a persuasive message to the public at large. That view has been proven to be over-simplistic by a whole range of eminent researchers, including Scott, Krugman, and Ehrenberg. But their theories, suggesting as they did that advertising doesn't receive much attention and doesn't change attitudes, were seen as inferior to persuasion. What these pioneers were not able to do was provide a plausible explanation for how advertising might work effectively *without* being persuasive.

Yet it is clear that advertising can work without being overtly persuasive. Three ads – two where the message was never recalled (O2, Renault Clio) and one where there was no message at all (Telma) – managed to build highly successful brands, and a fourth (Orange) managed to change attitudes despite no recall and no one knowing who it was for.

One reason it was so hard to explain how ads like these worked is that it is only in the last two decades that we have developed the necessary understanding of psychology. During this time we have transformed what we

Seducing the Subconscious: The Psychology of Emotional Influence in Advertising, First Edition. Robert Heath.
© 2012 Robert Heath. Published 2012 by John Wiley & Sons, Ltd.

know about how we learn, especially at low levels of attention, and how much we store in implicit memory. We have transformed our knowledge of the different mental processes we use when we are learning, and discovered fascinating defense mechanisms like counter-argument and perceptual filtering which can interfere with communication processing. We have transformed our knowledge of how we process emotion without attention, and even changed the way we view consciousness itself. And of course we now know that emotional communication plays a key part in decision-making and our relationships.

As a result, we are able to turn much of what was believed by the persuasion lobby on its head. For example, the idea that creativity makes us like and pay more attention to ads turns out to be wrong; if anything, we tend to pay *less* attention to creative ads because we don't feel threatened by them. But the less attention we pay, the less we counter-argue, so the *more* effective the subconscious communication of emotional influence is.

So, in a nutshell, what this new learning in psychology reveals is that we are extraordinarily vulnerable to emotive communication. I've identified three main ways in which emotive communication influences us, but there are very probably some others.

How Emotive Communication Influences us Subconsciously

The first way is via the agency of Emotionally Competent Stimuli (ECS). ECS can comprise any number of different entities, ranging from music, to slogans, to characters, to inanimate artifacts. What these all have in common is that when they are perceived they trigger a concept that is able to influence our emotions. On their own they have no effect on our behavior; it is only when we see or hear them repeatedly exposed in advertising alongside a particular brand that they take on any significance. When this happens the ECS becomes linked to the brand in our mind, and subconsciously conditions us to feel that the brand has the same emotional values as that generated by the ECS. It then becomes transformed into an Emotively Competent Brand Association.

The second way is by influencing the relationship we have with a brand. Although it sounds a little far-fetched, we feel a certain level of attachment to almost everything we use, from a pair of tweezers to a car. The extent of the emotional values of these attachments are usually subconscious, and that is why they can be so easily influenced subconsciously. Every piece of communication we receive, from a simple nod to a 90-second TV commercial, is packed full of elements that "qualify" the message that is being communicated. These elements are known as "metacommunication," and in advertising they can are generally known as Creativity. We are often not consciously aware of metacommunication, but our subconscious is extraordinarily sensitive to it. We can instantly sense if a nod is a happy nod, a cautious nod, a grumpy nod, or an angry nod, and so on. In the same way we are expert at subconsciously decoding creativity. So this creativity is able to covertly influence our brand relationships, which in turn covertly influence our brand attachment and make us more (or occasionally, less) likely to purchase the brand.

Our emotions also influence us in a third way, which is by acting as a subconscious gatekeeper to all our rational decisions. We are physically unable to make a decision if our emotions will not allow us to, and occasionally, when we are in a rush, our emotions can effectively make decisions for us via our intuition. So emotional content in advertising can subconsciously influence even our most rational and well-thought-out decisions.

To give you a better idea of how advertising "seduces" our subconscious I'm going to revisit some of the advertising case studies we looked at earlier in the book, but now I shall do so using the Subconscious Seduction model I developed in Part Four.

A Case Study Retrospective

Let's start with the O2 campaign. The way in which this worked is explained in a Gold Award-winning paper for the subsequent campaign, entered for the 2006 IPA Advertising Effectiveness Awards. The paper's authors make the following comment on the early campaign:

> O2 ... created ... a stylised universe built around blue and a stream of bubbles. This evoked freedom, clarity, and fresh air; O2 feels calm and serene, the antithesis to clutter and chaos, a contrast to the often frenetic world around mobile phones. (Maunder & Cook 2007: 106)

Using my book *The Hidden Power of Advertising* as a source, they go on to say "Emotional attachment to a brand is strongly enhanced by such non-rational non-verbal communication" (Maunder & Cook 2007: 106). And that's one aspect of the Subconscious Seduction model in a nutshell. It doesn't seem very likely to any of us that a calm and serene advertisement with no particularly relevant message can achieve much, because we expect advertising to be trying to get our attention and tell us something that will persuade us to do something. We are not that concerned when advertising just seems to be enhancing our emotional attachment, because that doesn't seem all that important. We are so in awe of our "thinking" brain that it never occurs to us that advertising might be quietly influencing what we buy by subconsciously seducing our "feeling" brain.

What about the Renault Clio campaign? You'll remember that this was the most successful small car launch ever in the UK, because of the Papa and Nicole advertising. I think it is easy now to see why. First, Papa and Nicole were the epitome of romantic sexiness: they were respectful of their lovers (kissing them and giving them flowers) and above all were French (and we all feel the French are the most romantic nation in the world). Second, Papa and Nicole were evidently a "class" act: they were good-looking, they had a magnificent chateau, and they wore beautiful clothes. That would have reinforced the marker everyone in the UK has that the French understand what style is all about. Seeing Papa and Nicole over and over again linked them inextricably (and consciously) with the Renault Clio, *subconsciously* conditioning us to feel that it was an exceptionally stylish and sexy little car.

The Clio advertising also explains why the Citroën Xsara ad was such a failure. Claudia Schiffer's striptease as she walks down the stairs may be sexy, but it isn't remotely romantic. The feeling this ad created was one of exploitation and *lack* of respect for women. That's the absolute opposite of what people want to feel their car stands for.

But from the point of view of subconscious seduction the most inspired part of the Clio ad is the message about big car luxury combined with small car nippiness. Not, I hasten to add, because it changed our beliefs or attitudes about the car. I'm pretty sure this message had little if any influence on our attitudes to the car, because our innate scepticism would automatically have counter-argued that all small cars are "nippy" by definition, and most of them are pretty comfortable. No, the clever thing about the message is just the fact that it was there. Because there was a message that *justified* all of Papa and Nicole's antics, it never really occurred to anyone that the ad might be working in any other way. No one regarded their sexy behavior and stylishness as forming any part of what was meant to be being communicated about the car. And so no one made any attempt to counter-argue the "sexy and stylish" conditioning, because we had no real idea it was going on.

It is perhaps a bit less easy to explain how the Telma Noodles advertising was such a success, because I can't show you the visuals or play you the music. You just have to take it for granted that the visuals portrayed joyful, vibrant, and slightly rebellious young people contrasted with their grumpy and irritable parents. These images, processed over and over again, would have exerted a powerful influence on the relationship between young people and the brand. Subconsciously, they would have felt it was on their side (not their parents' side) and as a consequence "their" sort of food brand. In addition to this, the music, repeatedly processed semi-consciously, would have acted not only to reinforce the feeling of fun and energy, but as a branding surrogate for Telma. We might speculate that if the music had not become famous, the ad might have simply sunk into anonymity. Lastly, the gibberish dialogue means that when you watch the ad you spend most of your time trying to work out what is being communicated in it, and that, like the message in the Renault Clio ad, takes your mind off the visuals and music and prevents them being counter-argued.

What of the Orange J.D. Power advertisement? This, you'll remember, was about how Orange had won the J.D. Power award for customer service for a second year running. This ad managed to influence attitudes towards the brand amongst those who recognized the ad, even though no one seemed to have much idea who it was for.

I suspect this worked in the same way as the O2 campaign. Many mobile phone buyers are young, and young people are very sensitive to having the coolest brand on the market. The black-and-white Orange J.D. Power ad was certainly very cool and stylish. It was beautifully shot and, like O2, had very hypnotic and serene music. I think these attributes might have been enough to make young people feel Orange was a little more "classy" than the others, and so feel more attached to it than the other brands on the market. A clue is that the positive attitude shift amongst those who had seen the ad was seen across most of the image dimensions, not just those relating to good service.

The British Airways advertising with its wonderful music we have dealt with in some detail. This is an example of a branded association that conditions us subconsciously to feel that traveling in the airline will be wonderfully relaxing and comfortable. Again, the clever thing is that the ad has a message, and that means we don't pay attention to or counter-argue the influence of the music, because we don't see it as being an important part of the communication.

The Andrex puppy advertising works similarly. The "soft, strong, and very long" message distracts us while the puppy subconsciously conditions us to feel that Andrex is a loving family-oriented company, and their toilet paper, like the puppy, is soft. But here again, as with Stella Artois, the ambition of the ad agency to adapt and change a proven successful formula has resulted in what I regard as a major miscalculation. First, the cute puppy was given a voice and allowed to talk, and then it was replaced by a computer-animated puppy. In my opinion neither of these artificial representations of the puppy are able to generate the conceptual values of softness and family love that the original did, so it will be interesting to see if over the next few years Andrex's sales start to decline.

The Hamlet ad is a little more complex. In this case there is no real message about the product itself, and the ads are ostensibly jokes which are being "sponsored" by Hamlet. That could be seen as having been an attempt by the brand to manipulate the relationship we have with it, using "like my ad, like my brand" mechanism. But this is very obvious and I think something that could easily be counter-argued. Much more likely I think is that the humor distracts us from realizing that the advertising is conditioning us to feel that smoking a cigar will relax us and drive away our worries.

What about the meerkats and Gio Compario? Do these seduce our subconscious? I'm not sure. Although the meerkats might seem cute and cuddly, they are not real meerkats, they are imaginary meerkats that talk. What you see – a rather daft invented story aimed at getting the name of the web site into your head – might well be all you get. There might be an element of goodwill generated by the meerkats, and that might encourage some people to feel more attached to Compare the Market than other sites, but so far that hasn't earned them market leadership in site traffic.

As for the others – Levi's, Cadbury's Gorilla, and the Michelin Babies – I hope I've explained how these work already. But these examples are just the tip of an iceberg. There are countless other advertising campaigns that use the Subconscious Seduction Model. A few, like the Hamlet ad and the Marlboro Cowboy, advertised products that we now know are harmful, and should clearly be proscribed. But the greater difficulty we face is how we decide if there is any harm in the rest.

For example, assuming Nike are a reputable company, why shouldn't they use their exceptionally potent tick-like swoosh as their logo? And why shouldn't they use the similarly potent phrase "Just do it" as their slogan? One might say the only people who suffer are their competitors.

And that's the tricky problem with advertising that seduces our subconscious. In many instances it is just a case of one company being fortunate, clever, or perceptive enough to latch onto a symbol, slogan, or advertising idea that others have overlooked. If Renault, Andrex, Cadbury's, Telma, Orange, Stella Artois, Michelin, VW, Tesco, Stella Artois, and Nike hadn't used this way of advertising, they would have been a lot less successful, and we would have missed out on some exceptionally clever and entertaining advertising.

A Force for Evil or Good?

Most of you reading this book will be grown-ups. In one area the dilemma is more important, and that is for children. Is it right that cereal manufacturers should be allowed to use advertising to create cartoon characters that appeal to children, when the products they are advertising contain significant quantities of added sugar? Is it right that video games makers should be allowed to use scenes of warfare and violence to advertise games to children that might encourage them into antisocial behavior? Given the dangers of addiction, should we allow brewers to advertise beer using funny ads? Does the Subconscious Seduction model mean we need to be a lot more vigilant about the sorts of campaigns that our children see? I suspect it does.

On this subject here is a fascinating story. After I had left advertising I did some consultancy work for a market research company. As part of my job I had to attend a research conference in London, where I met the person who was responsible for BMW marketing.

Over a drink at the bar our discussion turned to advertising. Using the slogan "The Ultimate Driving Machine," BMW produced outstanding advertising for over 30 years in the USA, and for at least 25 in the UK. During that time its sales in the USA alone increased by 17 times.[1] I asked, innocently, who the BMW advertising was aimed at, expecting the standard answer of "young men," and was astonished to learn that their target age range started at *6 years old*.

It was something of a revelation! Here was a major advertiser confessing that they were targeting people who wouldn't be able to afford a BMW for

[1] http://www.autoblog.com/2006/08/07/bmw-drops-ultimate-driving-machine/

20 years and wouldn't even be allowed to drive a BMW for 10 years or more. Why on earth would they do that?

And then the answer occurred to me. If you start advertising to people when they are aged 6, by the time they are 26 they will have been exposed to 20 years of advertising. Twenty years of beautiful imagery, 20 years of technical breakthrough, 20 years of "The Ultimate Driving Machine." Is it any wonder, then, that so many people in the world want to own a BMW?

Should this sort of thing be allowed? Probably the more important question is 'how can you stop it?'? You could exclude car advertising from children's programs on TV, but it's well known that children watch adult programs, and even if they didn't, they would see it on billboards by the side of the road, and in ads in newspapers and magazines left lying around. Should we ban advertising for cars altogether? Of course not: cars may damage the environment but they probably do us less harm than sweets, fast food, and fizzy drinks. If we banned car ads it would be a short step to banning advertising altogether. And if that happened, not only would most of our beloved media sources collapse in financial ruin, but advertisers would soon find another way to communicate with us. Remember the Marlboro clothing collection, and the slogan "Come to Marlboro Country."

But another way of looking at subconscious seduction in advertising is to see it as a force for good. Every year governments use advertising to try to make us live better. They warn us of the danger of HIV Aids and smoking, and they warn us not to eat too much sugar, salt, and fatty food. They warn us to drive more safely and considerately. Many of these campaigns are made using the defunct traditional model of advertising. They try to persuade us to behave correctly. And, of course, we find them all too easy to counter-argue.

Suppose this sector of advertising were to employ the Subconscious Seduction model when making their ad campaigns? And suppose they did it as effectively as the commercial brand marketers do. Might it not turn out to have a positive social role, not a negative one? Might it actually be a force for good not evil?

The answer is that I have no idea. But I do know that, by writing this book, a lot more people will understand the principles of advertising that seduces the subconscious. And I hope in due course a lot more ad agencies who work for the government will start to apply these principles to their advertising. So perhaps in a few years I will be writing a sequel to this book, exposing how clever the government has been in subconsciously seducing us with their advertising?

And Finally . . .

I think it is important that we all recognise the power advertising has to influence our choice of brands, both consciously and subconsciously. But I don't see how we can ban it. Our society is now dependent on commerce, and many businesses depend on advertising their brands in order to stay in business. On balance it is probably better to keep it and regulate it, rather than try to get rid of it.

But does that mean we have to live with our subconsciouses being seduced? I suspect it does, because there are only two ways I know to resist subconscious seduction. One is to exclude all advertising from your world: turn off commercial television and radio channels when the ads come on; don't watch programs with products placed in them; turn up at the cinema after the ads have finished; avoid buying newspapers and magazines; don't walk down streets where there are billboards; don't look in shop windows; and above all don't surf the internet. Pretty difficult, unless you're prepared to live like a hermit.

The other is the exact opposite. Pay attention to the ads on TV and radio; look carefully at billboards, internet banner ads, and shop windows; read the ads in magazines; most of all, watch out for those products placed in TV programs and films. The more you attend, the more you'll be able to counter-argue what you see and hear, and the less it will be able to influence you. It may be tedious, it may be annoying, and it won't be fool-proof. But at least you'll have the satisfaction of knowing you've substantially reduced the likelihood of being subconsciously seduced.

References

Allen, R. & Reber, A.S. (1980) Very long term memory for tacit knowledge. *Cognition*, 8, 175–185.

Ariely, D. (2008) *Predictably Irrational*, HarperCollins, London, UK.

Baddeley, A.D. & Hitch, G.J. (1974) Working memory, in *The Psychology of Learning and Involvement* (G.H. Bower, ed.), Vol. 8. Academic Press, London, UK.

Bargh, J.A. (2002) Losing consciousness: automatic influences on consumer judgement, behavior, and motivation. *Journal of Consumer Research*, 29 (September), 280–284.

Barnard, N. & Ehrenberg, A.S.C. (1997) Advertising: strongly persuasive or nudging? *Journal of Advertising Research*, 37 (1), 21–31.

Barry, T.E. & Howard, D.J. (1990) A review and critique of the hierarchy of effects in advertising. *International Journal of Advertising*, 9 (2), 121–135.

Barwise T.P. & Ehrenberg A.S.C. (1988), *Television and Its Audience*, Sage Publications, London, UK.

Beard, F.K. (2002) Peer evaluation and readership of influential contributions to the advertising literature. *Journal of Advertising*, 31 (4), 65–75.

Berger, J. & Fitzsimons, G. (2008) Dogs on the street, pumas on your feet: how cues in the environment influence product evaluation and choice. *Journal of Marketing Research*, XLV (February), 1–14.

Bergkvist, L. & Rossiter, J.R. (2008) The role of ad likability in predicting an ad's campaign performance. *Journal of Advertising*, 37 (2), 85–97.

Berlyne, D.E. (1960) *Conflict, Arousal, and Curiosity*, McGraw-Hill, New York, USA.

Berlyne, D.E. (1964) Emotional aspects of learning. *Annual Review of Psychology*, 15, 115–142.

Bernbach, W. (1989) *Bill Bernbach Said*, DDB Needham Worldwide, New York, USA.

Biel, A.L. (1990) Love the ad. Buy the product? Why liking the advertising and preferring the brand aren't such strange bedfellows after all. *Admap*, September.

Blackston, M. (2000) Pay attention! This advertising is effective. *Admap*, March, 31–34.

Boese, A. (2002) *The Museum of Hoaxes: A Collection of Pranks, Stunts, Deceptions, and Other Wonderful Stories Contrived for the Public from the Middle Ages to the New Millennium*, E.P. Dutton, pp. 137–138.

Bornstein, R.F. (1992) Subliminal mere exposure effects, in *Perception Without Awareness: Cognitive, Clinical, and Social Perspectives* (R.F. Bornstein & T.S. Pittman, eds), Guilford, New York, pp. 191–210.

Braun, K.A. (1999) Postexperience advertising effects on consumer memory. *Journal of Consumer Research*, 25 (4), 319–334.

Broadbent, D.E. (1958) *Perception and Communication*, Pergamon Press, London.

Brock, T.C. & Shavitt, S. (1883) Cognitive response analysis in advertising, in *Advertising and Consumer Psychology* (L. Percy & A.G. Woodside, eds), Lexington Books, Lexington, Massachusetts, pp. 91–116.

Brown, G. (1985) Tracking studies and sales effects: a UK perspective. *Journal of Advertising Research*, 25 (1), 57.

Carter, R. (1998) *Mapping the Mind*, Weidenfeld & Nicolson, UK.

Chandy, C. & Thursby-Pelham, D. (1993) Renault Clio: adding value in a recession, in *Advertising Works 7* (C. Baker, ed.), NTC Publications, Henley-on-Thames, UK.

Christiansen, S. (1992) Emotional stress and eye-witness memory. *Psychological Bulletin*, 112 (2), 284–309.

Clancey, M. (1994) The television audience examined. *Journal of Advertising Research*, 34 (4), 76–86.

Cohen, N.J. (1984) Preserved learning capacity in amnesia: evidence for multiple learning systems, in *Neuropsychology of Memory* (L.R. Squires & N. Butters, eds), Guildford Press, New York, USA.

Craik, F.I.M. & Lockhart, R.S. (1972) Levels of processing: a framework for memory research. *Journal of Verbal Learning and Verbal Behaviour*, 11, 671–684.

Cramphorn, S. (2006) How to use advertising to build brands: in search of the philosopher's stone. *International Journal of Market Research*, 48 (3), 255–276.

Damasio, A.R. (1994) *Descartes' Error*, G.P. Putnam's Sons, New York, USA.

Damasio, A.R. (2000) *The Feeling of What Happens*, Heinemann, London.

Damasio, A.R. (2003) *Looking for Spinosa*, Heinemann, London.

Day, R., Storey, R. & Edwards, A. (2005) British Airways: climbing above the turbulence, in *Advertising Works 13* (A. Hoad, ed.), World Advertising Research Centre, Henley-on-Thames, UK.

Dennett, D. (1993) *Consciousness Explained*, Penguin, London, UK.

Dijksterhuis, A., Smith, P.K., van Baaren, R.B., & Wigboldus, D.H.J. (2005). The unconscious consumer: Effects of Environment of Consumer Choice. *Journal of Consumer Psychology*, 15, 193–202.

Doyle, P. (1994) *Marketing Management and Strategy*, Prentice-Hall, Hemel Hempstead, UK.

Du Plessis, E. (2005) *The Advertised Mind*, Kogan Page, London, UK.

Duncan, T. & Moriarty, S. (1999) Brand relationships key to agency of the future. *Advertising Age*, 70 (10).

Ebbinghaus, H. (1885) *Über das Gedchtnis: Untersuchungen zur experimentellen Psychologie*, Leipzig: Duncker & Humblot. [English edition: Ebbinghaus, H. (1913) *Memory: A Contribution to Experimental Psychology*, Teachers College, Columbia University, New York, USA, Chapter 1.]

Ebbinghaus, H. (1902) *Grundzuge der Psychologie, Theil*, Veit & Co., Leipzig, Germany.

Ehrenberg, A.S.C. (1974) Repetitive advertising and the consumer. *Journal of Advertising Research*, 14 (2), 25–34.

Ehrenberg, A.S.C. (2004) My research in marketing: how it happened. *Marketing Research*, 16 (4).

Eysenck, M.W. (1978) Levels of processing: a critique. *British Journal of Psychology*, 69, 157–169.

Eysenck, M.W. & Keane, M.T. (2000) *Cognitive Psychology*, 4th edn, Psychology Press Ltd., Hove, UK.

Feldwick, P. (2009) Brand communications, in *Brands and Branding* (R. Clifton, ed.), Economist Newspaper/Profile Books, London, UK, pp. 127–145.

Festinger, L. & Maccoby, N. (1964) On resistance to persuasive communications. *Journal of Abnormal and Social Psychology*, 68, 359–366.

Fitzsimons, G.J., Hutchinson, J.W., Williams, P. *et al.* (2002) Non-conscious influences on consumer choice. *Marketing Letters*, 13 (3), 269–279.

Fletcher, W. (1999) *Advertising Advertising*, Profile Books, London, UK.

Franzen, G. (1999) *Brands and Advertising*, Admap Publications, Henley-on-Thames, UK.

Gladwell, M. (2006) *Blink*, Penguin Books, London, UK.

Goetzel, D. (2006) New data reveals virtually no viewers for time-shifted spots. *Media Daily News*, April 6.

Greenwald, A.G. & Leavitt, C. (1984) Audience involvement in advertising: four levels. *Journal of Consumer Research*, 11 (June), 581–592.

Grey Walter, W. (1963) Presentation to the Osler Society, Oxford University, in D. Dennett (1993) *Consciousness Explained*, Penguin, London, UK, p. 167.

Gunther, J. (1960) *Taken at the Flood: The Story of Albert D. Lasker*, Hamish Hamilton.

Hademan, J. (1945) *The Psychology of Invention in the Mathematical Field*, Princeton University Press, New Jersey, USA.

Hansen, C.H. & Hansen, R.D. (1994) Automatic emotion: attention and facial efference, in *The Hearts Eye* (P.M. Neidenthal & S. Kitayama, eds), Academic Press, San Diego, California, USA.

Haskins, J.B. (1964) Factual recall as a measure of advertising effectiveness. *Journal of Advertising Research*, 4 (1), 2–8.

Heath, R.G. (1993) Reassuringly expensive: a case history of the Stella Artois press campaign, in *Advertising Works 7* (C. Baker, ed.), NTC Publications, Henley-on-Thames, UK.

Heath, R.G. (2001) *The Hidden Power of Advertising*, Admap Monograph No. 7, World Advertising Research Centre, Henley-on-Thames, UK.

Heath, R.G. (2009) Emotional engagement: how television builds big brands at low attention. *Journal of Advertising Research*, 49 (1), 62–73.

Heath, R.G., Brandt, D. & Nairn, A. (2006) Brand relationships: strengthened by emotion, weakened by attention. *Journal of Advertising Research*, 46 (4), 410–419.

Heath, R.G. & Feldwick, P. (2008) 50 years using the wrong model of advertising. *International Journal of Market Research*, 50 (1), 29–59.

Heath, R.G. & Hyder, P. (2005) Measuring the hidden power of emotive advertising. *International Journal of Market Research*, 47 (5), 467–486.

Heath, R.G., Nairn, A.C. & Bottomley, P. (2009) How effective is creativity? Emotive content in TV advertising does not increase attention. *Journal of Advertising Research*, 49 (4), 450–463.

Hedges, A. (1998) *Testing to Destruction: A Critical Look at the Uses of Research in Advertising*, Institute of Practitioners in Advertising, London, UK.

Holbrook, M.B. & Batra, R. (1987) Assessing the role of emotions as mediators of consumer responses to advertising. *Journal of Consumer Research*, 14, 404–420.

Hopkins, C.C. (1923, reprinted 1998) *Scientific Advertising*, NTC, Lincolnwood, Illinois, USA.

Huey, E.B. (1968) *The Psychology and Pedagogy of Reading*, MIT Press, Cambridge, Massachusetts, USA (originally published 1908).

Hutton, S.B., Goode, A. & Wilson, P. (2006) Using eye tracking to measure consumer engagement during television commercial viewing. *Proceedings of the 5th International Conference on Research in Advertising*, University of Bath School of Management, UK.

Jacoby, L.L., Toth, J.P. & Yonelinas, A.P. (1993) Separating conscious and unconscious influences of memory: measuring recollection. *Journal of Experimental Psychology: General*, 122, 139–154.

James, W. (1890) *Principles of Psychology*, Dover, New York, USA.

Jones, J.P. (1990) Advertising: strong force or weak force? Two views an ocean apart. *International Journal of Advertising*, 9 (3), 233–246.

Kay, J. (2010) *Obliquity*, Profile Books, London, UK.

Kihlstrom, J.F. (1987) The cognitive unconscious. *Science*, 237, 1445–1452.

Kover, A.J. (1995) Copywriters' implicit theories of communication: an exploration. *Journal of Consumer Research*, 21 (4), 596–911.

Kroeber-Riel, W. & Barton, B. (1980) Scanning ads: effects of position and arousal potential of ad elements. *Current Issues and Research in Advertising*, 3 (1), 147–163.

Kroeber-Riel, W. (1979) Activation Research: Psychobiological Approaches in Consumer Research. *Journal of Consumer Research*, 5 (2), 240–250.

Krugman, H.E. (1965) The impact of television advertising: learning without involvement. *Public Opinion Quarterly*, 29 (Fall), 349–356.

Krugman, H.E. (1968) Processes underlying exposure to advertising. *American Psychologist*, April, 245–253.

Krugman, H.E. (1971) Brain wave measurement of media involvement. *Journal of Advertising Research*, 11 (1), 3–9.

Krugman, H.E. (1972) Why three exposures may be enough. *Journal of Advertising Research*, 12, 11–14.

Krugman, H.E. (1977) Memory without recall, exposure without perception. *Journal of Advertising Research*, 17 (4).

Kunst-Wilson, W.R. & Zajonc, R.B. (1980) Affective discrimination of stimuli that cannot be recognised. *Journal of Experimental Psychology: Learning, Memory, and Cognition*, 13, 646–648.

Langmaid, R. & Gordon, W. (1988) A great ad: pity they can't remember the brand. Proceedings of the MRS Conference, Brighton, UK.

Lannon, J. (1998) A Man with a Mission, *Market Leader*, 1 (2) 20–27.

LeDoux, J. (1998) *The Emotional Brain*, Weidenfeld & Nicolson, London, UK.

Lehrer, J. (2009) *The Decisive Moment*, Canongate Books, Edinburgh, UK.

Libet, B. (1999) Do we have free will? *Journal of Consciousness Studies*, 6 (8–9), 47–57.

Libet, B., Wright, E.W., Feinstein, B. *et al.* (1979) Subjective referral of the timing for a conscious sensory experience. *Brain*, 102, 193–224.

Lockhart, R.S. & Craik, F.I.M. (1978) Levels of processing: a reply to Eysenck. *British Journal of Psychology*, 69, 171–175.

Lockhart, R.S. & Craik, F.I.M. (1990) Levels of processing: a retrospective commentary on a framework for memory research. *Canadian Journal of Psychology*, 69, 87–112.

MacGill, F. & Gnoddle, K. (1995) BA: 10 years of the world's favourite advertising, but how much did it have to do with the world's most profitable airline? in *Advertising Works 8* (C Baker, ed.), Admap Publications, Henley-on-Thames, UK.

MacInnis, D.J. & Jaworski, B.J. (1989) Information processing from advertisements: towards an integrative framework. *Journal of Marketing*, 53, 1–23.

MacLean, P.D. (1952) Some psychiatric implications of physiological studies on frontotemporal portion of limbic system (visceral brain). *Electroencephalography and Clinical Neurophysiology*, 4, 407–418.

Maloney, J.C. (1962) Curiosity versus disbelief in advertising. *Journal of Advertising Research*, 2 (2), 2–8.

Martineau, P. (1957) *Motivation in Advertising: Motives that Make People Buy*, McGraw-Hill, New York, USA.

Maunder, S. & Cook, L. (2007) The best way to win new customers? Talk to the ones you already have, in *Advertising Works 15* (L. Green, ed.), World Advertising Research Centre, Henley-on-Thames, UK.

Mayer, M. (1991) *Whatever Happened to Madison Avenue? Advertising in the '90s*, Little, Brown and Company, Boston, MA.

McLuhan, M. (1964) *Understanding Media: The Extensions of Man*, McGraw Hill, New York, USA.

Meyers-Levy, J. & Malaviya, P. (1999) Consumers' processing of persuasive advertisements: an integrative framework of persuasion theories. *Journal of Marketing*, 63 (4), 45–60.

Meyers-Levy, J. & Peracchio, L.A. (1992) Getting an angle in advertising: the effect of camera angle on product evaluations. *Journal of Marketing Research*, 29 (4), 454–461.

Mick, D.G., Broniarczyk, S.M. & Haidt, J (2004) Choose, choose, choose, choose, choose, choose, choose: emerging and prospective research on the deleterious effect of living in consumer hyperchoice. *Journal of Business Ethics*, 52, 207–211.

Miller, G. (1956) The magical number seven, plus or minus two: some limitations on our capacity for processing information. *Psychological Review*, 63, 81–93.

Mittal, B. (1994) Public assessment of TV advertising: faint and harsh criticism. *Journal of Advertising Research*, 34 (1), 35–53.

Moore, T.E. (1982) Subliminal advertising: what you see is what you get. *Journal of Marketing*, 46, 38–47.

Norman, D.A. & Shallice, T. (1986) Attention to action: willed and automatic control of behaviour, in *The Design of Everyday Things* (R.J. Davidson, G.E. Schwarz & D. Shapiro, eds), Doubleday, New York, USA.

Ogilvy, D. (1983) *Ogilvy on Advertising*, Pan Books, London, UK.

Oxford Compact English Dictionary, 2nd edn. (1996) Oxford University Press, Oxford, UK.

Packard, V. (1957) *The Hidden Persuaders*, Random House, New York, USA.

Peracchio, L.A. & Meyers-Levy, J. (1997) Evaluating persuasion-enhancing techniques from a resource-matching perspective. *Journal of Consumer Research*, 24 (2), 178–191.

Petty, R.E. & Cacioppo, J.T. (1986) *Communication and Persuasion: Central and Peripheral Routes to Attitude Change*, Springer, New York, USA.

Petty, R.E. & Cacioppo, J.T. (1996) *Attitudes and Persuasion: Classic and Contemporary Approaches*. Westview Press, Boulder, Colorado, USA.

Phelps, E.A., Ling, S. & Carrasco, M. (2005) Emotion facilitates perception and potentiates the perceptual benefits of attention. *Psychological Science*, 17 (4), 292–299.

Pieters, R. & Wedel, M. (2007) Goal control of attention to advertising: the Yarbus implication. *Journal of Consumer Research*, 34 (2), 224–233.

Pinker, S. (1997) *How the Mind Works*, Penguin Books, London, UK.

Printers' Ink (1910) December 1, p. 74. In Barry, T.E. & Howard, D.J. (1990) A review and critique of the hierarchy of effects in advertising. *International Journal of Advertising*, 9 (2), 121–135.

Ray, M.L. & Batra, R. (1983) Emotion and persuasion in advertising: what we do and don't know about affect. *Advances in Consumer Research*, 10 (1), 543–548.

Rayner, K. (1998) Eye movement and information processing: 20 years of research. *Psychological Bulletin*, 124 (3), 372–422.

Reeves, R. (1961) *Reality in Advertising*, Alfred A. Knopf, New York, USA.

Rizzolatti, G. & Craighero, L. (2004). The mirror-neuron system. *Annual Review of Neuroscience*, 27, 169–192.

Rose, S. (1992) *The Making of Memory*, Bantam Books, Uxbridge, UK.

Rossiter, J. & Percy, L. (1998) *Advertising, Communications, and Promotion Management*, International Edition, McGraw Hill, Singapore.

Schachter, S. & Singer, J.E. (1962) Cognitive, social, and physiological determinants of emotional state. *Psychological Review*, 69, 379–399.

Schacter, D.L. (1996) *Searching for Memory*, Perseus Books Group, USA.

Schmitt, B.H. (1994) Contextual priming of visual information in advertisements. *Psychology and Marketing*, 11 (1), 1–14.

Scott, W.D. (1903) *The Psychology of Advertising in Theory and Practice*, Small, Maynard & Co., Boston, Massachusetts, USA.

Scott, W.D. (1904) The psychology of advertising. *The Atlantic Magazine*, January 1904.

Shapiro, S., MacInnis, D.J. & Heckler, S.E. (1997) The effects of incidental ad exposure on the formation of consideration sets. *Journal of Consumer Research*, 24, 94–104.

Shiv, B. & Fedorikhan, A. (1999) Heart and mind in conflict: the interplay of affect and cognition in consumer decision making. *Journal of Consumer Research*, 26, 278–292.

Shudson, M. (1984) *Advertising: The Uneasy Persuasion*, Routledge, London, UK.

Soley, L.C. (1984) Factors affecting television attentiveness: a research note. *Current Issues and Research in Advertising*, 7 (1), 141–148.

Soloman, M.R. (2006) *Consumer Behaviour*, 7th edn, Pearson Education, Upper Saddle River, New Jersey, USA.

Standing, L. (1973) Learning 10,000 pictures. *Quarterly Journal of Experimental Psychology: Learning, Memory, and Cognition*, 19, 582–602.

Starch, D. (1923) *Principles of Advertising*, A.W. Shaw Company, Chicago, Illinois.

Sunday Times (2011) The Andrew Davidson Interview (March 20, 2011), Business Section, p.6.

Sutherland, M. & Sylvester, A. (2000) *Advertising and the Mind of the Consumer*, Allen & Unwin, St Leonards, Australia.

Sutherland, S. (2007) *Irrationality*, Pinter & Martin, London, UK.

Tellis, G.J. (1998) *Advertising and Sales Promotion Strategy*, Addison-Wesley, Massachusetts, USA.

Thaler, R.H. & Sunstein, C.R. (2008) *Nudge*, Penguin Books, London, UK.

Trappey, C. (1996) A meta-analysis of consumer choice. *Psychology and Marketing*, 13, 517–530.

Tulving, E., Schacter, D.L. & Stark, H. (1982) Priming effects in word fragmentation completion are independent of recognition memory. *Journal of Experimental Psychology: Learning, Memory, and Cognition*, 8, 336–342.

Vaidya, C.J., Gabrielli, J.D.E., Keane, M.M. *et al.* (1995) Perceptual and conceptual memory processes in global amnesia. *Neuropsychology*, 10, 529–537.

Van Osselaer, S.M.J. & Alba, J.W. (2000) Consumer learning and brand equity. *Journal of Consumer Research*, 27, 1–16.

Watzlawick, P., Bavelas, J.B. & Jackson, D.D. (1967) *Pragmatics of Human Communication*, Norton & Co. Inc., New York, USA.

Wells, G.L. & Petty, R.E. (1980) The effects of overt head movements on persuasion: compatibility and incompatibility of responses. *Basic and Applied Social Psychology*, 1 (3), 219–230.

Wilson, T.D. (2002) *Strangers to Ourselves*, The Belknap Press of Harvard University, Cambridge, Massachusetts, USA.

Zajonc, R.B. (1968) Attitudinal effects of mere exposure. *Journal of Personality and Social Psychology Monograph*, 9.2 (2), 1–27.

Zajonc, R.B. (1980) Feeling and thinking: preferences need no inferences. *American Psychologist*, 35, 151–175.

Zhu, R. & Meyers-Levy, J. (2005) When background music affects product perceptions. *Journal of Marketing Research*, 42 (3), 333–345.

Website References

http://depts.washington.edu/uwch/katz/20022003/antonio_damasio.html Last accessed June 14, 2011.

http://en.wikipedia.org/wiki/Gorilla_(advertisement) Last accessed June 15, 2011.

http://en.wikipedia.org/wiki/Marlboro_(cigarette)#cite_note-6 Last accessed June 15, 2011.

http://en.wikipedia.org/wiki/Swoosh Last accessed June 15, 2011.

http://en.wikipedia.org/wiki/Whassup%3F Last accessed August 8, 2011.

http://finance.yahoo.com/news/McDonalds-says-no-way-Ronald-apf-1794463468.html?x=0 Last accessed June 15, 2011.

http://news.bbc.co.uk/1/hi/business/3188382.stm Last accessed June 15, 2011.

http://www.autoblog.com/2006/08/07/bmw-drops-ultimate-driving-machine/ Last accessed June 15, 2011.

http://www.dailymail.co.uk/news/article-494149/Where-did-wrong-beer-wife-beater.html Last accessed June 15, 2011.

http://www.guardian.co.uk/media/2010/jan/16/aleksander-orlov-price-comparison-ads Last accessed June 13, 2011.

http://www.guardian.co.uk/media/2010/jan/22/audi-vorsprung-durch-technik-trademark Last accessed June 15, 2011.

http://www.logoblog.org/nike_logo.php Last accessed June 15, 2011.

http://www.oxforddictionaries.com/definition/intuition?view=uk Last accessed June 15, 2011.

http://www.dove.co.uk/cfrb/self-esteem-fund/about.html Last accessed August 7, 2011.

Index

Seducing the Subconscious: The Psychology of Emotional Influence in Advertising, First Edition. Robert Heath.
© 2012 Robert Heath. Published 2012 by John Wiley & Sons, Ltd.